tear here

The Complete Idiot's Reference Card

Soundex Code

Letters		Numbers
B, P, F, V	=	1
C, S, K, G, J, Q, X, Z	=	2
D, T	=	3
L	=	4
M, N	=	5
R	=	6

Disregard the Letters

A, E, I, O, U, W, Y, and H

Rules for Soundex

A code always consists of one letter and three numbers: Johnson = J-525

The letter that starts the code is always the first letter of the name, regardless of whether that surname starts with a consonant or vowel: Edwards = E-363

When two or more letters with the same numerical value appear side-by-side in a name, code the first of these letters and disregard the adjoining letter(s) with the same numerical value: Jackson = 250

A name that yields no coded letters is assigned three zeros: Lea = L-000

Tips for Using the Federal Population Census

- The first federal population census was taken in 1790.
- Census records listed only the head of household by name until 1850. The others in the household were listed by age brackets.
- From 1850 the census included each person in the home by name, age, birthplace, and a variety of other information.
- Most of the 1880 through 1920 census has either a Soundex or miracode index, which indexes the head of the household by sound of the surname. (The exception is that several states in 1910 do not have a Soundex or miracode.)
- Most of the 1890 census was destroyed, though a large part of a special Civil War Union index taken at the same time exists.
- The most recent census now available to the general public is 1920.
- The 1930 federal population census will not be available until the year 2002 because of privacy restrictions.
- All the federal population schedules that are open to the public are available at the National Archives or its branches, and various other repositories.

Checklist for Abstracting a Deed

- Type of deed if shown (gift, trust deed, etc.).
- Name of the parties (grantors and grantees).
- Residences and occupations of the parties, if shown.
- Consideration "paid."
- A brief description of the property being sold, and acreage if given.
- Names of adjoining property owners mentioned.
- Any special clauses that might help in identification of the parties or the property (such as: "the land I received from my father by his will…").
- Signatures exactly as they appeared (exact spelling, or marks).
- Name of witnesses exactly as they appeared.
- Who acknowledged the deed in court and dower release if shown.
- Date and place the deed was acknowledged in court.
- Date of the deed and date the deed was recorded.
- Citation: County, state, volume, page number, etc.

Checklist for Abstracting a Will

- ✓ Name of the testator (person making the will) exactly as it appeared.
- ✓ Residence of the testator.
- ✓ Occupation of the testator.
- ✓ Item by item listing of all bequests and devises (of real and personal property). Show all names exactly as they appear. Also include designations such as my "aunt" Hattie, or "my eldest" son.
- ✓ Include any special clauses such as "my former wife," the "land I received from my father," etc.
- ✓ The name of the executor(s).
- ✓ Special clauses providing for apprenticeship of children, burial place if specified, any mention of religion, etc.
- ✓ Signatures as they appeared (exact spelling), and whether by signature (or by mark).
- ✓ Name of witnesses exactly as they appeared (with residences if included).
- ✓ Date of the will, and date the will was presented in court for probate.
- ✓ Citation: County, state, book, page, etc.
- ✓ Include (if known) if it is the original will, or clerk's transcribed copy.

The Complete Idiot's Guide™ to Genealogy

by Christine Rose, CG, CGL, FASG and
Kay Germain Ingalls, CGRS

alpha
books

A Division of Macmillan Reference USA
A Simon & Schuster Macmillan Company
1633 Broadway, New York, NY 10019

International Standard Book Number: 0-02-861947-1
Library of Congress Catalog Card Number: 97-073157

99 8 7 6 5

Interpretation of the printing code: the rightmost number of the first series of numbers is the year of the book's printing; the rightmost number of the second series of numbers is the number of the book's printing. For example, a printing code of 97-1 shows that the first printing occurred in 1997.

Printed in the United States of America

Publishing Brand Manager
Kathy Nebenhaus

Managing Editor
Jennifer Perillo

Development Editor
Faithe Wempen

Production Editor
Chris Van Camp

Copy Editor
Sandy Doell

Illustrator
Judd Winick

Designer
Glenn Larsen

Cover Designer
Mike Freeland

Indexer
Joelynn Gifford

Production Team
Tricia Flodder, Daniela Raderstorf, Laure Robinson, Megan Wade

Contents at a Glance

Contents

Part 2: Finding the Trail 51

5 Kissin' Kin: How to Find Them 53

6 A Rose by Any Other Name... 65

Foreword

You've been curious for quite a while. You've asked some questions of other members of your family, maybe poked around in the family papers, or even searched for others of your name on the Internet. But now you're serious about tracing your ancestors. However, just because you're serious doesn't mean you know how to tackle what seems like an unusual research project. That's why this book was written, to provide the background knowledge and skills necessary for successful genealogical digging.

Christine Rose and Kay Ingalls are both experienced genealogical researchers and teachers. They have done successfully for many years what they are teaching you to do—interviewed relatives, pored through volume after volume in libraries, poked through old or abandoned cemeteries looking for elusive tombstones, written letter after letter, searched in courthouses and archives across the country. Throughout this book they identify pitfalls to avoid and tips to assist your research—the fruits of their accumulated research wisdom.

Genealogical research is challenging, but it is not necessarily difficult. Like any acquired skill, it takes learning and practice. Every genealogical researcher, no matter how skilled or experienced, started out like you—with a little knowledge about the family, a few records, and a consuming curiosity. Don't feel that you have to know everything at the beginning. Read through the book once to start, but come back to it again as you progress in your research. It will be there for you as you tackle new record sources or new steps in your search.

As your research progresses, you will likely discover what many genealogists eventually realize—the searching is almost as much fun as the finding! You will find yourself making time to "do genealogy." Supper can wait so you can have just another half hour in the library; you give up watching television to stare at computer monitors; or you realize that since your family vacation plans take you so close anyway, maybe you can fit in a half day at a distant courthouse. And don't forget to share what you've found with your family. One find shared may stimulate further clues to investigate.

You will make discoveries along the way—and not just genealogical discoveries. You will learn more about yourself and the members of your immediate family. You will find ancestors that led quiet, ordinary lives. You may find scandals and secrets, or things our ancestors thought were scandalous but today hardly raise an eyebrow. You may find medical history details or hereditary factors that affect you and your family today. And you will find history much more interesting. Your view of the Battle of Gettysburg, the immigrant experience at Ellis Island or its predecessors, or the Salem witch trials is enhanced by the knowledge that your ancestors were participants.

Your ancestors are patient. However much time you put into searching for them, a couple of days vacation, one weekend a month, a few minutes whenever you can spare them, there will always be more you can do—another letter to write, another microfilm to scan, another book to check, another courthouse or archive to scour for clues. And when you do identify your fifth great-grandparents on your father's mother's side, each person in that distant generation had two parents waiting patiently for you to find them. You'll never run out.

James L. Hansen, FASG

Since 1974, James L. Hansen, FASG, has been the reference librarian and genealogical specialist at the Library of the State Historical Society of Wisconsin, where he assists thousands of researchers a year. He has taught genealogical research courses since 1975. Among his publications are articles on a variety of genealogical topics, a bibliography of territorial Wisconsin newspapers, and a guide to the library in which he works. He is a nationally-known speaker, having lectured at numerous conferences and seminars in the U.S. and Canada. He was the 1994–1995 president of the Association of Professional Genealogists, and is a Fellow of the American Society of Genealogists.

Introduction

We hope you will be swept along with us in our fascination with family history. As a little girl, one of us spent many weekends at the home of grandparents. Creeping out of bed, perched at the top of the stairs, she spent hours listening to the elders recount the family stories. "But why didn't Dad, who had grown up in the same tiny town, ever discuss his *own* mother and her family?" she wondered. Her curiosity was aroused and simmered for years. During these same years, the other one of us, sparked by family memorabilia, was consumed with a desire to know the people who shared bits of their lives in their diaries. Who played with the marbles in the old fashioned box, and who told stories of the bear whose tooth is still preserved? Who *were* these people? What were they really like?

Driven by our individual interests, we each picked up the same guidebook to genealogy and set upon a path that changed us forever. We didn't know each other then. In fact, we lived in different states. But we shared this passion for poking around courthouses, for solving the many puzzles we encountered, and for walking the ground our families walked before us.

During the years of research, we each made mistakes and learned from them. We read books, listened to countless lectures, and worked in the field. Then each of us, never losing the thrill of working with the dusty old records, obtained our certification from the Board for Certification of Genealogists and worked on the families of others, too. We still didn't know each other, but a move by one eventually brought us together in neighboring cities, and we began working as colleagues and enjoying a special friendship.

Now we have a rare opportunity to introduce you to the adventure and challenge of genealogy. And to share with you many tips we have acquired. Soon, every minute you can spare will be spent digging through the treasures of information left in your family long before you were born. You will enjoy the exhilarated feeling of finding that first document mentioning your ancestors, and then eagerly looking for the next, and then the next. You will be hooked.

With the guidance we provide on these pages, you will find many records and experience the thrill of holding a fragile and aged document that not only tells something about your ancestors, but may be the same piece of paper actually held by one of them. Your family tree will take shape as you uncover stories that surprise, inspire, and enthrall you. History will come alive. Your ancestors will become real. A record that includes height, weight, complexion, eyes and hair color, will enable you to visualize them. You'll learn if some were shoemakers or lawyers or farmers. You'll follow their moves as the frontier opened, and marvel at their sense of adventure (and their anxiety) as they moved with their large families. These pages give you the basics to start you on your adventure, and then continue with you as you develop a lifelong interest.

How This Book Is Organized

In this book we take you step by step through the process of genealogical research. You'll learn the techniques and resources to track down the information about your family's unique history.

Part 1, "Who Are You?" gives you a glimpse of the exciting adventure that is genealogy. We tell you how to begin gathering the information you need to start your search and how to keep track of what you've found.

Your ancestors left a trail, and in Part 2, "Finding the Trail," we teach you how to pick up that trail. You'll learn to connect with distant relatives, to track the correct surnames, and where to start looking for the evidence of your ancestors' existence in their hometowns and in libraries.

Part 3, "Following the Trail," guides you in the use of one of the most basic tools for finding your ancestors, the census, and how to research effectively from home by corresponding with individuals and repositories.

Part 4, "In Your Ancestors' Footsteps," takes you on the road to the exact places where your ancestors made their own history. We practically tell you how to pack your suitcase! (But if you can't travel now, don't skip this—the information here helps you even if you rely on searching from home.) We'll introduce you to the wonders to be discovered in courthouses and the information to be had from digging in cemeteries. Thought you knew how to read a newspaper? We'll show you new ways. And, some surprises are in store: You'll learn how wartime service provides peacetime information.

The "paper mountain" that grows from your research will be tamed in Part 5, "Making Sense of It All." This includes the sound practices of citing your sources and some techniques for writing your family history. You don't want just the dry dates of your ancestors' existence. You want to wrap them in the history of their times, so that they come alive to you and others. And, we'll help you over, under, around, or through the brick walls that every researcher hits.

Part 6, "Expanding Your Horizon," offers tips on getting the most for your money, and opens the door a crack to some advanced research opportunities, concluding with some dos and don'ts to keep in mind as you follow the crooked paths to knowledge of the past.

The appendices provide the names and addresses of some research repositories in every state, and the location of the National Archives and its branches. The appendices also contain abbreviations, definitions, and work sheets.

Extras

Within each chapter are some special boxed notes to call attention to things that will help you:

Tree Tips
These boxes contain genealogy gems to help your research.

Genie Jargon
Definitions of common terms as used in genealogy.

Pedigree Pitfalls
These sidebars offer cautions to help you avoid common mistakes.

Lineage Lessons

Notes covering extra information to enhance your study of genealogy.

Each chapter concludes with "Relative Resources," a list of the books or products discussed within the chapter, and some tips on the "Least You Need to Know."

You have an interest in your family's past. Our interest is guiding you through the excitement and challenge in your pursuit of your own personal history. We'll see you at the courthouse!

Acknowledgments

Many thanks to the staff of Macmillan (listed at the beginning of this book) who assisted us in so many ways—to Nancy Mikhail who was responsible for our agreeing to this project, and to Jennifer Perillo for overseeing it. We couldn't have brought it to you without the assistance of the editors: Sandy Doell (a latent genealogist) whose questions and suggestions resulted in many enhancements, and Faithe Wempen and Chris Van Camp who kept us on track with their fine-tuning. To all the others, the illustrators and the production team, our thanks, too. Though we didn't work with them directly, each had a hand in producing this book. You would not be reading it without this dedicated staff.

We thank our colleagues Kathleen W. Hinckley, CGRS, Virginia Sefton Meadowcroft, and Suzanne Renaud Miller for reading the manuscript chapter by chapter as it came off their fax machines. Their careful reading pinpointed areas needing clarification, and their interest in the project kept our morale high. Thanks, too, to colleague and technical editor, Patricia Law Hatcher, CG, for her detailed examination of the facts. Her constructive criticism was invaluable. We are grateful to James L. Hansen, FASG, for finding time to write the foreword. His scholarship and wit make him sought after in many capacities.

We are especially appreciative of our husbands, Seymour Rose and Don Ingalls, for years of enthusiastically aiding and abetting all our endeavors.

Trademarks

Part 1
Who Are You?

What's the fascination? A curiosity as to why Grandpa never spoke about his family? A yearning to know your ethnic roots? Whatever it is, Part 1 will get you going. Starting the search with your own family, you'll learn how to spot the significance of all the papers and memorabilia you are sure to find.

You'll also get the basics of recording what you find and an introduction into some of the charts, forms, and logs that will help you keep on track. You are laying the groundwork for a wonderful adventure.

Chapter 1

Why Genealogy?

In This Chapter

- Why you might be interested in tracing your history
- The benefits of making the effort
- Will you get what you expect?

Your friend is excited about the family reunion and the chart showing his descent from Pocahontas. You've just listened *again* to your mother's oft-recited tale of her grandmother's nomad existence with her itinerant preacher father. And this morning, when filling in your child's baby book, you realized how little you know of your family. Perhaps it was Alex Haley's *Roots* or a PBS series on ancestors that made you regret that you didn't quiz Aunt Mabel before she died about your French-Canadian antecedents. Whatever the reason, you now long to know about the people whose bloodlines you share. Is it possible, you wonder, to find your roots?

What's the Fuss About?

Genealogy is said to be the third largest hobby in the country. Just ask the librarians. They will tell you their walls are bursting with genealogy books. Tables that held two or three people on a Saturday are often now full, not only on Saturday, but all week long.

And no longer are they full of just women. Men have become just as obsessed. The fascination is hard to describe. Some enjoy "putting the pieces of the puzzle together." Some love history. If your great-grandfather served in the Battle of Gettysburg, instantly you connect to that historical battle site. If Great-Aunt Peggy was the first white child born in Monroe, Indiana, there is a bond to that town. Some are curious about a family story. Was Grandfather really expelled from college because he and some others hoisted a cow to the top of the belfry?

Genie Jargon

Genealogy, Webster tells us, is the account or history of a descent of a person, or a study of a person's family. Genealogy, the hobbyist will tell you, is a madness, an addiction, which will forever change how you spend your every spare moment!

Some embark upon the journey because of the need for a medical history. A disease or congenital condition may encourage a descendant to document the condition as it was passed down in the family. Another may be interested in a lineage society, and want to join the Society of the Colonial Dames or the Sons of the American Revolution. Whatever the reason, all who begin the journey of tracing their ancestry share a common opinion. It is addictive. All your extra time is spent writing relatives, searching documents, and placing queries everywhere to learn more. This addiction does have many rewards: new found relatives, friends in every part of the country, and fascinating bits of history and folklore to enrich your life.

All states have a major genealogy *repository*, and some have several. It could be within the state library or the state archives, or there may even be a special state library specifically for genealogy.

Genie Jargon

A **repository** is a physical location where things are placed for safekeeping. This could be a museum, library, archives, courthouse, or other similar place.

If you are a newcomer to genealogy, you will be amazed at the variety of information in a multitude of sources. Your first trip to a genealogy library will be overwhelming, as will a trip to a National Archives branch. "I can't believe there is really a book written about my family," you will exclaim when you find a genealogy published in 1875. You will feel excitement in finding your grandmother and grandfather in the 1920 census, with your mother as a small child listed in their home. With them, to your surprise, is an uncle you never heard about. What joy!

Lineage Lessons

There are thirteen branches of the National Archives in several states, in addition to the main Archives I in downtown Washington, D.C., and the new Archives II in College Park, Maryland.

Why the Effort?

With all the entertainment available, why would you want to spend your time writing letters, talking to relatives, and visiting libraries and cemeteries? A definitive answer defies all who attempt to explain. A sense of identity is foremost for many. Those who believe their family was too ordinary or too poor to be interesting are amazed to realize the sense of value they place on their family and heritage after delving into the family background. The tales of hardship, of endurance, will instill within you an understanding of the conditions under which they lived. My husband's grandfather would tell with pride how they were too poor to buy fruit, but his mother grew tomatoes and learned to make a wonderful sweetened green tomato pie. The courage and resourcefulness of your ancestors will bond you with them no matter what their station in life. You will feel their pain when they lost the little babies, and when the older children had to drop out of school because they had no shoes to wear.

Among reasons for interest:

- To determine ethnic origin
- To explain why your dad wouldn't talk about his family
- To find out if you are *really* descended from Paul Revere
- A passion for history
- To note traits in the family such as temperament and talent
- The need for a sense of identity
- Congenital health problems
- A desire to join a hereditary society
- To track down a family tradition
- An interest in migratory patterns
- To identify the owner of artifacts in the family
- To determine ancestors in a particular occupation
- To reclaim the family cemetery

Will It Really Grab Your Attention?

You have your own reasons for your interest. But, though the spark is there, you still wonder whether it is going to be worth the effort. "Why bother?" you think. "My ancestors are all gone. What difference does it make?"

It is hard to recognize, this early in your quest, that your search will affect positively not only your immediate family, but others as well. Within a short time you will experience the enjoyment it provides. When I developed my own interest in genealogy, my

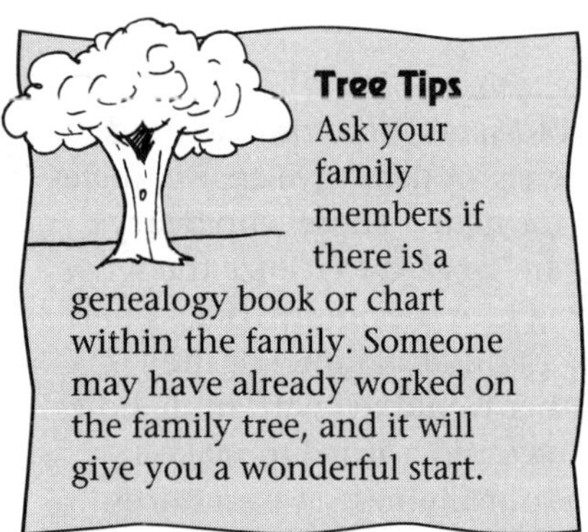

Tree Tips
Ask your family members if there is a genealogy book or chart within the family. Someone may have already worked on the family tree, and it will give you a wonderful start.

husband's grandmother was grateful that someone was interested enough not only to listen to all the stories, but to make sure the family mementos were not discarded: the locks of hair, the mother's pin worn during the war, the old postcards that were exchanged, and the very old letters that were written by family members. It brought her considerable peace to know these would be treasured and preserved. On another branch, our interest generated a family reunion, and relatives who had not seen each other for years were able to once again connect. An interest in family history touches many lives.

Starting Down the Road

My own adventure started about 1960. A small act was destined to shape the years that followed. My husband's maternal grandfather visited and brought with him some family papers. He thought we might like to look at them. That look changed the whole course for this family! I decided to write down the names of the grandparents and their parents, "just in case the children will ever be interested." My curiosity was immediately piqued when I noted that some of the spouses were unknown. "Who were *they?*" I wondered. Interest began to heighten.

The Path to Addiction

I went to the local library and borrowed a little book, *Searching for Your Ancestors*. I read it cover to cover. Our children were still young, and a hobby away from home was impractical. But here was something I could do in my spare time, from home, and with no time table. I could do as little or as much as I pleased, and whenever I pleased. No deadlines to meet—just write letters when I could, go to a library when I wanted—it was ideal. My interest in history also was appeased. While researching our ancestors' migrations from the east to the pioneer west, their service in various wars, their encounters with Indians and dry prairies, history came alive for me. I could (and did) spend hours going through family memorabilia and documents, becoming acquainted with each ancestor. The daily mail was the highlight, as I eagerly sought answers from county clerks, National Archives, fellow researchers, and relatives.

Who Is an Ancestor?

Perhaps by now you are wondering which of your many relatives are "ancestors." Whose bloodlines do you share? Your ancestors are those from whom you are directly descended. The term is usually used for someone earlier than your grandparent. Your aunts, uncles, and cousins are relatives, but they are not your ancestors.

Your great-grandfather is an ancestor; his brother is related to you but is not your ancestor. You have two parents, four grandparents, eight great-grandparents, sixteen great-great-grandparents, and so on. By ten generations (approximately 300–350 years), you have 1,024 ancestors. An impressive figure that will be more than enough to keep any searcher busy for a lifetime.

Lineage Lessons

A **maternal** ancestor is an ancestor on the mother's side of the family; a **paternal** ancestor is from the father's side of the family. Your father's mother was your paternal grandmother, while your mother's mother was your maternal grandmother.

This ancestor diagram starts with "You" at the left, and moves backward for three generations. The father's line moves at the top of the chart, with the mother's line at the bottom. See Chapter 4, "Keeping Track of What You Find," for another example of a pedigree chart.

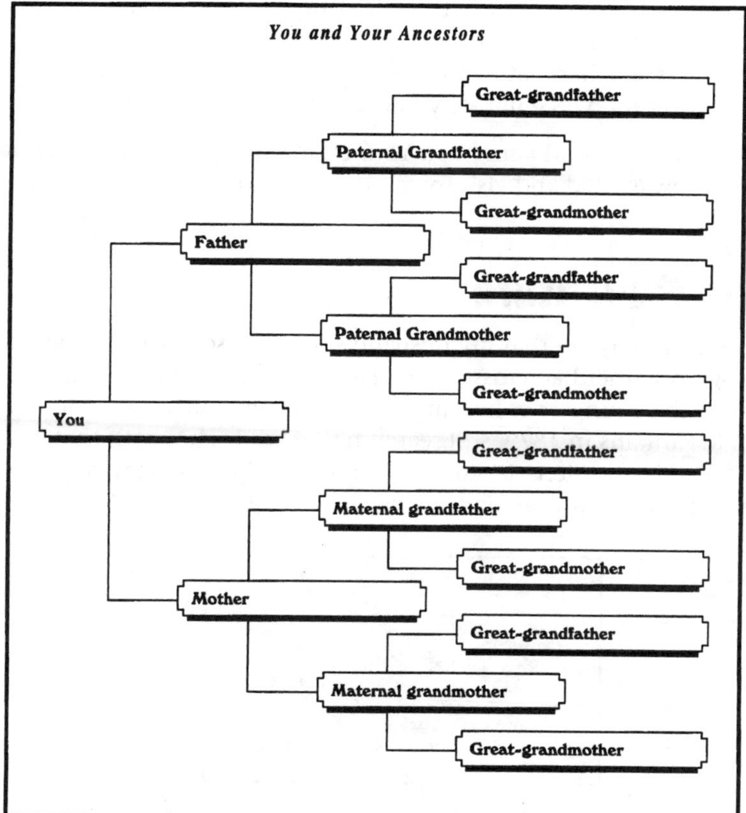

Ancestor diagram.

What Family to Trace?

You will, as you progress, need to make some decisions about which lines are of the most interest. Otherwise, you will be overwhelmed. Decide whether you will be content to trace those lines to the immigrant who arrived in America, or whether you will want to pursue some of them in their countries of origin.

The generations closest to you are the family names that first appeal to you. The name you bore at birth (your father's line), your mother's family, your paternal and maternal grandparents' families—these are familiar names and will influence your choice. As your search continues, other names will capture your attention. Perhaps the line that produced artists will fascinate you, especially if your child has some talent in that direction. The family that left their comfortable surroundings in Philadelphia and moved to the "wilderness" of Ohio bringing only meager possessions might stimulate your imagination.

What Will You Get from This?

Ask ten people what they get from genealogy, and the answers will vary widely. A distraught mother is sure to respond: "A messy house! Files overflowing." The young father may say, "the poor house" as extra funds go for books and purchasing documents. But what are the rewards? Meeting relatives you never knew. Making friends all over the country. A sense of completeness. Identifying with your ethnic background and someday visiting that country. Satisfying a passion for history. The list is endless. The rewards come not only to you as the researcher, but to all those you touch. Relatives will be forever grateful for your efforts and will embrace you eagerly when you meet.

Your interest will spark contacts beyond your own. Your children will become acquainted with relatives they never knew existed and visit towns and areas they would not otherwise have seen.

Embarking on the Adventure

When starting our own search, I found that my husband's paternal southern line was a real challenge. His great-grandfather had crossed the plains to California in 1856. My husband's grandfather was the youngest of his children, and he was only four when his father died in the Sierra Mountains in 1879, still searching for gold. The tooth that was saved from the bear he killed in the Sierra Mountains, shown in the following figure, is a reminder to his descendants of the frontier dangers he faced.

Bear tooth from bear killed in the Sierra Mountains.

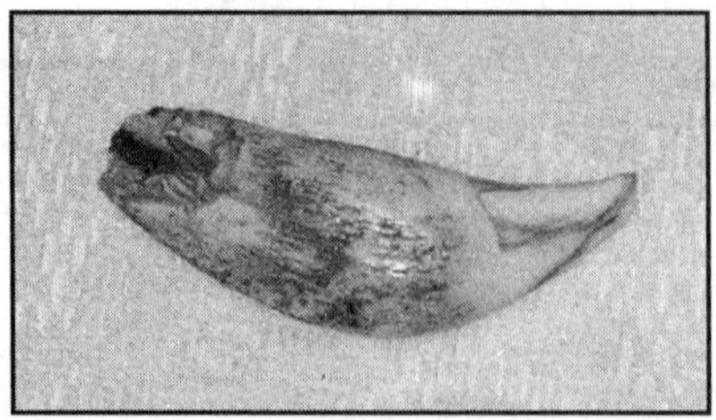

My husband's mother did recount a few stories, but she had not known her husband's family. Grandfather knew only that his father was from Alabama. The search seemed insurmountable. Then a family Bible turned up, and there was listed the county of his birth. I wrote some letters and located the family. What excitement to finally find these relatives!

Later we packed up four small children in a tiny trailer and undertook a trip with a great deal of trepidation. We knew not what to expect. It had been 112 years with no personal contact between the families. But what a warm and loving reception we received. Amid a huge family reunion, we met hundreds of relatives. We will always remember the ones in their 80s (first cousins of Grandfather) telling the stories they had heard about the final good-byes when their uncle left, never to be seen again, and the tears in their eyes when they met my husband, their first link to our branch. Everyone was wonderful.

Tree Tips
When meeting a large group of your family for the first time, ask each to sign a "Trip Memories" book for you. This would include their full name and address. You then have a way to get in touch with them later. If they add the names of their parents, it will also help you in identifying their branches as you become familiar with the family.

While we visited at an old farmhouse with its big front porch, large yard, and cornfields across the road, our relatives told us the stories we yearned to hear. They took us to the cemeteries, to other relatives, and treated us as their own. Others had us in their homes too. This was only the first of many visits. Going back to Alabama, walking the ground on which the ancestors lived, visiting their final resting places, we felt a part of their history and their lives. Until then, we had been isolated. Why genealogy? Because the joys are there.

You Won't Find Perfect People

The results of your search may surprise you. I had been told many times that one of our relatives was famous in the Revolutionary War. And indeed he was, on the other side! The supposed tie to a president may prove unfounded when you accumulate the facts. Grandpa's uncle perhaps never died young, as the family said, but instead was jailed for stealing a horse and branded as punishment, and the family never spoke of him again out of humiliation.

Pedigree Pitfalls
One common problem you will encounter in family stories is that many assumed the family was related to others of the same surname. If the name was Adams, they assumed a relationship to the two presidents carrying that name. If they carried the name Lincoln, they assumed there was only one Lincoln family.

Be prepared. Know from the beginning that you will not find all you expected. Be charitable, not judgmental. They made mistakes; they had weaknesses and strengths; they were human. Realize that you are not embarking on the research path to find perfect people.

You are seeking knowledge of their way of life and what made up the fabric of their character. The remarkable musical skill of your youngest child may be explained when you learn that three of the family were fiddling in the Blue Ridge Mountains at the age of four. There will be disappointments. Your hopes of joining the Daughters of the American Revolution may disappear when you cannot find any ancestors who participated in that war effort. But whatever disappointments the search may hold, they will be replaced hundredfold by understanding their lives and enjoying the friendships you make while on your search.

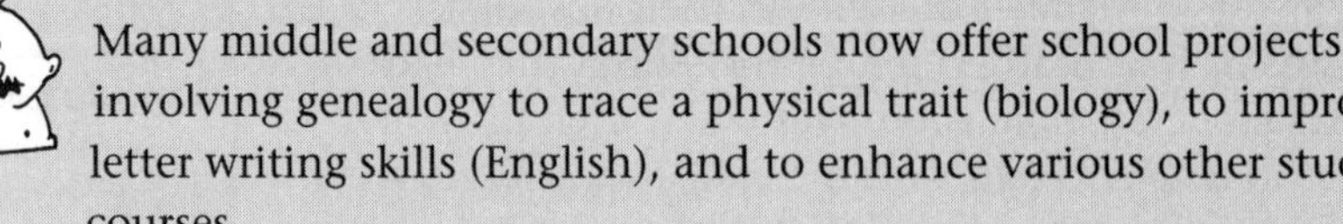

Lineage Lessons

Many middle and secondary schools now offer school projects involving genealogy to trace a physical trait (biology), to improve letter writing skills (English), and to enhance various other study courses.

Genealogy with Success

There are no guarantees that you will be able to trace your lines successfully. But certainly, out of the 1,024 direct ancestors in 10 generations, there are some whom you can trace to their entry into America. Be patient and follow all clues. Those who achieve the most success constantly follow all leads: church records, obituaries, vital records, war files, everything that could have a record created about their ancestor. They constantly restudy the material, as new data is found, to glean clues they may have missed previously. If you are systematic and use sound research techniques, you will be rewarded. No one is pushing. If you need to take two years off from the search to complete your college education, no one is demanding that you write genealogy letters. When you are ready, genealogy is there for you to pursue.

Tree Tips

Periodically reexamine the material you have accumulated. Today the name of "Elias Jenkins" in an old letter may mean nothing, but three months from now you may realize that had to be the son-in-law's name.

No Two the Same

Remember that every life is different. Each is important. Each had its joys and its sorrows. The stories of courtship, of moves by teams of oxen and early rail will enthrall you. When I learned that one great-grandfather left New York as a small boy and sailed the Great Lakes to Wisconsin, it led to a study of the great sailing era when hundreds of boats dotted the lakes. Finding that a great-great-grandfather was a "forty-niner" to California and had sailed around the Horn was almost as much fun to study as learning that within a couple of years his young daughter followed from the east, by way of the treacherous Isthmus of Panama crossing.

The Past Has a Personality

You will find opportunities along every step of the search to bring history alive for you and your family. The search is not about collecting names. It is about identifying, with certainty, each of your ancestors and learning enough about their lives to connect you to them. When you read a will written in 1715 and realize what few possessions they had and how they parceled them out, you will understand their lives of bare necessities. When you find the 1850 inventory of an estate that lists shoemaker's tools, you will realize that your shoemaker grandfather was following in the family trade. Opportunities to know your ancestors are endless. Enjoy them at every step of the search.

The Least You Need to Know

- Genealogy makes no demands; you are free to invest as little or as much time as you want.
- Reasons to trace the family are numerous.
- Your ancestors are those from whom you descend, the ones whose bloodlines you share.
- The only guarantee is that you will become totally absorbed in this fascinating pursuit.

Chapter 2

Start with Mom and Dad

In This Chapter

- What you need to get started
- Interviewing the relatives
- What you can find among the family mementos

A notebook and pencil get you started. That is one of the major appeals of genealogy—it requires only the basics, plus an inquiring mind and a sense of adventure. A tape recorder, though not essential, helps immeasurably to preserve the stories you hear. Someday those family members will be gone, and you will treasure the sound of their voices telling the tales of their past.

Later (in Chapter 4, "Keeping Track of What You Find") you will learn about genealogy charts. It is best, however, not to be confined by charts. You do not want to be restricted by a form that doesn't have adequate space for your notes. Use them only as a means of summarizing the information after you obtain it.

Get It Down on Paper

When you take notes, date the first page. Write the name of the person you are interviewing, your name as the person conducting the interview, and where the interview was conducted. You may think you will never forget, but after 10 such interviews you will. Years later, when your grandchildren find the notes, they will want to know these details.

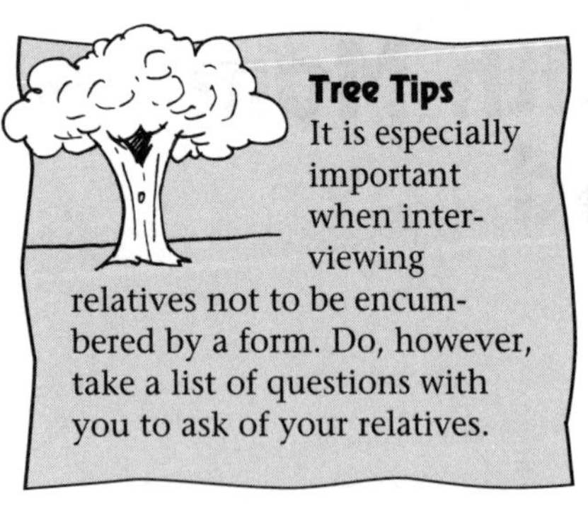

Tree Tips

It is especially important when interviewing relatives not to be encumbered by a form. Do, however, take a list of questions with you to ask of your relatives.

Keep your interview notes in a loose leaf notebook. You will refer back to this often. Section it by family, so you can instantly find them. If you have a computer, immediately after the interview transfer the notes to your word processor, entering them by family name for easy retrieval, or to the appropriate place in your genealogical software.

While you are querying your relatives for dates and locations of family events, also ask about the personalities and physical appearances of your ancestors. You want to know whether your ancestors were kindhearted, quiet or boisterous, or big-framed with a flowing beard—not just when and where they were born.

When talking about women, always ask, "Was that the maiden name?" Uncle John told you his grandmother was Martha Jackson when she married his grandfather. Later you find her obituary and puzzle for weeks over why it shows she was born Martha Smith. You finally visit Uncle John again and ask him. "But of course," he says, "she was born a Smith but married first to Joseph Jackson." Ask the right questions!

Pedigree Pitfalls

If Aunt Hattie says "Grandma was a Scott before her marriage…" ask her *which* Grandma. It is easy (especially for older people) to switch sides of the family as they relate the tales, without making that switch clear.

Questions help the family remember. They trigger recollections of incidents and people older relatives haven't thought about for years. Give them time for those memories to return. Don't rush through your questions; encourage them slowly. You won't get all your answers in one day. If you sense that the memory is confused, and your relative is getting flustered trying to remember, go to another subject. Later, on another visit, come back to it.

If you traveled a long distance to visit elderly relatives, you may need to get as much information as you can on one visit. Proceed gently. If they are confused, turn to other questions. Later in the interview you can return to the previous subject.

Don't Be Too Pushy

Watch for signs that Grandma is reluctant to give details. Don't press. If she says, "I don't want to talk about it," let it go for now. There may be a "secret" and pushing too hard can silence her for good. Be patient. The "secret" may be nothing more than a divorce, which was scandalous indeed in 1850. Don't ridicule or discount a family member's reluctance to discuss it further. Some family rifts have existed for years; feelings run deep.

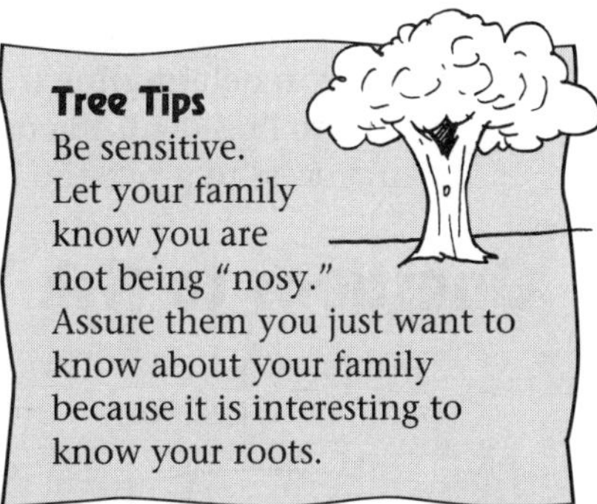

> **Tree Tips**
> Be sensitive. Let your family know you are not being "nosy." Assure them you just want to know about your family because it is interesting to know your roots.

Remember that times have changed. Behavior that is tolerated today was shameful then. Deep hurts could have resulted when Great-Grandma married two weeks after she was widowed, to a man half her age, or because Great-Uncle Al enjoyed playing cards on the riverboat. And heaven forbid if there was a shooting or jail term.

These obstacles can slow a search, but getting the information is often crucial to continued success. If you don't know there was a second marriage, you may not know under what name your grandmother was buried when you try to find her tombstone. Be patient. Ask the same questions of a number of relatives; you are likely to get the needed information in time, although you may never get the full details from the family.

If you suspect a notorious scandal, check the local newspaper instead of pressing the family too hard for details.

Don't Believe Every Story You Hear

As a child it was fun to play the game of gossip. Two lines were formed, a story was whispered into the ear of the first person in line, and traveled by whispering to the end of the line. The end person in each line recounted what he or she had been told, and the one closest to the beginning story was the "winner." How often was it even close to the same tale? Even with only five or six people in each line, the original story was often unrecognizable. How can we then expect a story, or *family tradition*, to be accurate after five or six generations?

> **Genie Jargon**
> **Family traditions** are those stories handed down from generation to generation, usually by word of mouth.

Be cautious of the tradition that the immigrant came disguised as a little girl to hide him from kidnappers, as an extraordinary number of families have similar stories. Another common tradition is that "three" immigrants came: "one went north; one went south; and one went west." All family traditions should be carefully noted, but effort must be made to document them before you, as the genealogist, can accept them. Don't ridicule the family traditions, even when you suspect they are false. Respect the feelings of those who believe them. You can tactfully correct them as you accumulate evidence.

As you learn the techniques of tracing your family, you can examine various documents to assist in determining if a family tradition is correct. The tradition that your family was related to President Adams or to Jesse James can be confirmed or discarded after a step-by-step process to prove the family's lineage.

Questions to Ask Your Family

The best way to start is with your own family. Ask lots of questions. Not just of Mom and Dad, but of everyone: aunts, uncles, cousins, and especially all the older relatives. Write down all their answers fully. The purpose of the questions is to give you a beginning point for the search. You need to know the names of those you are seeking, some idea of dates so you will know which records to search, and very importantly, the various locations in which they lived. Make a list of questions. These might include:

> **Pedigree Pitfalls**
> Don't be confrontational if you know the information being told is incorrect. Memories can be faulty, and age might be a factor. You will be taking steps to verify all you learn.

- What was Grandpa's full name? Nickname?
- When and where was he born?
- What was his father's name?
- What was his mother's maiden name?
- Did Grandpa have brothers and sisters? What were their names? When were they born? Where were they born?
- Where did they live? Did they always live there? Where else might they have lived?
- What were the names of Grandpa's aunts and uncles?
- What did Grandpa look like?
- Does anyone have any photos of him?
- What did Grandpa do to earn a living?
- Where is he buried? Is there a tombstone?
- Did Grandpa ever serve in one of the wars?
- What church did he attend?
- Did he have a trade? A hobby?
- Did he own land?
- What was his nationality?

These basic questions will get you started. Ask the same questions about your grandmother. The answers will lead you to more questions and to the records your ancestors left. Until you know approximate dates and locations, there is no track to follow.

Roamin' the Attics and the Basements

Remember those old trunks and boxes you saw when playing around the attic and basement as a child? When you asked, Mom said they were just "family things." Hmmm…but Mom now lives 100 miles from you. How about spending a weekend with her and Dad, and asking a few questions?

Ask Mom to go through the attic with you. Make sure you have plenty of time. Don't hurry her. She hasn't seen these things for a long time, and as they are lovingly removed from boxes, memories will come flooding back. Have a pencil and paper handy to make notes. Get the stories behind the items.

Have a tape recorder handy as you go through the boxes and trunks. Record descriptions and ask questions regarding the objects. Be sure to announce on the tape the date, location of the interview, your name, and whom you are interviewing. Leave it running; you don't want distractions caused by turning the recorder on and off.

The little doll—who owned it? It was wrapped with such care—it had to be very important to a little girl at one time. The little toy soldiers at the bottom of the trunk; they are sure to stir memories of the little boys who played with them endlessly. Who were they?

A little china doll like this one, packed with loving care, can stir up a lot of memories with your interview subject.

The Objects with Tales to Tell

What about the objects that are going to help tell you about your grandpa, and those before him? How can you find them in that old trunk? But, look. There is a batch of old

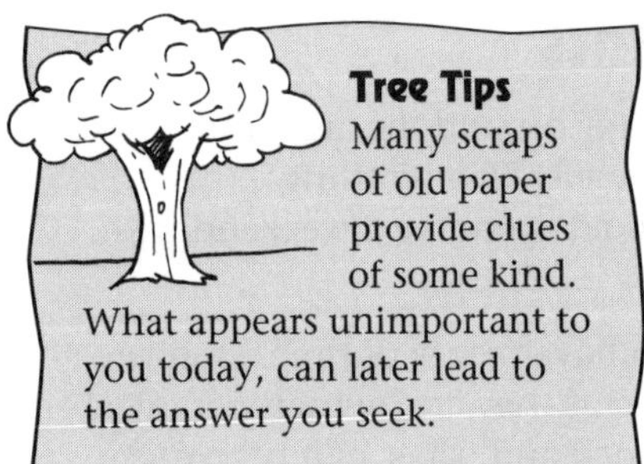

Tree Tips
Many scraps of old paper provide clues of some kind. What appears unimportant to you today, can later lead to the answer you seek.

letters, with a ribbon carefully tied around them. They are still in good condition after all this time. You open them, and read in amazement. There is a letter from Great-Grandpa, written in 1889, when he went to Texas to look for a piece of land. He wrote back that he was getting discouraged, that he missed the family, and was about to come home. But then, three weeks later, another letter. He finally found what he wanted. He described the land, and the little farmhouse on it. He promised to be back home soon to bring the family to Texas. Uncle George found a place too. They will be living nearby. George's wife Mary is already starting to fix theirs. Now you have some names and locations. These will prove important as you search.

Family members, when queried, will often say, "But I don't have anything that would help." It is not that they are reluctant to assist; they just don't realize the significance of what is stored in the old boxes.

Among the family mementos to look for:

- Photographs
- Bibles
- Documents such as deeds
- Letters
- Applications for lineage societies
- Scrapbooks and news clippings
- Funeral cards
- Account books
- Diaries and journals
- Baby books
- Christmas lists and address books
- Greeting cards
- Needlepoint samplers

Genie Jargon
Within a family, **memorabilia** are those items with a significance to the family. This may be the first baby shoe, the wedding announcement, or any other items that evoke memories of the family.

These are but a few of the *memorabilia* that hold some clues. Perhaps there is a yearbook, a letter from an alumni association, or an invitation to a school reunion. Be alert to anything that will give you an idea of where you might find further information.

Picture the Past

Likenesses of your ancestors are treasures. They may be faded *daguerreotypes* or hardly recognizable *tintypes*. But hopefully someone has included a note as to who they were. (A good photo shop can restore them with amazing results.) Many of the old black-and-white photographs are remarkably preserved, especially if they have not been subjected to light. Examine each for names and dates. Note too the city of the photography studio where the photo was taken; it can provide a location for the family.

> **Genie Jargon**
> **Daguerreotypes** and **tintypes** are early photographic processes with the image made on a light-sensitive, silver-coated, metallic plate or made directly on an iron plate varnished with a thin sensitized film.

When you visit relatives, take some photographs with you. It will bring back memories. If you have a scanner attached to your computer, scan some photographs and take copies to leave, or make photocopies. The family will be thrilled. And they may be able to identify some of the people in old photographs for you.

> **Tree Tips**
> If you can leave copies of the photographs on your visits, your relatives may study them and later be able to identify them by the dress or other identifying features.

Sometimes it is possible to connect two branches of your family by the photographs they own. Your Ohio branch and the Missouri branch may have lost touch 75 years ago. If both have the same photo of the original family home in Ohio, the photo in common can assure you they are of the same family. The photos belonging to your relatives can also assist you if they have the same photograph, which was unidentified on your family's copy, but identified on theirs. Your photograph of an unidentified Civil War soldier may be the same photo in another branch, with identification.

The Old Family Bible

Have you ever really looked at the old family Bible? Take a good look now. Surprised to find that there is a section of family records? This was not only common, but often is the only written record of the births and marriages in a family. Examine it carefully. Some of the old style script can be difficult to read. The flourishes render the capital letters especially hard to decipher, and numbers can be a problem too. But as you improve your *transcribing* skills, you will be able to read many styles of handwriting.

> **Genie Jargon**
> **Transcribing** is to faithfully duplicate the exact wording, spelling, and punctuation of the original.

Pedigree Pitfalls

Entries in the Bible made sometime after the event are more apt to have errors. Entries copied into a newer Bible from an older Bible are subject to error too, because of a possible misreading of a name or date, or the omission of an entry.

Genie Jargon

A **deed** is a legal document used to transfer title; a **mortgage** is a pledge to repay money borrowed.

Get a photocopy of the Bible pages (or a photograph if it is too fragile to copy), and be sure to include the title page to show when and where the Bible was published. "Why would I want to know that," you wonder. It is important to establish when the entries were written. If the Bible was printed in 1850, but the first entry is 1775, you know the entries were either copied from an older record or are based on some other source. They are subject to errors from copying or transcribing the older record.

Knowing the publication date may help you resolve discrepancies when comparing the Bible with other documents. If the Bible was printed in 1850 and the first entry is the marriage in 1852, followed by births of the children in the order they were born, the entries were probably made at the time of the event and are therefore more apt to be correct. Pay particular attention to the handwriting. Were all the entries in the same hand? Were some of the dates added with a ball-point pen in a later, more modern hand? These observations will help you evaluate the accuracy. Try to find out not only the name of the present owner, but all the previous owners of the Bible.

"This Deed Dated the..."

Scattered among those family papers you may find old *deeds, mortgages,* and perhaps even an Army discharge. The names and locations they mention can reveal many clues and may even have others of the family mentioned. Other documents of value might be a will that was never discarded after a new will was made, or a life insurance policy with family background. Take careful notes. List the documents so in the future you can refer to them as you learn new search techniques.

Letters: Speaking from the Grave

Faded and hard to read, once deciphered, those old letters can capture a bit of your family's life. A letter written to a sister in 1855, "My wife Mary died and I have no one to help with the little ones...can you come and help for a while?..." or "We just arrived at the mines in Placerville, where the people are fighting for a spot to camp...," written from California in 1850, points you to events, locations, and individuals to find. It will be frustrating when the letter is written to "Dear Sister," or "Dear Son" with no further identification of the recipient. But as the search progresses, the identity may emerge. The names within the letter then become valuable new leads.

Lineage Lessons

When you transcribe the old letters, follow them word by word in the exact spelling and punctuation. Do not be concerned with the errors they made in writing. The fact that they could even write, when schooling was so scarce, was an accomplishment. It is important to retain the transcription exactly as it is in the original.

Also take note of the envelope that accompanied the letters: to whom it was addressed, the manner in which it was addressed, and the dates.

Pedigree Pitfalls

Beware of salutations such as "Cousin" Joe and "Aunt" Hattie. Relationships were sometimes stated loosely. "Cousin" could really mean second cousin or another relationship; "aunt" may be a great-aunt or step-aunt. Rarely did anyone include the "great" in a relationship when speaking of another. Also watch for "Sr." and "Jr." for they were not necessarily father and son. They were often used in letters and in legal documents only to distinguish between two people with the same name, living in the same town. They might be related, as uncle and nephew or in some other manner, or not related at all. If they were related, when Sr. died, Jr. often became Sr. If the latter also had a son by the same name, the son (probably previously known as III) would have become Jr. Watch for this switch.

"Ancient and Honorable...": Lineage Societies

Joining lineage societies was very popular in the first half of the 20th century and remains so. The societies are based on descent from veterans of various wars, from pioneers, from specific trades (such as tavern keepers), and many more. Watch for these applications. Information the applicants provided about their ancestors can assist in the search. Though most lineage societies' documentation requirements were looser in earlier years than now, the application can provide valuable clues. Also note the names of the *sponsors*. They knew the applicant and might be leads to further records.

Genie Jargon

Sponsors were those people who vouched for the suitability of the applicant to be admitted to the society.

Membership in these organizations has grown and flourished; currently there are hundreds of such groups. Some have published their member lineage records. If you suspect someone in your family joined such a group, obtain the society's address and write for the member's application.

In order to gain as many clues as possible from lineage papers, be sure to ask the organization for a copy of its membership requirements. This can help you understand the records connected with the application. Daughters of the American Revolution, for example, will admit descendants not only for revolutionary service of the ancestor but also if the ancestor provided supplies for the war effort.

Account Books: Not a Penny More

Account books, kept by the father of the family to record money transactions and other miscellaneous notes, often include the cash advances made to the children to purchase a farm, buy equipment, purchase household items, or for any other reason. And they were just that: advances recorded faithfully, to be settled at the time of death of the father if they were still due. When he made his will, he often meticulously listed the cash advances, down to the penny. He made sure that those advances were accounted for against the child's portion of the estate when he died. The account books may contain various other transactions: money put out to interest; implements purchased; and perhaps even a family birth, death, or baptism. Scrutinize them carefully for clues on occupation, too.

Lineage Lessons

The sons in the family often were given more than the daughters. They inherited the land, farm implements, and most of the stock. The daughters usually received beds and bedding, perhaps a horse or cow, slaves (in the south), and personal items, unless the father had sufficient land to give to all.

"Dear Diary"

Did a member of the family travel west or take a train trip through seven states? Travel back to "the old country"? The traveler may have left a journal. A careful reading might reward you with the names of relatives visited on the trip and perhaps some interesting sidelights.

It was especially popular to write diaries during the Gold Rush to California and during the several journeys west to Oregon, Wyoming, Colorado, and other points. The Civil War also produced numerous journals, though many did not survive. Those who were unable to write during the war period often put their recollections on paper after their return home.

Diaries can tell you much about the people and their daily lives. From the prairie, you hear about the heat, the dust, the deaths. And yes, the births, and the fun the little children had, and the fear when they were unexpectedly visited by Indians. Your ancestors' writings during the war tell you of the loneliness, the fear, the pain of losing comrades. But they also tell you of their hope for the future and of the pride in serving for a cause in which they believed. Your ancestors will come alive to you as you read their penned words.

Popular in the 19th century, charming autograph books contained poems, short writings, and eulogies. The following poem was inscribed at the bottom "Selected for Belina Adams by her Grand Father in the 77th year of his age A Webster Lebanon Aug 30th 1828." Besides genealogical value, there is some historic interest, because her grandfather A. [Abram] Webster of Lebanon, New York, was a brother of Noah Webster, of dictionary fame. Look among your family's papers and you too are bound to find such treasures.

How vain are all things here below
How false and yet how fair
Each pleasure has its poison too
And every sweet a snare
The brightest things below the sky
Give but a flatt'ring light
We should suspect some danger nigh
Where we possess delight
Our dearest joys and nearest friends
The partners of our blood
How they divide our wavering minds
And leave but half for God
The fondness of a creatures love
How strong it strikes the sence
Thither the warm affections move
Nor can we call them thence
Dear Saviour let thy beauties be
My souls eternal food
And grace command my heart away
From all created good

Selected for Belina Adams
by her Grand Father in the 77th year of his age
Lebanon Aug 30th 1828 A Webster

From an old autograph book of Belina Adams, daughter of Isaac Ward and Eunice (Webster) Adams.

Baby Books: A Mom and Pop's Joy

Baby books so lovingly written are wonderful to read. Mom's excitement when the first tooth poked out; Dad's pride when first steps were taken. Besides the list of gifts, which might name relatives, there could be notations: "He has deep blue eyes like Grandpa Smith." Or, "Everyone says she looks just like Aunt Margaret." Now you know there was an Aunt Margaret! Watch too for baptismal dates, new addresses, and other listings that point to more records.

Address Lists, Samplers, and Other Treasures

Look for old address books, Christmas lists with addresses, and invitations to a 50th wedding anniversary. Old greeting cards also are helpful for names and addresses, and family news. You want to find anything that might give a lead to a relative or a town in which they lived.

Don't overlook the cross-stitch sampler. A popular pastime was to create one with the names and birth dates of all the family members. Friendship quilts created by a bride's friends as a wedding present may feature embroidered names in each square.

Tree Tips
Look also for engraved silverware. The initials may give a clue to a husband's or wife's name.

No Longer Junk

Those boxes and trunks have now taken on new meaning. No longer "junk," they are the means by which you are going to know your family, and the lives they led. It takes weeks to adequately search the memorabilia in your family, among the aunts and uncles and grandparents. Once you have, you are ready for the next steps in the path to your family's roots.

The Least You Need to Know

- Start your genealogical search with your own family members, not only your parents, but also aunts and uncles.
- Be sensitive; don't press when the family is reluctant to talk about an episode in the past.
- Thoroughly exhaust all the family mementos. Most will help in some way in your search.
- The old family Bible often is the only written record of a family.

Chapter 3

You're Hooked, Now What?

In This Chapter

- Getting the right information into your notes
- How to create logs to help keep track
- The importance of transcribing and abstracting
- Learning the language of old documents

As you gather the odd-shaped pieces of the puzzle of your family history, your excitement mounts. Eager to find the missing pieces and to fit them into the picture, you want to rush ahead. But before you plunge into the wonderful world of records and documents waiting to be discovered, pause for a few minutes and learn how to get the information you need from your research. This chapter and the next explain some tools and techniques to assist.

What Are You Looking For?

What are you trying to learn as you go through the family papers, interview family members, and research in libraries or archives? For each ancestor and other relative, you want to know:

- A full name (and nickname if there was one)
- The date and place of birth
- The date and place of marriage
- The date and place of death
- The name of parents

These dry facts don't give much insight into your ancestors' existence, their joys, hardships, or relationships. You need these basics, however, to know where to look for the records that will help you to visualize them as individuals.

Genie Jargon

A **collateral relative** is someone with whom you share a common ancestor but who is not in your direct line. Your mother's brother is a collateral. Your grandfather's uncle is a collateral, as are your cousins, because you and they share a common ancestor.

You read in Chapter 1 that your ancestor is one from whom you are descended. The siblings of your ancestors are related to you, but they are not your ancestors. Your ancestors' cousins are related to you, but they are not your ancestors. Nonetheless, it is important to learn as much as you can about these *collateral relatives* because they may lead you to information on your ancestors.

It is important to collect the same information for your collateral relatives that you collect for your ancestors. It is especially important when you are at a brick wall. For example, I thought my great-great-grandfather, George Marvin, was the son of Sylvanus Marvin, but I could find no proof. There was no mention of George in Sylvanus' will, though several daughters (including Harriet Bush) were named. I started looking for the records of these collateral relatives, and eventually found Harriet's will. In it she named her brothers and sisters, (including George), and willed to them her share of her father Sylvanus Marvin's estate. Because of the record she left, I could now connect another generation in my pedigree.

What Should I Use to Take My Notes?

When you become interested in genealogy, you quickly accumulate pieces of paper with family stories and details. Even if you use a computer to keep track, much of what you do involves note taking with paper and pencil.

Tree Tips

Always use the same standard size paper for all your notes. It facilitates filing the notes. Standard size paper (8.5 × 11 or 8.5 × 5.5) fits standard notebooks.

Avoid the temptation to take notes on any handy piece of paper: the backs of envelopes, credit card receipts, and odd size note pads. They will get lost. Take your notes on loose leaf paper, or in tablets or spiral notebooks. Loose leaf paper is particularly advantageous. There are no ragged edges, and the notes can be neatly filed under a variety of topics. I made the mistake of starting with a nonstandard notebook (9 × 15) and soon found that most forms did not fit the notebook, custom paper was expensive (if it could be found), and the notebook was cumbersome to take to research facilities.

Develop a system of note taking that works for you. I like to put this information in the top right corner of each sheet of paper:

- The surname of the family
- The location of note taking (for instance, someone's home, a specific library, county courthouse, or other repository)
- The date the notes were taken

With these headings, I can tell at a glance what family I worked on, and when and where.

Use separate sheets of paper for different surnames, even if the information is from the same person. If your mother recites family stories about her mother and father, put the information on two sheets of paper—one with the father's family and one with the mother's family. It is easy to get so involved in note taking that information pertaining to several surnames ends up on the same sheet. This can create a confusing situation as you attempt to study each individual surname.

Whatever system you devise for yourself, keep it simple, and be consistent. However, be flexible enough to change your system if you read about or observe another that you think will work better for you.

Tree Tips
Use only one side of the sheet of paper for note taking. If you want to refer to something in a group of clipped together sheets of paper, it is much easier to shuffle through them.

Always try to take notes in a manner that minimizes recopying. Each time they are copied, the chance of error multiplies.

After you label your note paper, write a full *citation* for the source you are using. (For more on the correct format for citing sources, see Chapter 18, "Doing It Right.") You may get so excited about a "find" that you forget to write down where you found it. Undocumented information, that is, information with no source citation or an incomplete source citation, cannot be successfully used to prove your line.

Genie Jargon
A **citation** is the authority or source from which the information was taken, added for support of the facts. In genealogy, every fact needs at least one citation.

Additionally, complete references to sources are needed for other reasons. In cases of conflict in information, you need to know the sources to properly evaluate which is most likely to be correct. You can't do that unless you know the source on which the information is based. Equally important, you may find that you neglected to get all the information the source offered and need to find it again.

Writing It Right

Once you have labeled your paper and written the source citation, you are ready to take notes. While your notes should be complete, you can use standard and recognizable abbreviations, arrows, and symbols. They should be clear to you or to anyone reading your notes. Don't be too brief. It is better to have too much information than not enough. Something that seems inconsequential now may be crucial as the search progresses.

> **Genie Jargon**
> A **given name** is the first name; the name given to a child at birth. It is sometimes referred to as the Christian name.

Write out the full names of individuals. If you know the middle name, include it. If there is a nickname, indicate that by putting the nickname in quotes after the *given name*. Do not use parenthesis to show the nickname. Parenthesis between a given name and surname is used to enclose the maiden name, and it will be confusing to use it for nicknames too.

What's in a Person's Name?

If someone is known by more than one name, put the alternate name or names in parenthesis after the surname, preceded by "a.k.a." (also known as). As an example, John Smith (a.k.a. John Taylor). This situation might occur, for instance, when John Smith had been adopted by a Taylor and was known by both names.

Write down all the names by which a person was known. If he was known by his middle name, or known by initials only, note that too. Laurence William Holmes has been known as Bill, Will, and Willie. It will be important one day for his descendants to know that, for he may be listed under any of those.

Always note the spelling variations you find. They can be insignificant, a reflection of times when names were spelled phonetically, or they can be important, suggesting that you have information on two different individuals rather than one. (See Chapter 6, "A Rose by Any Other Name...," for more on spelling variations.)

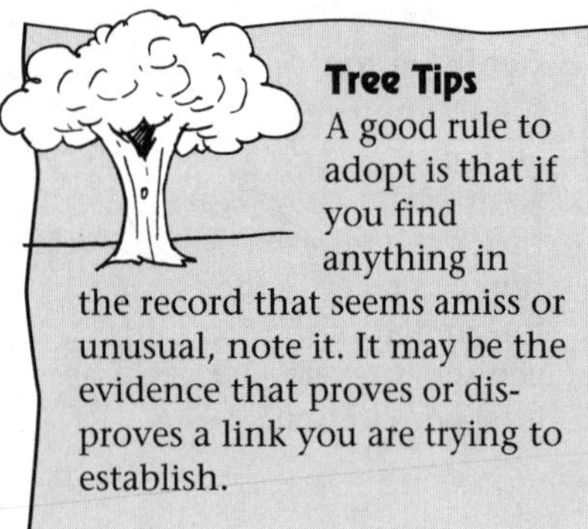

> **Tree Tips**
> A good rule to adopt is that if you find anything in the record that seems amiss or unusual, note it. It may be the evidence that proves or disproves a link you are trying to establish.

For names that can be either male or female (such as Gale-Gail, Gene-Jean, Marion-Marian, Frances-Francis, Leslie-Lesley) indicate whether the individual was a man or woman if you can determine that from the document. It eliminates confusion.

If you find an individual with a name usually given to someone of the opposite sex (remember the Johnny Cash song, "A Boy Named Sue"?), be sure to indicate that in your notes. In early times there were a number that have now fallen into disuse: Eleanor, Mildred, Beverly, and Valentine (to name a few) were often male names as well as female.

Women and Their Changing Surnames

Women's names present a special problem. You may find women under their maiden (birth) or married name, or even the name of a prior husband. You want to establish a woman's birth name in order to identify her parents, for they are your ancestors, too. List her by that maiden name, and indicate the names of her husbands. In your notes, list Mary Jordan (her maiden name) and show that she was married first to John Jackson and then to Frank Swift. Her full name would properly be shown as Mary (Jordan) Jackson Swift, listing first her given name, followed by her maiden name in parenthesis, followed by the surnames of her subsequent husbands with the latest at the end.

Lineage Lessons

Though the proper full name of a woman includes her maiden name, and all married names, when you refer to her in your narrative, use the name she was known by at the time of the event. If she was already married to Frank Swift when she and her husband moved to Indiana, you would say "Mary Swift and her husband Frank moved to Indiana."

When you are recording a female on charts, but do not have her maiden name, insert only her first (or given) name. In the preceding example, if you did not know Jordan was her maiden name, show her as Mary ( ). If you need to refer to her in your notes, show her as Mary ( ) Jackson Swift, indicating by the blank parenthesis that her maiden name is unknown. When her maiden name is established, you can fill in the blank.

Be careful with women's surnames. The name you find in documents can be a maiden name or a married name. If a woman is widowed (or divorced) and remarries, the surname in the marriage record may be that of the previous husband. Sometimes this is distinguished by the record: Mrs. Margaret Smith married Richard Carter indicates that she had a previous marriage to a Smith.

Place Names Can Be Tricky, Too

Place names should be fully identified by writing down the town, county, and state (or the equivalent divisions for foreign countries). These geographic divisions are important in genealogy because many of the records you need are in the towns and counties where your ancestors lived. Because many states have towns and counties of the same name, be sure your notes always indicate the state, too.

Lineage Lessons

As your ancestors moved west, they often named the new area after their old home area. If you don't know their prior residence and they were pioneers to that area, the name of the new town might provide a clue. Among those original settlers of Granville, Licking County, Ohio, were people from Granville in Massachusetts. If your ancestor was one of the first settlers, the name of the new town, named in honor of the old, would be an important clue to a possible prior residence.

If the records you find mention landmarks or geographic features such as creeks or hills or roads, include them in your notes. They may help to distinguish between two different families in the area with the same surname. Abbreviations of place names (except for states) can be confusing later, so write them out.

Dating Problems

When you insert dates in your notes, use the format of day, month (spelled out), and four-digit year: 10 January 1988. If you write the date 10/1/88 or 1/10/88, later you or others will not be sure if the date was January 10th or October 1st, and whether the year was 1888 or 1988.

Sometimes the record is unclear as to the date, or the date is given in two places in the document and there is a discrepancy. Be sure to include these discrepancies in your notes. They may be important later in your research.

Did You Miss Something?

A final word about your notes. Review them at the end of any research session or interview. Check to see if there is anything in your notes that is not clear. You may not have access to that source again; you want to be sure you have it right.

Beyond Notes: The Other Papers You Need

You'll want to keep more than just your interview and research notes on paper. You'll also want to create some lists to keep track of the sources you check and the information you find when you do your research. You can create your own or use commercially printed forms. These lists, or logs, can be a help in organizing your finds, in deciding the next steps, and in eliminating duplication.

Two kinds of logs are especially useful. One is the Research Calendar; the other is the Correspondence Log.

The Research Calendar

The Research Calendar is labeled with the surname and problem you are researching and has at least four columns: the date of the research, the repository, a description of the record searched, and a brief summary of the findings. You can add other columns (time period, library call number, and more). The Research Calendar shows you at a glance what records (documents, films, or books) you have used. It is not, however, the place to record the more expansive notes taken during your research.

____
Surname

RESEARCH CALENDAR

Search focus (brief statement of research problem)

Date	Repository/call no.	Source	Findings

Example of a Research Calendar.

Correspondence Log

The Correspondence Log is a record of the letters you've written and the replies received. The log should have a blank for the surname at the top and five columns with space for the date the letter was sent, the name of the person to whom the letter was addressed, a brief statement of the information desired, the date of the reply, and a brief note of the results. Some researchers also like to include a column to list any fees paid to get the information.

CORRESPONDENCE LOG

Date Sent	To Whom	Request	Reply Date	Results (Positive, Negative, Burned)

Example of a Correspondence Log.

Word by Word: Transcribing and Summarizing Documents

The logs mentioned previously summarize your research activity. In addition, you will have your notes, analyses, and photocopies of what you found. Your notes contain all the details that do not appear on the logs. These notes include *transcripts* and *abstracts* of documents. Transcribing and abstracting are particular kinds of note taking.

Learning by Transcribing

Genie Jargon

A **transcript** is a word-for-word exact copy of the text in a document. Nothing is changed; everything is written just as it appears: errors, punctuation, misspellings, and all.

An **abstract** is a summary of the text of a document, retaining all its essential details.

Transcriptions are most useful when the document is very difficult to read (due to content or condition). It is also helpful when you are unfamiliar with the type of document, or when you have a particularly complicated or unusual document. You will be forced to transcribe if the fragile condition of the document restricts photocopying.

When you begin your research, it is helpful to transcribe all the documents you find relating to your family. The practice will assist you in becoming familiar with the old handwriting and will help you learn to recognize common phrases in similar documents. As your familiarity increases, you can switch to abstracting the documents except in selected cases.

Abstracts: Summarizing the Document

For an abstract, you extract every detail that might shed light on your research problem. You are looking for *all* names, dates, places, and events. Examine documents carefully for unexpected information. A document may have a name that doesn't mean anything now, but may turn out to be a relative. Note any mention of a location; it may lead to other records.

Tree Tips

Read a document several times before you begin to transcribe or abstract. Difficult words or handwriting may become clear after several readings, making it easier to take notes.

Although an abstract is a summary and does not include every word and punctuation mark in the document, it does include names and places just as they appear. If you think there is an error in a name or place (or anything else significant), you can include your correction or explanatory remarks in square brackets after the word. The brackets enable others to easily distinguish what was actually in the abstract, and what you added. It is permissible to correct simple words in the abstract; "funrale" may be corrected to "funeral." It is important however to distinguish that some simple words can be corrected in the abstracts, but in the transcription the spellings are retained as they are in the original.

In the following figures you see a will from an actual probate file, followed by the transcript and abstract of the document. Compare the transcript and the abstract to the original document and then to each other. The transcript includes every word from the original; the abstract is a summary of the important information.

Pedigree Pitfalls

If the name appears as Jas., do not convert it to James. The abstract is not the place for the interpretation. After you have examined all the records, then you can determine if the person is actually James. What looked like an "a" might turn out to be an "o," and Jos. is the abbreviation for Joseph.

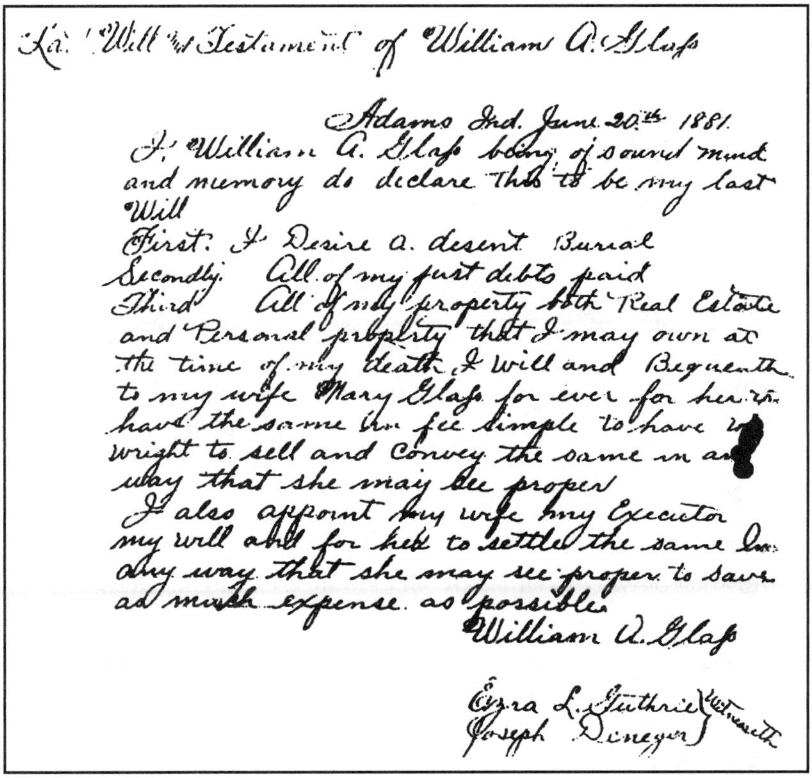

Last Will and Testament of William A. Glass

Adams Ind. June 20th 1881.
I, William A. Glass being of sound mind and memory do declare this to be my last Will
First: I Desire a desent Burial
Secondly: All of my just debts paid
Third All of my property both Real Estate and Personal property that I may own at the time of my death I Will and Bequeath to my wife Mary Glass for ever for her to have the same in fee simple to have [illegible] wright to sell and Convey the same in a[illegible] way that she may see proper
I also appoint my wife my Executor my will and for her to settle the same in any way that she may see proper to save as much expense as possible
William A. Glass

Ezra L. Guthrie }
Joseph Dineger } Witness

Will of William A. Glass. Note the blotch and how it is treated in the transcription in the next figure.

The brief will of William A. Glass, filed in Decatur County, Indiana, in Will Book 5 page 182.

> La[st] Will & Testament of William A. Glass
>
> Adams Ind. June 20th 1881.
>
> I William A. Glass being of sound mind and memory do declare this to be my last Will
>
> First: I Desire a desent Burial
>
> Secondly: All of my just debts paid
>
> Third All of my property both Real Estate and Personal property that I may own at the time of my death I will and Bequeath to my wife Mary Glass for ever for her to have the same in fee simple to have t[he?] wright to sell and convey the same in a[ny?] way that she may see proper
>
> I also appoint my wife my Executor of my will and for her to settle the same in any way that she may see proper to save as much expense as possible
>
> William A. Glass
>
> Ezra L. Guthrie }
>
> Joseph Dineger } Witnesseth

Did you think the name in the will was Glap? The last two letters are the "tailed s" and an example of how documents can be misread if there is not some familiarity with old handwriting. All spelling and punctuation are retained. When a word is not entirely legible or partly gone (as are two words in this document), brackets are used.

Abstract of the brief will of William A. Glass.

> [Abstract of will of William A. Glass, Will Bk 5 p. 182, Decatur County, Indiana.]
>
> Adams Co., Ind. June 20, 1881, William A. Glass, all property real and person to wife Mary Glass in fee simple. Appoints wife Executor. Signed: William A. Glass. Witnesses: Ezra L. Guthrie and Joseph Dineger. [If the copy shows the date it is proved in court by the witnesses, that would also be included in the abstract.]

Although there are fill-in forms available for use in abstracting, they are constraining. I prefer to shorten the original while retaining the order of information in the document as closely as possible. When trying to adapt the information to a form, omissions might occur or clues in the wording and order might be lost.

> **Tree Tips**
> If ever in doubt as to whether something belongs in your abstract, include it. If it is something extra, it doesn't matter. If it is something you later need and don't have, it matters a great deal.

Learning the techniques for transcribing and abstracting is essential. Both are an integral part of genealogy research. Practice constantly, and examine various books of abstracts at the library when you are there. (See Chapter 13, "Courthouses: Gateway to the Past," for further discussion.)

It Says WHAT?

> **Tree Tips**
> It can be helpful to enlarge the writing with a photocopier, especially if the quality of the original is poor.

Because you start your research with yourself and work backward, the first documents you are likely to research are more recent ones. These are usually not too difficult to read because they are in a more modern hand. But as you move back in time in your research, you will find many documents that are difficult because of terminology and handwriting.

You Can Read It, But What Does It Mean?

The terminology that baffles you may be complex legal phrases or obsolete clauses. It could just be a peculiarity in the writing of the individual who created the record. Working with the official documents of a specific place and time, you will learn the terminology and recognize standardized words or sentences that aren't important to the interpretation of the document. But when you begin, if you transcribe the complete document as suggested, (including all words and punctuation), it won't take you long to recognize the common statements that you can ignore.

Until you become familiar with standard terminology or legal phrases in documents, read and copy everything in the document.

"Strange" Old Words

As you do your genealogy research, you will encounter many unfamiliar words. Customs change, laws change, word meanings change. Occupations become obsolete, ethnic groups assimilate, and new inventions require new words. Language is constantly changing through usage.

Sometimes you can determine the meaning of a word through the context of the words around it. Or through the interpretation of other documents. Sometimes you'll find the

Tree Tips
A common phrase may have variant meanings. "Meeting house" could refer to a New England town hall, or it could be a Quaker place of worship. The difference could affect your research.

words defined in your regular dictionary. (The Oxford English Dictionary is particularly useful because it includes many archaic terms.) You can also consult a genealogical dictionary. An excellent resource is *What Did They Mean By That? A Dictionary of Historical Terms for Genealogists,* by Paul Drake, J.D. In addition to definitions, this book includes documents that will help you become familiar with the kinds of things you'll encounter in your research. It reproduces two ledger sheets from the mid-1700s. You can practice your skills by reading the items in these documents and then looking at the compiler's lists to see if you interpreted them correctly.

Latin for Genealogists

Legal documents and court records are full of Latin terms that need defining. It is important for you to know that when an index lists a name followed by *et al*, there are other names connected with this document in addition to the name that is indexed; or that *et uxor* or *et ux.* means "and wife." The best source for legal terms is a law dictionary. Consult *Black's Law Dictionary*, whenever you encounter legal terms you do not understand.

Lineage Lessons

The term *et al* is shortened from *et alii*, a frequently used legal term meaning "and others." When you encounter it in an index, pursue the full record to determine the names of the additional individuals. Often they are family members. Also seen frequently in an index is *et ux.*, shortened from *et uxor*, meaning "and wife." An examination of the document will probably disclose her name.

Abbreviations

A number of abbreviations common in early documents are rare today. You will often see "inst" as an abbreviation for "instant." That will help to establish a correct date if you know "instant" was the term used to indicate that the date referred to was in the same month as a mentioned date. Thus, in a response on December 28th to a letter dated December 4th, the letter writer might say, "In responding to your letter of the 4th instant," which is to say, "I'm replying to your letter dated December 4th."

"Ultimate," as a contrast to instant, refers to the previous month. An obituary in the newspaper of 25 July stating that the deceased died the 20 ult. would indicate he died June 20th.

Making Sense of Chicken Scratches

The handwriting in some documents may be nearly impossible to decipher at first glance. However, with practice and careful examination you will learn to read many styles. Even neat, clear handwriting will reflect the contemporary style or usage and can leave you wondering about some words. It helps to seek references with illustrations of letter combinations and writing styles. Consult *The Handwriting of American Records for A Period of 300 Years* by E. Kay Kirkham. In it are large illustrations of the manner in which letters of the alphabet were written through the years, as well as the abbreviations for selected names. The book also has some transcriptions. You can attempt to transcribe the same documents and then check your work against the published transcriptions.

The chapter "Reading Handwritten Records" by Raymond A. Winslow, Jr., pp. 97–105, in *North Carolina Research* has a good illustrated discussion of peculiar letter forms, symbols, and abbreviations that you may see in old documents.

Now that you've learned a little about how to extract information from your research, go on to the next chapter to learn how to manage that information.

Relative Resources

Here are some books that can help you with the tasks covered in this chapter:

Black, Henry Campbell. *Black's Law Dictionary*. Revised 6th edition. St. Paul, Minn.: West Publishing Company, 1990.

Drake, Paul J.D. *What Did They Mean By That? A Dictionary of Historical Terms for Genealogists*. Bowie, Md.: Heritage Books, Inc., 1994.

Kirkham, E. Kay. *The Handwriting of American Records for A Period of 300 Years*. Logan, Utah: Everton Publishers, Inc., 1981.

Leary, Helen F.M. *North Carolina Research*. Raleigh, N.C.: North Carolina Genealogical Society, 1996.

The Least You Need to Know

- You need to establish the name, and the approximate dates and places of birth, marriage, and death to start searching.
- When making notes, add full details of where you got the information.
- Note carefully full names, nicknames, and variations.
- Transcribing documents will help you learn to read the old writing, and to understand the terminology.

Chapter 4

Keeping Track of What You Find

In This Chapter

- Using charts to keep track
- Computer genealogy programs for record keeping
- Computer-generated reports

Genealogy research is a little like the connect-the-dots pictures you did as a child; if you did not connect the dots in the right order, the emerging picture wasn't quite right.

To help connect your genealogy dots in the right order, you will use genealogy charts and family group sheets to record the research data. You can use these basic structures with pencil and paper or with a computer.

The two general types of genealogy charts are *ascendant* and *descendant* charts. In addition to the charts, a Family Group Sheet is used to keep track of individual families.

An *ascendant* chart starts with you and moves back through the generations of all your ancestors. A *descendant* chart starts with an individual and comes down through the generations listing that individual's descendants.

These charts are not your finished genealogy. They are research tools, reminders of where you are in your genealogy research.

Pedigree or Family Tree Charts

The chart you begin with is a *pedigree chart*, an ascendant chart. On it you start with yourself and work back in time, generation by generation, filling in your parents, grandparents, great-grandparents, and so on, as far back as you can.

> **Genie Jargon**
> A pedigree chart starts with you and shows the line of your direct ancestors. It is sometimes called a family tree, lineage, or ancestry chart.

Think of the pedigree chart as a shorthand master outline of your bloodline. A quick glance at it alerts you to the blank spots in the information you are gathering. This in turn helps you develop your research plan. When you notice that Great-Grandma Diana's maiden name is blank or that there is no marriage date or place for Grandpa Guy, you have a clear picture of the information you still need.

A pedigree chart begins with a subject and works back through the generations.

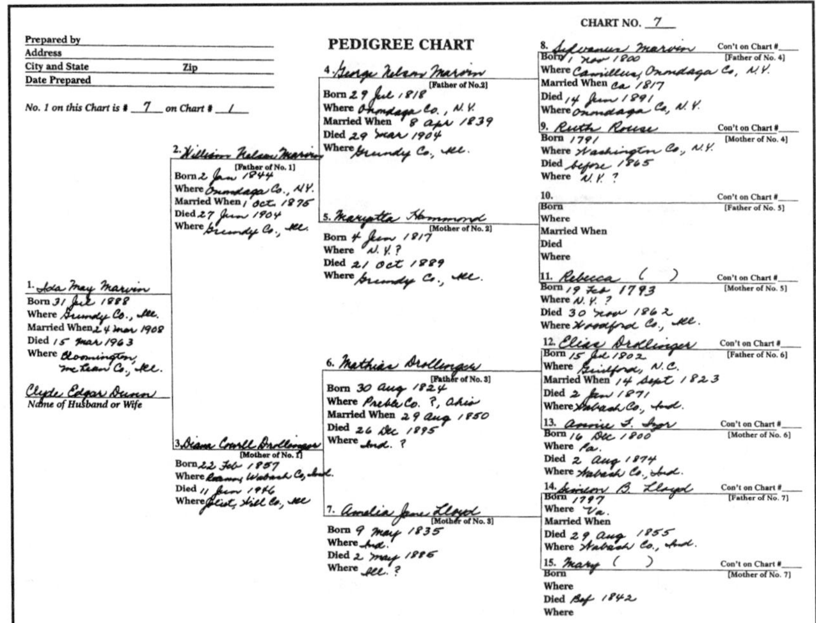

CHART NO. 7

PEDIGREE CHART

Prepared by
Address
City and State Zip
Date Prepared

No. 1 on this Chart is # 7 on Chart # 1

1. Ada May Marvin
Born 31 Jul 1888
Where Grundy Co., Ill.
Married When 24 mar 1908
Died 15 mar 1963
Where Bloomington, McLean Co., Ill.

Clyde Edgar Dunn
Name of Husband or Wife

2. William Nelson Marvin [Father of No. 1]
Born 2 Jan 1844
Where Onondaga Co., N.Y.
Married When 1 Oct. 1876
Died 27 Jun 1904
Where Grundy Co., Ill.

3. Diana Cowell Drollinger [Mother of No. 1]
Born 22 Feb 1857
Where Lagro, Wabash Co, Ind.
Died 11 Jun 1946
Where Joliet, Will Co., Ill

4. George Nelson Marvin [Father of No. 2]
Born 29 Jul 1818
Where Onondaga Co., N.Y.
Married When 8 apr 1839
Died 29 mar 1904
Where Grundy Co., Ill.

5. Maryetta Hammond [Mother of No. 2]
Born 4 Jan 1817
Where N.Y.?
Died 21 Oct 1889
Where Grundy Co., Ill.

6. Mathias Drollinger [Father of No. 3]
Born 30 aug 1824
Where Preble Co. ?, Ohio
Married When 29 aug 1850
Died 26 Dec 1895
Where Ind. ?

7. Amelia Jane Lloyd [Mother of No. 3]
Born 9 may 1835
Where Ind.
Died 2 may 1886
Where Ill. ?

8. Sylvanus Marvin — Con't on Chart # — [Father of No. 4]
Born 1 Nov 1800
Where Camillus, Onondaga Co, N.Y.
Married When ca 1817
Died 14 Jun 1891
Where Onondaga Co, N.Y.

9. Ruth Rouse — Con't on Chart # — [Mother of No. 4]
Born 1791
Where Washington Co., N.Y.
Died before 1865
Where N.Y. ?

10. — Con't on Chart # — [Father of No. 5]
Born
Where
Married When
Died
Where

11. Rebecca ( ) — Con't on Chart # — [Mother of No. 5]
Born 19 Feb 1793
Where N.Y. ?
Died 30 Nov 1862
Where Woodford Co., Ill.

12. Elias Drollinger — Con't on Chart # — [Father of No. 6]
Born 15 Jul 1802
Where Guilford, N.C.
Married When 14 Sept 1823
Died 2 Jan 1871
Where Wabash Co., Ind.

13. Annie S. Igor — Con't on Chart # — [Mother of No. 6]
Born 16 Dec 1800
Where Pa.
Died 2 aug 1874
Where Wabash Co., Ind.

14. Simeon B. Lloyd — Con't on Chart # — [Father of No. 7]
Born 1797
Where Va.
Married When
Died 29 aug 1855
Where Wabash Co., Ind.

15. Mary ( ) — Con't on Chart # — [Mother of No. 7]
Born
Where
Died Bef 1842
Where

The format of a pedigree chart is always the same: your name (or the individual whose ancestry you are tracing) is on the first line, your father's name (or the subject's father's name) is on the upper line, your mother's on the lower line. The upper track in a pedigree chart is that of the father's (paternal) line. The lower track is the ancestral line for the mother's (maternal) line. You are number 1 on this chart. Your father is assigned number 2 and your mother number 3. On a pedigree chart the numbers for men are always even numbers, and the numbers for women are odd.

As you can see, you quickly run out of space for all your ancestors on a four-generation chart. To list the additional generations, you must create additional charts.

In numbering the pedigree chart, you are number 1 on chart 1. One of your great-grandfathers is number 8 on chart 1. You will need to make a new chart to continue with his ancestors. That great-grandfather (who is number 8 on chart 1) will become number 1 on chart 2. Be sure to make a reference on chart 2 that he is also number 8 on chart 1, so you can easily follow the line in connected charts.

Large or Small, They Chart Your Family

Blank pedigree charts accommodating 4 to 15 generations can be purchased. The four-generation pedigree chart is the most convenient to work with in your day-to-day research. The more generations on the chart, the less room there is for data about individuals.

Some decorative pedigree charts are suitable for framing. They can be fan shaped with the lines radiating out from you at the center. Some are in the form of a tree with limbs and branches representing family lines. Still others have spaces for photographs. While attractive as wall art, these charts are too large to be useful as research aids.

> **Pedigree Pitfalls**
> Pedigree charts have no space for source citation. Therefore, they should not be disseminated unless accompanied by an attached sheet with full citations keyed to the information on the chart, or a family group sheet, which does have citations.

Filling in the Pedigree Chart

Completely fill in as many of the spaces on the pedigree chart as you can. If you know an individual's middle name, write it out rather than use the initial. Put nicknames in quotation marks after the given name. Use women's maiden names, and if they are not known, use a blank parenthesis, such as ( ). When known, geographic places should indicate the town or township, county, and state. Write the dates with the day first, the month written out next, and all four digits for the year.

Because the pedigree chart is an instant guide to your research, keep it up to date so you can follow the clues. Add new information as you find it, and correct the information as you uncover errors.

Pedigree charts cannot stand alone as evidence of your ancestors. They are research tools, not the end result of your research. Look at the pedigree charts as notes to yourself to show at a glance where you are in your pursuit of your family history.

> **Genie Jargon**
> The **family group sheet** is the form used to record information on a family unit. It is neither an ascendant chart, nor a descendant chart. It is merely a form on which all the members of one family can be listed (not just your ancestors).

Family Group Sheets

Each of your ancestors was a family member, first as a child and then as a mother or father. You collect information about the entire family in order to learn more about your ancestors. The information on the whole family is recorded on a *family group sheet.*

They Keep You Organized

Family group sheets are the foundation for organizing everything you learn about your ancestors. The layouts of family group sheets may vary, but the categories of information are basically the same.

Family group sheet. Form for recording information on a family unit.

FAMILY GROUP SHEET NO. ____

HUSBAND [Full name] William Nelson Marvin
BORN 2 Jan 1844 AT Warners, Onondaga Co., N.Y
CHR. AT
MAR. 1 Oct 1875 AT Joliet, Will Co., Ill.
DIED 27 Jun 1904 AT
BURIED AT Braceville-Gardner Cemetery, Grundy Co, Ill.
FATHER George Nelson Marvin MOTHER [Maiden Name] Maryetta Hammond
OTHER WIVES
RESIDENCES RELIGION
OCCUPATION Farmer MILITARY

SOURCES: Brief listing.
No. 1. 1900 Census
No. 2. Death Certificate
No. 3. 1880 Census
No. 4. Obituary
No. 5. Marriage Return
(Complete source citations on reverse)

[Use separate forms for each marriage]

WIFE [Full maiden name] Diana Courll Drollinger
BORN 22 Feb 1857 AT Roanoke,
CHR. AT
DIED 11 Jun 1946 AT Joliet, Will Co., Ill.
BURIED AT Braceville - Gardner Cemetery, Grundy Co., Ill.
FATHER Mathias Drollinger MOTHER [Maiden Name] Amelia Jane Lloyd
OTHER HUSBANDS

Sex	Children	Day-Month-Year	City/Town County State	REF. No.
F	1. Myrtle Olive Marvin	b. 12 Oct 1879	at Grundy Co., Ill.	Ref. 3,1
	Spouse: Jack Redmond	m.	at	Ref.
		d. 8 May 1941	at Evergreen Park, Cook Co., Ill.	Ref. 2
F	2. Emma Grace Marvin	b. 21 Dec 1882	at Grundy Co., Ill.	Ref. 1
	Spouse: Don C. Ritchie	m. 4 Apr 1905	at Joliet, Will Co., Ill.	Ref. 5
		d. 30 Dec 1943	at Detroit, Wayne Co., Ill.	Ref. 2
M	3. Sylvanus Jay Marvin	b. 6 Apr 1885	at Grundy Co., Ill.	Ref. 1
	Spouse:	m.	at	Ref.
		d. 25 May 1947	at Joliet, Will Co., Ill.	Ref. 2,4
F	4. Ida May Marvin	b. 31 Jul 1888	at Grundy Co., Ill.	Ref. 1
	Spouse: Clyde Edgar Dunn	m 24 Mar 1908	at Joliet, Will Co., Ill.	Ref. 5
		d. 15 Mar 1963	at Bloomington, McLean Co., Ill.	Ref. 2
F	5. Etta Jane Marvin	b. 20 Jun 1892	at Grundy Co., Ill.	Ref. 6
	Spouse:	m.	at	Ref.
		d. 18 Oct 1893	at Grundy Co., Ill.	Ref. 6
F	6. Sarah Bernice Marvin	b. 21 Jul 1895	at Grundy Co, Ill.	Ref. 1
	Spouse: Rodney McKell	m. 11 Apr 1911	at Salt Lake City, Salt Lake Co, Utah	Ref. 5
		d. 28 Jun 1981	at San Dimas, Los Angeles Co, Calif.	Ref. 2
	7.	b.	at	Ref.
	Spouse:	m.	at	Ref.
		d.	at	Ref.
	8.	b.	at	Ref.
	Spouse:	m.	at	Ref.
		d.	at	Ref.
	9.	b.	at	Ref.
	Spouse:	m.	at	Ref.
		d.	at	Ref.
	10.	b.	at	Ref.
	Spouse:	m.	at	Ref.
		d.	at	Ref.

PREPARED BY OTHER MAR. OF CHILDREN
Address Use reverse for additional marriages
City and State Zip
Date Prepared:

b.=born m.=married d.=death ch.=christening List references at top and use ref. numbers on items. Use reverse if necessary.

The top section of the record is for recording the names of the husband and wife and the following information about each:

- ➤ Birth dates and places
- ➤ Christening dates and places
- ➤ Marriage date and place for this couple
- ➤ Death dates and places
- ➤ Burial dates and places
- ➤ Occupation, military, religion
- ➤ Names of their parents
- ➤ Names of other spouses

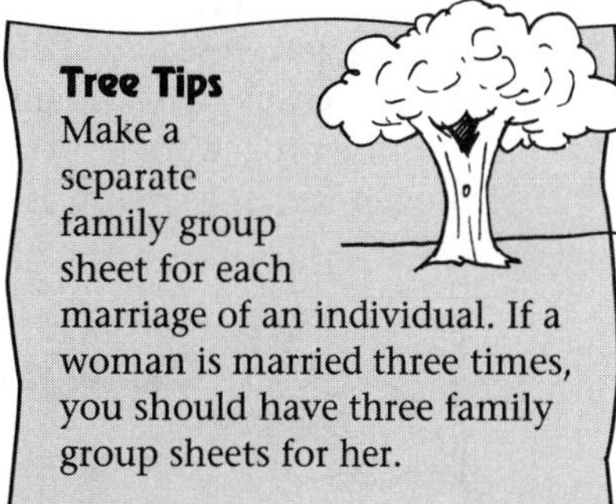

Tree Tips
Make a separate family group sheet for each marriage of an individual. If a woman is married three times, you should have three family group sheets for her.

Following this information, the children of this marriage are recorded with their birth dates and places; marriage dates and places and spouses names; death dates and places. If the family is a large one, the list of children should continue on a second page.

When you gather information, collect it on whole families, your ancestors and their siblings. Each person on your pedigree chart should be on two family group sheets: once as a child with parents and siblings, then as a mother or father with children.

Family Group Sheets and Sources

Each fact on the family group sheet must be linked to a full source citation. If all the information came from the same source, the family group sheet notation might read:

> All information on this family from 1860 U.S. Census, Population Schedule, Noble County, Indiana, Perry Township, Ligonier, page 105, dwelling 84, family 84.

As your research progresses, your information on the family will come from several sources. The same information may be in two or more documents. For example, the birth date of Mary Smith, 2 March 1846, might be based on both a family Bible and her tombstone. When you enter her birth on the family sheet, list those two sources, and key them to her birth date. You want users of the family sheet to immediately understand on what you base the date. (When you do enter the citation, be sure that you give sufficient information to properly identify it. See Chapter 18 for more on citations.)

Each fact on the family group sheet should be documented by a specific source citation. It is not enough to just add a list of sources to the group sheet with no indication as to which facts they document. Those using the information need to know where you obtained the information on each individual fact: every birth, every birthplace, every marriage, and so on. Use both sides of the paper if necessary.

Descendant Charts

Other charts are useful for genealogy research. You will more often use descendant charts later in your research. These charts start with an individual and list that person's descendants. Because descendant charts begin with a progenitor, you must do some research to find the progenitors in your lines. Descendant charts include all the descendants of the progenitor, or as many as can be identified.

Genie Jargon

A **progenitor** is an ancestor in a direct line. When genealogists refer to a progenitor, they usually mean the earliest proven person in a line. If the earliest proven person in your paternal line is your grandfather, he is the progenitor for that line. When you can go back one more generation and prove who your great-grandfather is, he becomes the progenitor. Each of your lines has a progenitor.

A text-based descendant chart.

DESCENDANT CHART

```
George Nelson Marvin (1818 - 1904)
 └ Maryetta Hammond (1817 - 1889)
   ├ George W. Marvin (1840 - 1889)
   │ └ Julia ( ) ( - dec.)
   │   ├ Mary A. Marvin ( - dec.)
   │   ├ Edward H. Marvin ( - dec.)
   │   ├ Charles N. Marvin ( - dec.)
   │   ├ Ada E. Marvin ( - dec.)
   │   ├ Jesse D. Marvin ( - dec.)
   │   ├ Dora M. Marvin ( - dec.)
   │   └ Frank L. Marvin ( - BEF 1908)
   ├ Emma Marvin (1842 - 1917)
   │ └ Augustus C. Van Horne (1844 - 1924)
   │   └ Alfrieda Van Horne (1882 - 1924)
   ├ William Nelson Marvin (1844 - 1904)
   │ └ Diana Courll Drollinger (1857 - 1946)
   │   ├ Myrtle Olive Marvin (1879 - 1941)
   │   ├ Emma Grace Marvin (1882 - 1943)
   │   ├ Sylvanus Jay Marvin (1885 - 1947)
   │   ├ Ida May Marvin (1888 - 1963)
   │   ├ Etta Jane Marvin (1892 - 1893)
   │   ├ Sarah Bernice Marvin (1895 - 1981)
   │   └ William Manfred Marvin (1898 - 1909)
   └ Sylvanus Marvin (1845 - 1862)
```

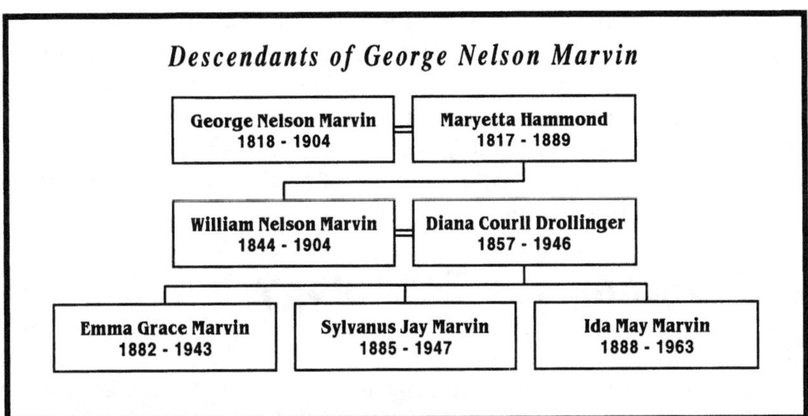

This is also a descendant chart, but it is graphical rather than text-based.

Drop Charts

A variation of the descendant chart is the *drop chart*. Sometimes called a box chart, the drop chart is a clear representation of one line of descent.

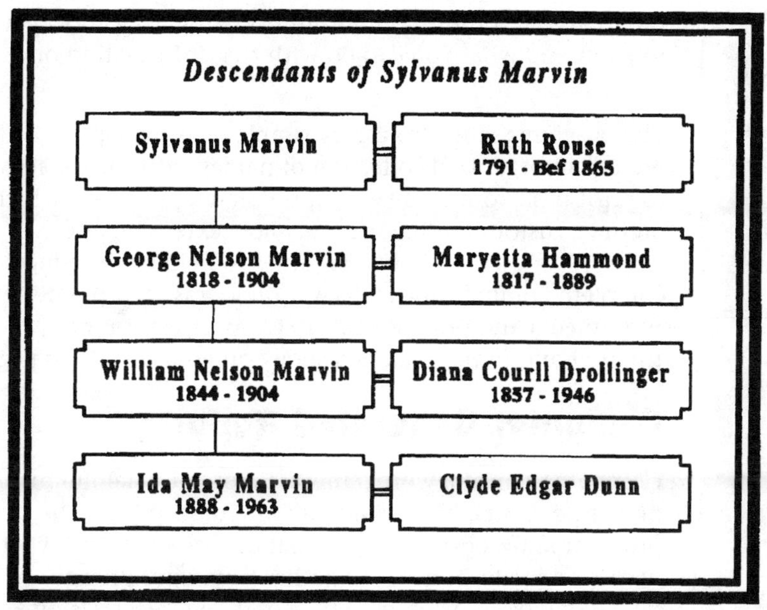

Direct descendant chart or drop chart.

Notice that the last three figures use individuals from the pedigree chart and the family group sheet (pictured earlier in this chapter) to illustrate the various ways to treat your genealogy information. The first is a descendant chart for individual number 4 on the pedigree chart. The next figure is a graphic descendant chart for this individual, one of his sons, and some of his grandchildren. The last figure in the group is a drop chart showing the direct line connection from individual number 8 on the pedigree chart to his great-granddaughter, number 1 on the pedigree chart.

Using Computer Programs for Genealogy Record Keeping

If you have a computer, consider using a computer genealogy program to manage your genealogy information. These programs give you great flexibility in compiling and analyzing your research, as well as making it easier to share data.

Genie Jargon

A **drop chart** connects two people generation-by-generation through their direct line. Starting with the ancestor, the chart then lists one child of the ancestor, say a son; then it lists one of the son's children, the ancestor's grandchild, and so on down the line. It does not include all the progenitor's descendants, only those in one direct line.

Pedigree Pitfalls

You should avoid computer genealogy programs that do not provide adequate space for source citations. Look for programs that advertise full documentation with complete sources for each piece of your information.

After entering the data into the computer once, you can arrange it in many ways. All the programs use a family group sheet format to keep track of your information, and all print pedigree charts. The differences in genealogy programs lie in the amount of information they allow you to enter and what you can do with that information once it is entered.

The programs range from very simple ones, which are merely an organized collection of names with the capacity to print basic forms, to very sophisticated programs, which produce customized reports and allow extensive research notes, footnotes, and bibliographies to help you produce complete family histories. Newer programs incorporate multimedia and provide tools to connect you to the Internet and to put your genealogy on your own Web page.

Computer-Generated Reports

Computer genealogy programs are especially helpful for preparing charts, both ascendant and descendant. The program knows from the information you enter just what names and dates it needs to gather from your lineage-linked database to compose the chart you select. Using a computer program makes it easy to print new, correctly numbered charts as you add newly found information.

Putting together a complete descendant chart by hand is tedious work. You must scour your files for all descendants, and group them by generations. This is a task well suited to computers. In moments the computer searches through all the material you entered and finds everyone connected to the person you designate as the starting individual. It then creates a descendant chart based on your preferences.

Having all your data in a computer program makes it easier to write research reports for yourself and to share information with others working on your lines. A good computer program allows you to enter everything you find. It provides space to write evaluations of your data and sources and space for remarks to yourself, such as "Check the 1850 census of Indiana to find sibling's family."

Computer Searching: What Do You Want to Know?

With a good computer program you can search your data for nearly anything. You can look for all individuals in your database born before 1900 in Grundy County, Illinois; get a list of every person in your database who had military service; or find the average age of marriage for all the females in your database. Just creating a list of all the marriages in your database can be helpful.

Many computer programs let you view your materials in many ways, making the work of connecting people much easier. You can search for patterns or interesting statistics: How many men died of heart disease before age 60? Find all the women in your database for whom you need maiden names. How many relatives share your birthday?

You can determine your relationship to everyone in your database. How are you related to all the individuals you've researched so far? (If you collect records on several hundred people, you will have difficulty figuring this out without a computer.)

Lineage Lessons

Most commercial programs have a built-in conversion program, so that if you switch to another genealogy program, you do not have to reenter your data. Look for GEDCOM-compatible (Genealogical Data Communications) programs. However, these conversions are not fail safe; you will have to carefully check your data for possible errors introduced during the conversion process.

Multimedia

Computer technology allows some sophisticated programs to store the photographs of your ancestors. All those charming photographs you have gathered, Aunt Lizzie on her first bicycle or Grandma tending her garden, can be stored on the computer and used to enhance your family histories.

Distant family members may not have seen the photos you can now incorporate into your genealogy. Pictures of the rude log cabin or the primitive sod house add immeasurably to descendants' understanding of what life was like in the early days of our country. Imagine the children's glee as they look at the very bushy eyebrows on third Great-Grandmother Harriet and discover the origin of their own eyebrows.

Some programs can incorporate audio clips with the material you gather. Grandpa recollecting his capture in the Battle of the Bulge or your cousins in Germany explaining the original pronunciation of your name add color to your family history.

Computer programs bundled with CD-ROMs of resources, indexes, or family trees are rapidly becoming available. Many of the lineages bundled with computer programs on CD-ROMs have no source citations, however. Though helpful as clues for further research, you'll need to research and document the information to be sure it is correct. The CD-ROMs that consist of indexes to official records or extracts of the information in those records (such as the Social Security Death Indexes) are the most useful. Although helpful in the research process, none of the CD-ROMs are substitutes for traditional research in libraries and repositories.

How to Find a Good Computer Program

If you are interested in buying a computer genealogy program, you can compare their features by reading *Genealogical Computing*, published quarterly, or the National Genealogical Society's *Computer Interest Digest*, published in the *NGS Newsletter* bimonthly. Many local genealogy societies have computer interest groups that meet regularly for demonstrations and discussions of various programs. You can read about available programs at the various genealogy sites on America Online, CompuServe, or Prodigy. Computer programs change constantly, so make your choice based on the latest information you can find.

Relative Resources

Following are some sources for charts and forms and periodicals with information on genealogy software:

Genealogical Computing. Salt Lake City, UT: Ancestry, Inc. Published quarterly. (P.O. Box 476, Salt Lake City, UT 84110-0476)

NGS Newsletter. Arlington, VA: National Genealogical Society. Published bimonthly. (4527 17th St. North, Arlington, VA 22207-2399)

Sources for Charts and Forms

American Genealogical Lending Library (AGLL), P.O. Box 329, Bountiful, UT 84011-0329

Ancestry, Inc., P.O. Box 476, Salt Lake City, UT 84110-0476

Everton Publishers, Inc., P.O. Box 368, Logan, UT 84321

Hearthstone Bookshop, 5735-A Telegraph Rd., Alexandria, VA 22303

The Least You Need to Know

- There are ascendant and descendant charts to assist in record keeping.
- A valuable chart for recording the whole family is the family group sheet.
- Charts and forms are tools to use in your research. They are not your finished genealogy.
- Computer programs allow you to generate reports in many ways.
- CD-ROMs bundled with computer programs are an aid to traditional research, not a substitute.

Part 2
Finding the Trail

By this time you are searching for the relatives you never knew. Part 2 will make a detective out of you, guiding you in techniques to find your kin.

So that you won't be led astray, you'll be introduced to the variations in the names you will be searching. Then, you'll head for the library and find a whole world that you didn't know existed.

You'll even take another look at your family's hometown, seeing it from a new perspective. Now the town is a hunting ground—a place where there are potential clues for you to follow. All you have to do is find them!

Chapter 5

Kissin' Kin: How to Find Them

In This Chapter

- The lost relatives
- How family associations and reunions can help
- Using the Social Security Death Index
- How you can use the Internet to find relatives

You learned in earlier chapters how to start your search with your own relatives. But what about those relatives with whom you have lost touch? Now you are going to get a chance to do some digging. To do so, you'll need to learn about a few records. If you have a bit of detective in you, get it working. Start with:

- Telephone listings
- Libraries
- Newspapers
- Queries (published inquiries about the family)
- Family associations
- Family reunions
- Social security
- Internet forums

Ma Bell Comes to the Rescue

Your local library's reference department may have a collection of current telephone directories covering the whole United States, or at least a few states. List the relatives who may still be living, and spend an evening at the library. If you cannot find the specific person you're searching for, list all those by the surname in the area you believe the person lived if the list is not too lengthy. For common names such as Smith or Jones you'll need to narrow the list by looking for familiar family given names. Prepare a letter giving some details of your family and your purpose. Send it to each. If the phone book does not provide the ZIP codes for the addresses, check the library while you are there for their ZIP code directory. You can also obtain the ZIP codes through the Web site http://www.usps.gov/ncsc/lookups/lookup_zip+4.html. Look for other Web sites or services that provide names and addresses (including ZIPs). Some provide it at no cost; others have a fee.

If your library does not have an extensive collection of telephone books, inquire at the local telephone company. They may maintain an archive.

Tree Tips
If you do not have your own computer or CD-ROM drive, your library may have one that is available for public use.

Several commercial companies have issued CD-ROMs of residential and business telephone numbers. Their databases vary, but they are collected from a variety of sources such as utility companies, mail-order houses, voter registers, and telephone books. The margin of error is great; people move often, and the lists are quickly outdated. Nonetheless, they are valuable. Some can be searched quickly by name, area code, state, address, or a combination of parameters.

Your state or city library or historical society might have a collection of old telephone directories for selected areas. The series is rarely complete, but it will help. When the listing disappears from the directory, it could signify death or removal from the area.

In recent years the absence of the names cannot be easily interpreted, for the parties may choose to keep their number unlisted.

After obtaining the address of a possible relative, resist the temptation to pick up the telephone. A letter can assure them you are related, and may elicit more information than a surprise call. If you don't get a response, follow the letter with a telephone call. Your letter will have introduced you and your purpose.

The lack of a response to a letter does not necessarily indicate disinterest. Your relative may hate to write. Your initial letter will serve its purpose in introducing you, however.

Consult Your Local Library

The local library's holdings depend upon the size of the area. Although they may be too small to have books that would directly pertain to genealogy (see Chapter 7, "Getting the

Most from Libraries"), they will no doubt have a number of traditional reference books that will be useful. Check the reference section: Besides the telephone books already mentioned, look for other types of directories that could prove useful in your search.

City Directories

Become acquainted with city directories, found in your library's reference section. You will use these extensively, in a variety of ways, as your research techniques develop.

Although city directories are very useful for tracing the earlier generations of your family, for now you'll use them to help locate those who are living. Directories list the residents alphabetically and often include a cross reference by street address. This provides the names of neighbors. If the neighbors still live there, they may have known your family. If they were close friends, they may even have kept in touch and might provide you with current addresses.

> **Genie Jargon**
> SASE (or S.A.S.E.) is a Self Addressed Stamped Envelope. Due to cost, many organizations (and individuals) will not answer inquiries if one is not provided.

Many larger cities have now changed the format of their directories. They continue to provide a listing by street (called a householder's index), but they have eliminated the alphabetical name listing. Instead, they usually provide a cross index by telephone number. Although some towns still retain the old style alphabetical format, you will lose that aid to your research in many areas.

Write to the library of the town or city where you believe your family lived. Ask them to search the current issue or to photocopy the pages with the surname or street you are seeking. Offer to pay the costs, and enclose an *SASE.*

To obtain the addresses of libraries to which you can write, contact the reference librarian at your local library and ask him to check the *American Library Directory*.

Elizabeth Petty Bentley's *The Genealogist's Address Book* can assist with addresses too, although the libraries listed in that source are only those with genealogical holdings. Many of the small town local libraries are not included.

> **Pedigree Pitfalls**
> Never send a notice with writing on both sides because it cannot be properly displayed. Be sure it includes your name and address. (Your phone number is optional.)

Post It

In determining ways in which you might find your lost relatives, consider the library bulletin board. The librarian may be willing to post a notice. Mention that your research is for genealogy and enclose a separate notice for posting. Keep it brief, but give enough details to identify the family you are seeking.

Ask the librarian if the library maintains files of letters from people who have written the library for information. A letter from your second cousin, also interested in genealogy, could be in that file, waiting for you to find it!

Sign In, Please

Visitor registers are popular in the genealogy section of the library. A bound volume (or loose leaf, or even 3 × 5 cards) is placed prominently for visitors to enter their names and addresses and the surnames of their interest. The librarian may be willing to search it for others who are searching the same names you are researching.

If you are visiting any facility with a guest register (courthouse, museum, library, historical attraction), take a few minutes to add your name. It can reward you with a letter or telephone call from a distant relative.

The Hometown News

To locate living relatives, consider subscribing to the hometown paper. You will be amazed at the leads it can provide, particularly if it is a small community. Watch for family names in the social news, school news, church news, and even the advertisements. All will be of interest and might eventually lead to contact with relatives.

Don't overlook obituaries, particularly the part about "the survivors include...." It is common to include brothers, sisters, aunts, uncles, and children, and often their city of residence. This will help immensely.

Also try a "Letter to the Editor" of the hometown newspaper. This is especially successful in smaller communities. Make your letter brief but show clearly that it is a family local to their area, and that your interest is for genealogy.

Sample of Letter to the Editor for inquiring to the newspaper about living relatives.

> Dear Editor,
>
> My great-uncle John Jackson died 15 September 1925 in your town. At that time his obituary stated that he left two sons, Joseph and George, and a daughter Mary Jefferson. I am interested in contacting them as we are compiling our family genealogy. Can some of your readers put me in touch with them?
>
> Thank you for your help.
>
> Sincerely,
>
> [Your name and address here.]

If all else fails, don't overlook the use of the classified section. An advertisement under "Personals" may be seen by those who know your family. Give a few details so the family can be quickly identified; ask to reach your relatives. Mention your interest in genealogy.

After School: Alumni Records

Does someone remember that cousin Harry was a graduate of the state college? His brother attended Harvard? Check the telephone directories or city directories for schools, as well as the various college directories on your library's reference shelves. Address your letter to the attention of the Alumni Director. The school may have alumni records with an address. Some periodically publish alumni directories. Local schools may be willing to give information too, especially if they've known the family for a long time.

Literature on school reunions may help; the newsletter after the event could include your relative's new location.

The Genealogical Societies

When you have determined in which county your relatives lived, obtain the name of the county's genealogical society. There are a number of directories that could assist. *The Genealogical Helper* publishes annually, in their July–August issue, a list of genealogical societies. Some societies are listed in Everton's *The Handy Book for Genealogists*; *Ancestry's Redbook*, or Ancestry's *The Source*; Elizabeth Petty Bentley's *The Genealogist's Address Book*; and a variety of other publications. Examine these publications for addresses of societies in other areas.

Consider joining the genealogical society in the county in which your relatives lived. As a member of that society, you will have privileges. You may find an interested volunteer who will assist you. If the organization publishes a newsletter, ask them to publish a notice in their *query section*. One of your relatives may even be a member of the society. Many societies solicit family charts from members. Ask if they will search those charts for others working on your family names.

Genie Jargon
A **query section** in a genealogical publication refers to a specific section of the magazine set aside for submitted inquiries. Almost all periodicals have such sections, as do some newspapers that carry genealogy columns. They may limit the length, or have other restrictions.

Periodicals Galore

Thousands of genealogical periodicals are published each year in the United States. In addition to those in the county you are researching, place queries in those that are published statewide or nationwide. Inquire about cost and whether they require membership or subscription to use that service. Make some choices depending upon your budget. Mention enough about the family so that readers can identify them.

Sample of query to submit for publication in genealogical periodicals.

> Seeking descendants of John Masters
>
> b. 15 April 1858 in Monroe Co., NY, m. there in 1888 to Mary Adams. They moved about 1910 to Perry County, IL and had 3 ch., John b. 1912, Joseph b. 1915, and Agatha b. 1918 (who m. John Davis). Wish to contact descendants.

Genie Jargon

"**b.**" is used for born, "**m.**" for married, and "**ch.**" for children. These are standard abbreviations used in queries to reduce space. See Appendix C for other abbreviations commonly used.

A number of national journals are connected to a society and are part of the society's membership benefits. These include The New England Historical and Genealogical Society's *Register (NEHGR)*, The National Genealogical Society's *Newsletter,* The New York Genealogical and Biographical Society's *New York Genealogical and Biographical Record (NYGBR)*, and others.

Some national periodicals are subscription only, that is, not associated with a society. Three that have query sections are *Everton's Genealogical Helper* (the largest), *Reunions Magazine,* and *Heritage Quest.* Some subscription journals focus on articles but do accept a limited number of queries from members. *The American Genealogist* (known as *TAG*) is among them.

Families That Stay Together

A valuable resource in your effort to locate relatives is a family association dedicated to the particular family name you're researching. These operate under a variety of names—society, clearinghouse, or others. Their purpose is to collect information on the family. They may publish a newsletter, maintain a database for researchers, or offer search services. They are eager to hear from descendants. They may be able to supply the addresses of others in your family. If they publish a magazine, ask them to insert a query.

There are thousands of family associations, but many are short-lived. Others are so ill-manned that they often do not reply. But there are also many hundreds who maintain extensive archives and are eager to assist. Do not let the lack of a reply from one group influence your decision to contact another. They often have valuable records and sometimes are the only source for a particular photograph, a family Bible, or an old letter.

Locating a Family Association

Although there are some directories listing groups, none are complete. Try the March–April annual issue of *Everton's Genealogical Helper.* Two directories are included in that issue: "Family Associations and Their Leaders" (for those who paid for the listing), and "Family Periodical Publications." The latter includes only those who submitted a copy of their publication during the year, so it is not complete. It is, however, current because listings are not included without such a submission.

Elizabeth Petty Bentley compiled a useful *Directory of Family Associations*. The disadvantage in using Bentley's *Directory*, is that it includes many organizations no longer in existence, and in some instances, individuals who collect a name but who are not family associations. Despite this drawback, it can be helpful.

Tree Tips
If you have difficulty locating an association, insert a query in a national periodical inquiring whether an association for that surname exists.

A Rose Is a Rose Is a Rose

In using the resources of a family association, an understanding of their focus is important. They differ considerably. They may include descendants of an ancestor who is not the immigrant, descendants of the immigrant, or descendants of the surname.

Those focused on the descendants of an ancestor who is not the immigrant, for example, may include all the descendants of the great-grandfather and his wife who settled in Des Moines, Iowa. In this case the association is probably named after that couple. Those devoted to descendants of an immigrant carry the surname in their title and include all the male and female descendants of that immigrant. In the third type, the surname organization, anyone bearing the surname is traced. They may have no relationship to each other. Members do not have to bear the surname, but have in common that each trace someone carrying that surname.

Even surname organizations have differences. One may search all of the surname in the United States, regardless of nationality. Another may focus on an ethnic group, such as those of Scottish ancestry or those of German ancestry.

Upon ascertaining the existence of a family organization, write to them. Be specific in your request. Identify the family briefly (names, dates, locations, spouses, children), and ask if they can put you in contact with members of that family. Inquire also about queries.

Tree Tips
Although most family associations do not require your membership to be of assistance, ask for a copy of their membership brochure. You may find it beneficial, depending upon their goals and services, to join the group.

We'll Meet on the 4th Sunday...

Thousands of families hold family reunions each year; these range from a picnic in the park to a major gathering in a large hotel. Watch for announcements in genealogical publications. No magazine includes all the reunions, only those for which they have received an announcement. Try to attend if possible. The contacts you make will evolve into wonderful friendships, and you will hear many stories you have yearned to know.

The reunion might be small, organized by a local branch, or it could be nationwide, involving hundreds of descendants. Some even plan overseas trips to the ancestral home.

Using Social Security to Find Your Kin

In 1935 the Social Security Act was enacted. It generated an enormous amount of paper records, some of which can be used to locate your relatives.

The Death Index

One especially useful resource is the Social Security Death Index, available on CD-ROM. It does have limitations. It does not include all those who died with a social security number, only those whose deaths were reported to the Social Security Administration. Usually this occurred when the family applied for a benefit at the death of their relative. If the death was not reported to the Social Security Administration, the individual is not listed in this database.

> **Pedigree Pitfalls**
> Although some of the CD-ROMs are titled "Social Security Death Index," the database includes deaths that were *reported,* whether or not survivors actually received benefits.

Most of the deaths included in this database occurred after 1962, when the Social Security Administration started keeping this information on their computer.

The information contained usually includes:

- Social Security number
- Name (last and first)
- Birth date
- Death date
- Issuing location of the original card (by code)
- ZIP code of last known residence
- ZIP code of recipient if a lump sum payment was made

Locating an entry on the Social Security Death Index can help find living relatives. For example, follow up on the date of death provided by obtaining the death certificate. The death certificate can in turn lead you to living relatives by providing the place of death and the name of the informant who may be related.

Lineage Lessons

A small fee ($7.00 at present) is possible to get a microprint of a deceased person's social security application. The microprint will supply the birth date and place of the applicant and name of parents. This would not help in finding living relatives, because only applications of deceased persons can be obtained. It can, however, be tremendously helpful in tracing the family. Provide the social security number of the deceased, proof of death (such as a death certificate), and the required fee, and mail to: Freedom of Information Officer, Social Security Administration, 6401 Security Blvd., Baltimore, MD 21234.

The Internet: Finding Cousin John

There is an explosion of activity on the Internet that can help the genealogist. Many *forums* (usually connected with services such as CompuServe and America Online) are available in which users can post a notice of interest in certain families. Others can respond. If you are on the Internet, use these forums to seek relatives. Some report astounding results, locating lost branches of their family they had never expected to find.

As always, be specific. Asking to locate the relatives of "The Taylor family who lived in central Ohio" is too brief. It will be ignored, or will bring overwhelming responses asking for clarification. Inquire instead with precise details.

Use of extensive abbreviations in posting notices on the Internet is acceptable, but be sure you don't sacrifice readability. You want everyone to understand. See Appendix C for acceptable abbreviations.

Genie Jargon

A **forum** on the Internet is an electronic meeting place where messages can be exchanged.

Not the End of the Tale

As your search progresses, you will constantly discover new ways in which you might locate living relatives. A letter written by a descendant may be part of the military pension file in the National Archives, and provide you with a location of family members. The state may maintain a statewide property index, and allow its search. The voter registers may be open to the public. The possibilities are endless. You will be thrilled when your scouting turns up the people you have been seeking. Every success will energize you, and will make you understand the satisfaction of following clues. You're now on your way to the same addiction afflicting the rest of us!

Relative Resources

American Library Directory 1996–97. 49th ed. New Providence, NJ: R. R. Bowker Co. Vol. 1 & 2.

Bentley, Elizabeth Petty. *Directory of Family Associations*. Baltimore, MD: Gene. Publ. Co. 1993–4 ed.

———. *The Genealogist's Address Book*. 3rd ed. Baltimore, MD: Gene. Publ. Co., 1995.

Eicholz, Alice, Ph.D., CG. *Ancestry's Redbook*. Revised ed. Salt Lake City, UT: Ancestry, 1991.

Handy Book for Genealogists, The. 8th ed. Logan, UT: Everton Publ., 1991.

Szucs, Loretto Dennis and Sandra Hargreaves Luebking. *The Source: A Guidebook of American Genealogy*. Revised ed. Salt Lake City, UT: Ancestry, 1997.

Addresses

American Genealogist, The. [TAG]. Demorest, GA.: priv. publ. Published quarterly. [P.O. Box 398, Demorest, GA 30535-0398.]

Everton's Genealogical Helper. Logan, UT: Everton Published bi-monthly. [P.O. Box 368, Logan, UT 84323-0368.]

Heritage Quest. Bountiful, UT: AGLL, Inc. Published bi-monthly. [P.O. Box 329, Bountiful, UT 84011-40329.]

National Genealogical Society Quarterly. [NGSQ]. Arlington, VA: Natl. Gene. Soc. Published quarterly. [4527 Seventeenth Street North, Arlington, VA 22207-2399.]

New England Historical and Genealogical Society Register, The. [NEHGR]. Boston, MA: New England Historic Genealogical Society. Published quarterly. [101 Newbury St., Boston, MA 02116.]

New York Genealogical and Biographical Record, The. [NYGBR]. New York, NY: New York Genealogical and Biographical Society. Published quarterly. [122 East 58th St., New York, NY 10022-1939.]

Reunions Magazine. Milwaukee, WI.: Reunions Mag. Published quarterly. [P.O. Box 11727, Milwaukee, WI 53211-0727.]

Social Security Administration, Freedom of Information Officer, 6401 Security Blvd., Baltimore, MD 21234. [Microprint of Social Security application of a deceased person.]

The Least You Need to Know

- Your library has telephone directories, city directories, and other items to help search for your living relatives.
- Your hometown newspaper can assist in the search.
- Use the genealogical societies and family associations, which can help locate living relatives.
- The voluminous social security records are a wonderful source of information.

Chapter 6

A Rose by Any Other Name…

In This Chapter

- Surnames change through time
- Changes—deliberate and accidental
- Spelling variants
- Handwriting complications
- Naming patterns

Surnames evolved to help distinguish one person from another. They were descriptive of relationships such as Thomasson (Thomas's son); of physical characteristics such as Petit (small) and Schoen (beautiful); of place names (Hill, Lea, Meadow); or of occupations (Carpenter, Hunter, Miller). Many of us are known by surnames that would surprise our immigrant ancestors. Surnames are not static through time, nor are they necessarily the same for an individual throughout a lifetime.

The spelling of names is phonetic, and the way the letters were arranged depended on the person writing the name. Most of us descend from people who were illiterate. Our ancestors couldn't write and didn't know how their names were spelled. They only knew how to pronounce their names as spoken by their families and neighbors.

Variations Aplenty

Outside influences, unusual events, naming patterns, spelling variations, and misinterpretations by transcribers determined the surnames of our ancestors. Before searching for documents, consider that your ancestors' names may be different from what you were led to believe. The same surnames may be spelled so many different ways as to be unrecognizable by someone trying to trace the line. For example, in the following figure, each of these surnames was used by at least 100 people at the time of the census.

Examples of name variations found in the first United States federal census, 1790. Taken from A Century of Population Growth.

Fitzgerald, Fichgerrel, Fitchgearald, Fitchgerrel, Fitsgarrel, Fitsgerald, Fitsgerel, Fitsgorrel, Fitsjarald, Fitsjerald, Fitts Gerald, Fitzarrell, Fitzgarald, Fitzgarrold, Fitzgearld, Fitzgeral, Fitz Gerald, Fitzgerrald, Fitz Gerrald, Fitzgerrel, Fitzgerrold, Fitzjairald, Fitzjarald, Fitzjerald

Rawlings, Raling, Rallins, Raulens, Raulings, Rawlins, Rollens, Rollin, Rolling, Rollings, Rollins

Sinclair, Saintclair, St. Clair, St. Clear, St. Clere, Senkler, Sinekler, Sinclar, Sinclare, Sinclares, Sinclear, Sincleer, Sincler, Sinclere, Sinclier, Singclair, Sinklar, Sinklear, Sinkler

Ministers, recording clerks, ship captains, and census takers wrote what they thought they heard. And what they heard was based on their knowledge and background. Language and spelling were not standardized even among the educated. Many times a name was spelled several different ways in the same document.

Handwriting Further Obscures the Names

Tree Tips
Sometimes looking at other documents or entries written in the same hand makes the letters easier to read. Comparing the names in the county as written by two different people, say the county clerk and the tax assessor, may clear up problems.

Letter formation often leads to difficulties in reading and interpreting surnames. Flourishes and curlicues can render letters nearly indecipherable. The letters I and J sometimes look very similar. A poorly written G can resemble an S. The letters R and K are often written similarly, and a capital B that is not closed at the bottom can be mistaken for an R. Other letters can be confused: M and N; N and H; V and U.

Indexers had difficulty interpreting the letters too, so the name you are looking for may be alphabetized under the wrong letter. If you don't find Seemon in the "S" section, look under "L."

Immigrating Changed Lives and Sometimes Names

Immigrants changed their names by accident or by design. Other languages had letter combinations not found in English, or letters pronounced as other letters in the English language. *F* sounded like *V*, so Freer was written Veer. *W* sounded like *V*, so Werner was listed as Verner. A guttural pronunciation made *G* sound like *K*. Letters were slurred, an *H* dropped. *Sch* sounded like *Sh*, so the *c* disappeared.

Finding It by Pronunciation

According to the 1850 census, Diana Drollinger's grandfather was born in North Carolina about 1800. A search of the North Carolina census and other records turned up no Drollinger/Drolinger/Drullinger families. Although census information is sometimes incorrect, other sources also suggested a North Carolina birthplace. The key to the puzzle was in the microfilmed pension records at the National Archives. Henry Drollinger states in his pension deposition that his name was Drollinger, pronounced Trollinger in the German style. A check of North Carolina records for Trollingers uncovered numerous families, and eventually, Diana's great-grandparents.

The Wish to "Sound American"

Occasionally, the immigrant shortened or changed his name, but more often, the children of these immigrants Anglicized their names to better assimilate: Petrasovich became Preston; Noblinski became Noble; Savitch became Savage; Madsen became Madison.

Sometimes finding their names "different," immigrants chose to translate their names to the English equivalents. Blau and Bleu became Blue; Weiss, Blanc, and Bianco all became White. Occupational names were changed with Schmidts becoming Smiths and Küfers becoming Coopers.

If you are unfamiliar with the language of the immigrant, look for a dictionary that has both the foreign language and English. Perhaps the foreign language equivalent for the surname will be the one you need to further your research. Knowing that "Weaver" translates to "Weber" in German may be just the clue you need to find an earlier generation.

A wish to disassociate from "foreigners" made some families make the change. In Pennsylvania, Frank Nicotera felt the pressure of his Italian name. When he married a Collins, he registered at the union hall as Frank Collins. When his little brother was ready to go to work, Frank took him to the union hall where everyone assumed he was Nick Collins, not Angelo Nicotera. The family today goes by the name Collins. The grandchildren are unaware that the family's surname was Nicotera only three generations ago.

The following sample Declaration of Intention is an example of the name changes that often happened. The subject was born 20 October 1892 in Casal Velino, province of Salerno, Italy, according to his birth certificate, which names him as Florigio Cicerelli. He first immigrated (under that spelling) in 1910 with his father Saverio on the *USS Berlin*, arriving in New York City with a destination of San Jose, California. Returning to Italy, he was married under that spelling in 1922 to Carmela Spagnuola. When Florigio returned in 1930 from his fourth and final trip to Italy, the Arrival Certificate in New York shows him as Cicierelli. Three years later, when he filed to become a citizen, his name is shown as Ciciarelli. In the meantime, he also had adopted the more American sounding "Frank," and was known throughout the rest of his life as Frank Ciciarelli. His children's names bore that spelling, too. Similar changes occurred in thousands of families.

A Declaration of Intention form filed in 1933.

TRIPLICATE (To be given to declarant) No. 5135

UNITED STATES OF AMERICA

DECLARATION OF INTENTION

(Invalid for all purposes seven years after the date hereof)

State of California } ss: In the Superior Court
County of Santa Clara } of California at San Jose, Calif.

I, Florigio Ciciarelli (Full, true name, without abbreviation, and any other name which has been used, must appear here)
now residing at Route 2, Box 5, Los Gatos, Santa Clara, California (Number and street) (City or town) (County) (State)
occupation Barber, aged 40 years, do declare on oath that my personal description is:
Sex Male, color White, complexion Medium, color of eyes Blue
color of hair Brown, height 5 feet 8 inches; weight 165 pounds; visible distinctive marks
None
race Italian, North; nationality Italian
I was born in Casal Velino, Italy (City or town) (Country), on October 22, 1892 (Month) (Day) (Year)
I am - married. The name of my wife or husband is Carmela Ciciarelli
we were married on Oct. 2, 1923 (Month) (Day) (Year), at Casal Velino, Italy (City or town) (State or country); she or he was born at Casal Velino, Italy (City or town) (State or country), on July 17, 1900 (Month) (Day) (Year), entered the United States at New York, N. Y. (City or town) (State), on Jan. 16, 1930 (Month) (Day) (Year), for permanent residence therein, and now resides at Los Gatos, California (City or town) (State or country). I have two children, and the name, date and place of birth, and place of residence of each of said children are as follows: Ranato, born Dec. 7, 1929, at Naples, Italy; and Angela, born Apr. 27, 1932, at Los Gatos, Calif.; both residing at Los Gatos, California.

I have - heretofore made a declaration of intention: Number -, on Aug. 3, 1923 (Date)
at San Francisco, California, (City or town) (State) in the U. S. District Court. (Name of court)
my last foreign residence was Casal Velino, Italy. (City or town) (Country)
I emigrated to the United States of America from Naples, Italy (City or town) (Country)
my lawful entry for permanent residence in the United States was at New York, N. Y. (City or town) (State)
under the name of Florigio Ciciarelli, on August 23, 1910 (Month) (Day) (Year)
on the vessel Berlin (If other than by vessel, state manner of arrival)

I will, before being admitted to citizenship, renounce forever all allegiance and fidelity to any foreign prince, potentate, state, or sovereignty, and particularly, by name, to the prince, potentate, state, or sovereignty of which I may be at the time of admission a citizen or subject; I am not an anarchist; I am not a polygamist nor a believer in the practice of polygamy; and it is my intention in good faith to become a citizen of the United States of America and to reside permanently therein; and I certify that the photograph affixed to the duplicate and triplicate hereof is a likeness of me: So HELP ME GOD.

Florigio Ciciarelli

Florigio Ciciarelli (Original signature of declarant without abbreviation, also alias, if used)

Subscribed and sworn to before me in the office of the Clerk of said Court, at San Jose, Calif. this 7th day of August anno Domini 33. Certification No. 22-12153 from the Commissioner of Naturalization showing the lawful entry of the declarant for permanent residence on the date stated above, has been received by me. The photograph affixed to the duplicate and triplicate hereof is a likeness of the declarant.

Henry A. Pfister
[SEAL] Clerk of the Superior Court.
By R. Korleil, Deputy Clerk.
14—2023

Form 2202—L-A
U. S. DEPARTMENT OF LABOR
NATURALIZATION SERVICE

Families make unpredictable decisions that cause research problems for genealogists. Letters are added or dropped. Perhaps the name had a prefix that was later dropped: St. Martin became Martin; Van Hoorn became Horn. A generation later, someone chose to reinstate the suffix. One branch of the family may decide the name would be more aristocratic with a slight change. Even simple names are changed. Names abound where an "e" is added or removed: Brown/Browne, Green/Greene, Germaine/Germain, Low/ Lowe.

Lineage Lessons

There are families in which brothers have different surnames though they have the same father. One has decided to keep the old spelling, while the others have adopted a new spelling.

This can lead to two branches of the same family having very different surnames. In another case, a divorce in New York City in the 1820s resulted in the wife resuming her maiden name and her younger children taking that name, while the adult children retained the father's name.

Talk to Yourself

You may need to be creative to find other spellings of the surnames you are tracing. Think of the many ways a name could be pronounced and then think of the spellings. Say the surnames out loud and spell them phonetically. Look for records under any of those spellings. Could Stone be spelled Stoan? Charette could mutate to Shorett, Cayeaux to Coyer. To help you think of the spelling variants, examine the compilation of names from the 1790 census mentioned above. As you speak the names, you may get new ideas on how to spell the surnames you are researching.

Tree Tips
Ask your friends and associates how they would spell the surname you are tracing, based on its pronunciation. Ask children, who are much more phonetic and unbiased than adults. You may come up with some new ideas on variant spellings.

Names were often corrupted as immigrants interacted with their neighbors. Perhaps the individual giving information to the census taker was not your ancestor, but a neighbor who happened to be home when your ancestor wasn't. The census taker took the information the neighbor gave rather than revisiting your ancestor. And so Mr. Justice became Mr. Justis or Jean Christien became John Christian.

Pedigree Pitfalls
Never assume that the surname you are researching has stayed the same through the generations or even through a lifetime. How many times have you had to correct the spelling of your own name? Perhaps some of the misspellings will survive to someday confuse your descendants.

Different Record, Different Spelling

The name might undergo several transformations before it takes the familiar form you know. When the immigrant Weir/Weer accumulated enough money to buy a house, he recorded the deed in the county clerk's office where he became Wiere. Weir/Weer/Wiere moved West, bought some land, and this time the clerk wrote Wear. Meanwhile, his account at the general store was under the name Ware, and that's the name the children learned to write when taught by the 18-year-old schoolmarm. So your grandfather is George Ware, but his grandfather was Samuel Weir.

Naming Patterns

Patronymics were widely used in forming surnames. This was used to sort out the individuals in a community, such as Richard's son or Thomas's son.

Genie Jargon
Patronymics are names derived from a father's name or paternal side of the family. For example, if your father was named "Tom," your surname might end up "Tom's Son" or "Tomson," which in turn might turn into "Thompson."

Patronymics were particularly prevalent in the Scandinavian countries. At first it seems confusing to know that Mr. Jensen's sons all have the surname Ericssen. But as soon as you know that the surname is formed by adding *sen/son* to the first name, you can see how Eric Jensen's sons came to have the surname Ericssen. Daughters would have *datter* added to the father's first name, thus Eric Jensen's daughters would use Ericsdatter as their surname.

Other countries used the son suffix also, Williamson, Jameson, (also expressed as just Williams or James), but did not change the surname with every generation.

Other prefixes and suffixes were used to denote sons or daughters, among them, *O*, *Ab* or *Ap*; *Mac* or *Mc; Fitz, ich* or *itch; ev,* or *off*. The resulting names were sometimes altered with O'Brien becoming Obrien or Bryan, Ab Owen abridged to Bowen.

Religious Naming Customs

In some religions, it is customary to name children for dead relatives in a specific order. In other religions, it is the custom to name the first boy for the maternal grandfather and the first girl for the paternal grandmother. In others, it is the custom to name the first boy after his paternal grandfather and the first girl after her maternal grandmother.

Individual Naming Patterns

Some families devise a naming pattern of their own that persists for several generations. The first male in every family is named Henry, perhaps, or James. Each generation perpetuates the tradition. When there are 3 or 4 first cousins all named William Smith, it can be difficult to sort them out, especially if all remain in the area throughout their lives. It may also be the family custom to name a child the same name as an older sibling who died in infancy.

Tree Tips
When working on a family you know to be a specific religion or nationality, learn the naming patterns common to that group.

Mother's Name Preserved

A mother's maiden name is frequently used as a middle name for either boys or girls. Other family surnames are used as well. Clark Stone Phillip's middle name is his paternal grandmother's maiden name. Mary Catherine Smith may be shown as Mary C. Smith in a record, but when she married John Jordan, she may be shown as Mary Smith Jordan, or Mary S. Jordan.

Pedigree Pitfalls
Never assume you have the correct person if there are two or more individuals in the same area with the same name. It is necessary to gather the facts for each event they are connected to and make comparisons.

If your ancestors were creative, you may have to be creative.

Strange things happen in genealogy. A contemporary family has two girls and two boys. The boys carry their mother's maiden name as their surname because the mother is from a family with no boys and she wants the name to be carried on. The girls have their father's surname.

Pedigree Pitfalls
Don't assume that a child's surname-sounding middle name is a surname in your direct line. I once found a child whose name was Diana Courll Drollinger. Courll was not Diana's mother's maiden name, as originally thought. Instead, she was named for her married aunt: Diana Drollinger Courll.

Given Names Give Us Trouble

It is not only surname variations that befuddle us, but first names also. Is Katharine Shimmin the same person as Catherine Shimmin? This name could also be spelled Kathryn. First names could also be Anglicized. Katharine may have been Katrina or Katja or Catherina, Katrintje, or Tryntje.

Five Children, Same First Name!

German children often had two given names, but were called by the second. Frequently, all the boys in the family had the same first name, or a variation of the same name, such

Pedigree Pitfalls
Many family names, Reese, Morgan, Lawson among them, may be used as first names, and provide clues to the surnames in a line. However, sometimes a name is chosen because it sounds good, or is the name of a good friend, although it has no history within the family.

as Johann/Hans, but were called by their second names. And the girls in the family might all have the first name Anna or Maria. The children may be referred to with both names or just the second. Different documents may use different names for the same child. You will wonder if you are dealing with one person or three, as you sort out Maria Elizabeth, Maria Christena, and Maria Caterina. This can be further confused by an adult returning to his first given name after being known by his second as a child.

Today parents-to-be thumb through books of names looking for ideas for the baby's name. Although there have always been trends in first names, your ancestors didn't rely on book lists. They thumbed through the Bible, or they named their children for friends and relatives or famous people. Hundreds of boys went through life carrying the first and middle name of George Washington or Benjamin Franklin.

The romance of the West inspired parents in the naming of their children. The little girl Sierra Nevada is enumerated as Nevada one time, Sierra another, and on her marriage license, she is Vada. As far as can be determined, her parents were never west of Indiana.

He Was Called Billy; She Was Called Abby

Pedigree Pitfalls
Don't assume that because your ancestor carried the same name as a famous person you are connected to that famous person. The name may only reflect the hero worship of the time.

Nicknames can throw you off the trail. If you always knew your great-aunt as Polly, you may be surprised to find her name was really Mary. The Sally in a will may be the Sarah on a deed. William could be Bill, Billy, Will, or Willie. Bert can be a shortened form of Albert, Gilbert, Robert, and others.

Finding the name that the nickname stood for is not always obvious. This is especially true when the nickname is encompassed within a name, such as Gus for Augustus, Gum for Montgomery, or Fate for Lafayette. You may need to do some reading to know what names to look for.

Tree Tips
A good reference for nicknames is *Nicknames Past and Present*. It includes cross references by given names and nicknames.

Double Trouble

It has been said that everyone has a double, someone else in the world who looks just like him. The same thing is true of names. In a recent election, a man who had voted regularly since 1979 was cut from the rolls. John P. Taylor called the Registrar of Voters and found he had been cut because he was listed at two different addresses. The computer matched the John P. Taylors' month, day, and year of birth, found them to be the same, and deleted one from the rolls. But there were actually two different John P. Taylors with the exact same birth date; one was John Paul and one was John Phillip, but they had both registered as John P.

Almost no one has a unique name. Names that are no longer common seem exotic to us, and we think the individuals will be simple to isolate. You may think that Tryphena Atherton should be easy to identify because, to you, the name is unusual. Early Vermont records have several Tryphena Athertons. You may think that the common name of Davis pared with Caleb is unique. In that case, you would be surprised to learn there are at least four Caleb Davises on the 1840 census in New York.

Your ancestors went by many names, just as we do today. Some have different names at different stages of their lives. Some women change their names when they marry; some do not. Siblings may spell their surnames differently. In some families, one woman may hyphenate her maiden and married names, while others may not.

Which Do You Pick?

When you begin to do genealogy research, you have the option of tracing any one of numerous surnames. How do you choose the one you want to work on? For many, this is a personal decision; for others, it is a matter of practicality. I began working on my maiden name because my father would never talk about his family, and I was very curious as to who they were. As I began to gather information from many family sources, I became interested in other lines because I had more information and a better chance of success.

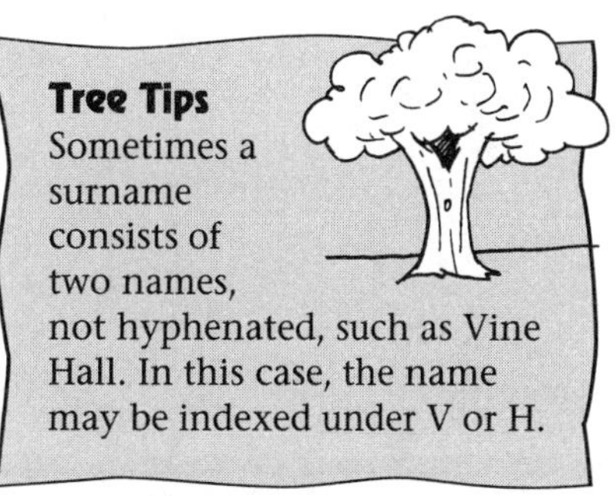

Tree Tips
Sometimes a surname consists of two names, not hyphenated, such as Vine Hall. In this case, the name may be indexed under V or H.

Some may choose a surname to follow because of a family tradition connected with it: "Our family is related to Kit Carson." "Our family is connected to President McKinley." Maybe you have a desire to prove you are a Mayflower descendant, or the descendant of a Revolutionary War patriot. Maybe you seek admission to the Sons of the Republic of Texas. Perhaps you are eager to prove that you are a descendant of a Native American, a French trapper, or are eligible for a pioneer descendant certificate offered by many states.

Whatever surname you decide to pursue, one of the first things to do is consider the different ways the name could be spelled.

Relative Resources

Century of Population Growth: From the First Census of the United States to the Twelfth 1790–1900. Reprint. Orting, Wash.: Heritage Quest Press, 1989. orig. printed Washington, D.C., U.S. Government Printing Office, 1900.

Rose, Christine. *Nicknames Past and Present.* 2nd edition. San Jose, Calif.: Privately printed, 1995.

The Least You Need to Know

- Names could be spelled in a variety of ways.
- Ancestors may have translated their foreign name, or shortened it.
- Different branches could be using different variations of a surname.
- Customs among ethnic and religious groups can affect naming of the children.

Chapter 7

Getting the Most from Libraries

In This Chapter

- Finding the genealogical collections
- Using the catalogs and indexes
- Finding family histories
- The different types of libraries

The previous chapter acquainted you with the diversity of written names. Now you're ready to tackle some of the repository research. Libraries differ. So do their holdings. The small town library has a limited budget to purchase books for special interests. But if the local genealogy society is enthusiastic, their fund raisers and contributions provide needed funds. As a result, even small libraries usually have at least a few books on the subject.

If your own county has little on genealogy, check the surrounding area. You may discover collections in nearby towns or cities, or an excellent regional repository in an adjoining county.

The Bigger the Better

All states have a major repository. It may be a state library, a state genealogical society library, a state archives with a library, or a state historical society library. Some lucky states have all four. Each will have a particularly strong collection. It may be extensive holdings of newspapers or manuscripts or an extraordinary number of family histories. Become familiar with all the collections in the geographic area of your search. The larger facilities should have an inventory or guide book, or at least a leaflet describing important aspects of their holdings. Though the state repositories will have larger collections, don't overlook the local and regional libraries.

Genie Jargon

An **on-line catalog** refers to a database that can be accessed by computer.

Genie Jargon

A **consolidated index** is an index combined from more than one source. The indexes to five county histories might be consolidated into one, or the census index of a county from 1850 through 1900 consolidated into one index.

Making Your Way Around

It's important to understand the library's cataloging system. You may be familiar with the standard card catalog with entries by subject, title, and author. But look also for catalogs of newspapers, schools, photographs, and other specialties.

Many libraries now have their catalogs on computer. Ask for assistance if necessary. The library staff will be glad to help. If you have access to a computer and a modem, you can also search the *on-line catalogs* of many libraries from your home or office. Ask for instructions on how to access them from your computer. You can even connect to many major catalogs (such as universities), by using the Internet.

Also inquire about special indexes. Volunteers may have indexed all the obituaries before 1920. Other projects might include a *consolidated index* to names in the county histories or one of all the town officers for the first 100 years. Consolidated indexes are valuable to your search. (And to your sanity when seeking a name among thousands!)

Winding Your Way with Books

One fundamental book to seek out is Val Greenwood's *The Researcher's Guide to American Genealogy, 2nd revision*. This classic is often used as a textbook for genealogy classes. It devotes chapters to various categories of records. Definitions of terminology, lists of records available, recommended reference materials, and some advice on handling problems are included.

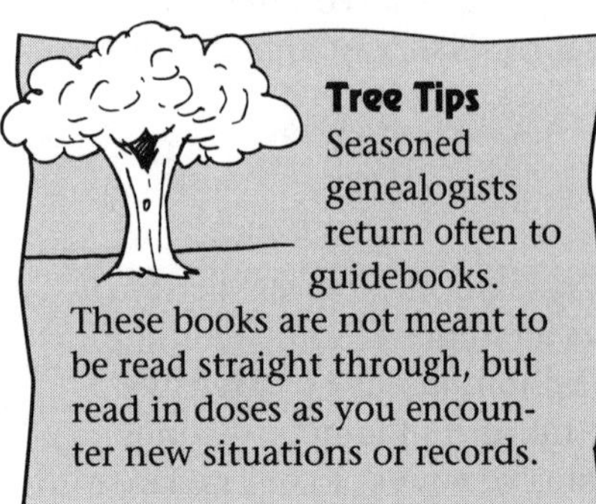

Tree Tips

Seasoned genealogists return often to guidebooks. These books are not meant to be read straight through, but read in doses as you encounter new situations or records.

A more comprehensive aid to research is Loretto Dennis Szucs and Sandra Hargreaves Luebking's *The Source, A Guidebook of American Genealogy*, revised edition, which covers record types in detail. You will turn to this massive book again and again as questions arise and you need more help.

An excellent treatment of regional and state records can be found in the two-volume set of *Genealogical Research: Methods and Sources*. Volume I includes such general information as interpreting the documents, genealogical evidence, family records, and others, as well as regional geographic sections. Volume II continues with regional records (including overseas), heraldry, study of surnames, and others. The two volumes used together are valuable for the insight and advice they give.

Your Family on Its Pages

Probably the books that will surprise you the most, when you start this pursuit, are family histories. I was astounded the first time I saw one among our family's books. I was so excited; I couldn't believe that anyone ever put the time and effort into such a project. My surprise turned into amazement when I visited my first genealogical library and realized that this book was not unique. There were hundreds, no, thousands, of similar books. These histories are usually devoted to one specific family (the Adams family, the Webster family) or a combination of families.

Because no collection is complete, you should check a number of repositories for a family history on your family. Ask your reference librarian for assistance as you search for books on your ancestors.

Catalogs to Help

Look for various catalogs listing books in print. Many major libraries (Newberry in Chicago, New York Public Library, and others) have published catalogs. An example is the *Genealogies Catalogued by the Library of Congress Since 1986*, over 1300 pages, listing hundreds of books. None of the catalogs contain every genealogy published. They will be limited by time period, the library's collection, or other considerations.

Another helpful source is the series *Genealogical and Local History Books in Print,* published since 1975. It lists thousands of books, but you'll need to check each of their volumes.

Lineage Lessons

When you find a family history on the surname you are searching, don't assume that everything in it is correct. Being in print doesn't make it true. The authors may not have had access to the records now available. If there are no citations included upon which you can judge the reliability, you'll have to do some independent searching to establish that the facts are indeed true. You don't want to proceed for 20 years on someone else's word, and then find you have been following the wrong family!

Magazines and Journals: Not at the Corner Newsstand

Family histories are not confined to books. Many periodicals and journals, particularly those national in scope, publish compiled genealogy articles. In some cases these are extensive and might be serialized in several issues. Others may be limited, perhaps covering just the immigrant and one or two generations. Significant finds (proving the English ancestry of a Mayflower passenger, the maiden name of the immigrant's wife) appear often on their pages. Libraries frequently have a section of "newly arrived periodicals" in the genealogy department. Spend some time examining these to become familiar with what is published. They will not be available at your local newsstand or even your local bookstore. Seek them out in the library's collection; then consider subscribing to those of most interest. In some instances you will obtain the magazine by joining the associated organization.

Crammed with Articles

There are hundreds of genealogy periodicals with thousands of articles. How to find the articles that might lead to information on your family? Consult *PERSI* and *GPAI.*

PERSI is the *PERiodical Source Index* published by the Allen County Public Library in Fort Wayne, Indiana. Their massive indexing project covers hundreds of periodicals in their library. Retrospective indexes in 16 volumes cover periodicals published from 1847 through 1985. Articles were indexed by subjects, locations, and surnames. Every year since 1986 *PERSI* has published an annual supplement of periodicals published during that year. Planned for release in 1997 or 1998 is a CD-ROM version, which will include all of the indexes.

Also valuable in locating articles is *Genealogical Periodical Annual Index* or *GPAI,* published since 1962. It indexes genealogies, lineages, Bible records, source records, and book reviews that appear in various periodicals. Use both PERSI and GPAI to get a broad coverage. When you examine these for the surnames and the regions of interest, you will be astounded at what is in print. If you cannot locate the magazine once you have determined there is an article, the Allen County Public Library provides a copying service for a small fee.

Lineage Lessons

In addition to the comprehensive periodical indexes, there are numerous consolidated indexes to specific periodicals, such as *The Virginia Genealogist* and *New England Historical and Genealogical Register.* The indexes to these two are not only in print but also available on CD-ROM. As the use of CD-ROMs increases, many more are expected to be become available in this form.

Not Always Bound

Libraries can hold a variety of *original material,* some of it unbound. In a visit to The State Historical Society of Wisconsin, I located a Bible record from an early family of New England. The original pages, torn and deposited in the society's collection, were probably from a Bible that made its way west in one of the many migrations. It listed the father born in 1782, and the mother in 1779, with their full birth dates, their marriage date, the wife's maiden name, their children, and much more. Letters written by early pioneers have made their way into similar collections. The business papers of a local businessman, a thesis for a college degree, original sheet music composed by an ancestor, a genealogy chart sent from the old country—any of these and much more can be found.

Genie Jargon

Original material, when referring to manuscripts, can be loose papers, letters, photographs, diaries and other items. It may be maintained in a separate manuscript section of the library with a separate catalog.

The Wonderful World of Reference

If you first visited the library's genealogy section, don't stop there. Check the reference section too. Nationwide directories of funeral directors; of newspapers (with addresses, date formed, and other important details); of schools; and many others are on the shelves. You'll need these when you start writing for information. The reference section also holds the multivolume biographical dictionaries such as *Dictionary of American Biography,* (New York: Charles Scribner's Sons, 1937, 20 vol.), *Lamb's Biographical Dictionary of the United States,* (Boston: James H. Lamb Co., 1900, 7 vol.), and others. These have marvelous biographies and pen sketches, and often signatures as well.

Pen sketches and signatures adorn the pages of the biographical dictionaries, gazetteers, and atlases.

In the preceding figure, this pen sketch and signature illustrate the marvelous reproductions you can sometimes obtain from biographical dictionaries. They often include details that help in tracking the families.

Lamb's *Biographical Dictionary of the United States,* from which the previous sketch was taken, will tell you that Charles Triplett O'Ferrall, governor of Virginia, was born at Brucetown, Virginia on 21 October 1840, a son of John and Jane Lawrence (Green) O'Ferrall, and grandson of Dr. John C. Green. The sketch also provides information that his father was of Irish descent, a soldier in the War of 1812, justice of the peace, sheriff, representative in the state legislature, and clerk of the court. Upon his father's death in 1856, Charles was appointed temporary clerk of the Morgan County Court and elected to that position in 1858. He served in the Confederate cavalry and was made sergeant and then captain of Company I, 12th Virginia cavalry. He was wounded several times and twice left for dead on the field. He studied law at Washington College in Lexington, Virginia, and graduated in 1869. He practiced law in Harrisonburg and was a representative in the state legislature for Rockingham County. He later was Governor of Virginia from 1893 through '97.

All this appears in his biographical sketch, together with information on his two marriages, including his wives' names and their parentage. Other interesting facts of his life are also included. Because he was still living at the time his biography was prepared, it is assumed that it is accurate, though as always, undocumented information should be verified. The biographer could have erred in setting down the facts, or typographical errors could have occurred when it was published. This short biography demonstrates the multitude of leads in these books. Each of the mentioned items could have generated records.

Webster Was Never Like This

In the reference section you will find numerous dictionaries besides the standard Webster's. Consider the multivolume *Oxford English Dictionary* when faced with archaic terms. This explains many words and phrases no longer in use that you may encounter, including tools, implements, diseases, and others. You'll find numerous other specialized dictionaries on a wide range of topics.

A Library Is a Library Is a Library

Wrong! The types of library vary considerably. Among those you will use:

- Public libraries
- Private libraries
- Genealogical and historical society libraries
- Lending libraries
- University and college libraries
- Ethnic and religious libraries
- Lineage society libraries

Public Libraries

These can be very small on the local level or very large on the state level. Most public libraries have books that can be checked out, though that service may be restricted to residents. Usually reference books, which may include genealogical material (or fragile or irreplaceable books), are not allowed out of the library.

Private Libraries

Some excellent collections are severely restricted in use. Manuscripts can only be accessed by certain individuals, though the librarians will usually assist by mail. However, many private libraries do make their collections personally accessible to the general public.

Genealogical and Historical Society Libraries

The genealogical or historical society library may be public, or it may be the private collection of a genealogical or historical society. If it is the latter, restrictions may apply. In some cases, members have *open stack* privileges, while nonmembers do not. If it is closed stack, the books must be requested and then retrieved by the staff. There can be a delay (usually 15 minutes to an hour) before the book is delivered. Most libraries that are considered closed stack do have some of their more commonly called-for books available on shelves.

Genie Jargon
Open stack refers to the use of the books. If the library has open stacks, patrons may freely examine books on the shelves.

Lending Libraries

Genealogy libraries usually do not allow patrons to borrow the books, but there are exceptions. California's Sutro Library in San Francisco, for example, will allow some books out on *inter-library loan*. The Library of Virginia in Richmond will allow inter-library loan of county materials on microfilm. There are others.

Though inter-library loan is an advantage for those who cannot travel, it should be taken into consideration if you are making a long trip to the library. Patrons often express disappointment at not finding the book they intended to consult when they arrive. Inquire first; the book you want might be out on loan.

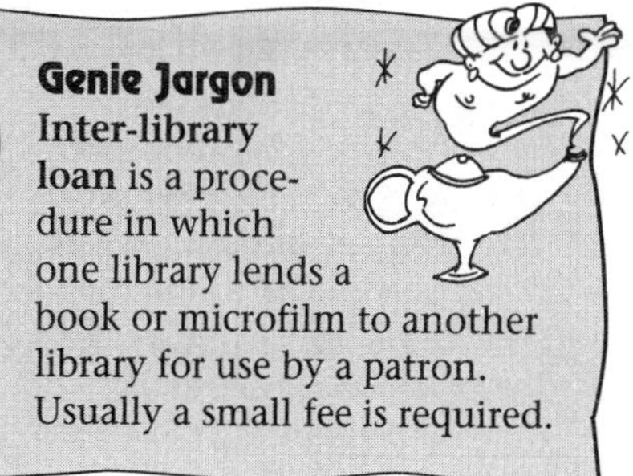

Genie Jargon
Inter-library loan is a procedure in which one library lends a book or microfilm to another library for use by a patron. Usually a small fee is required.

The New England Historic Genealogical Society in Boston maintains a lending library, as does the National Genealogical Society in Arlington, Virginia. Both loan to members only. If you are interested in borrowing books by mail, examine the list of lending libraries in Elizabeth Petty Bentley's *The Genealogical Address Book,* pages 515–516. Some are not based on membership. For a fee and a deposit, anyone can borrow the books. Some will also lend microfilm or microfiche.

If you are searching for a specific book, ask your reference librarian for assistance. The librarian can help in determining which repository has it, and whether it is available for loan.

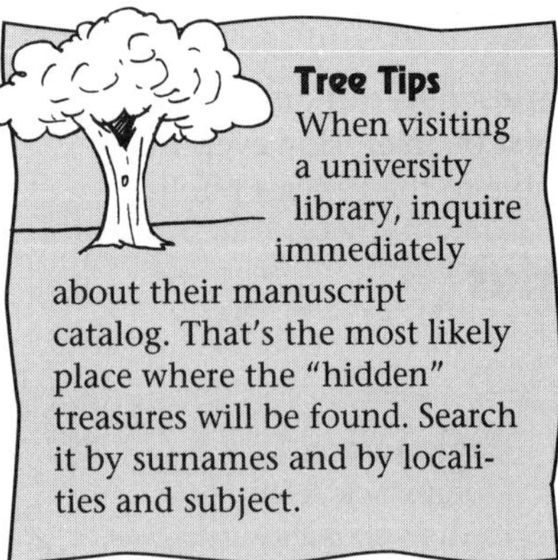

Tree Tips
When visiting a university library, inquire immediately about their manuscript catalog. That's the most likely place where the "hidden" treasures will be found. Search it by surnames and by localities and subject.

University and College Libraries

Among the least used libraries in genealogy, although some have rich genealogical holdings, are those of the universities and colleges. In the collection of the Colson Library, University of West Virginia in Morgantown, I located fragments of an original deed that had not been recorded. This indisputably proved the parentage of a Virginian born in the mid-1750s. At the Bancroft Library at the University of California in Berkeley, I was thrilled to hold in my hands an account book written in the 1700s giving valuable information on the Thomas Jefferson family.

Family History Library

The Family History Library is maintained by the Church of Jesus Christ of Latter-day Saints (Mormon) in Salt Lake City. As a result of their religious convictions, their genealogical collection is immense. It is not limited to use by members of the church; the materials are available for research by anyone. Their microfilming projects extend worldwide. Their computerized library catalog and other computer projects make access to many of their records relatively easy. They maintain over 2,500 Family History Centers across the country, in many localities. Anyone can order microfilm for use in these branches.

A variety of finding aids have been compiled to assist patrons. The Family History Library's immense collection called FamilySearch® is a collection of several genealogical databases. It includes the Family History Department's Ancestral File™, their International Genealogical Index™, their Family History Catalog™, and others. These are on CD-ROM and are updated regularly. Ancestral File™ is a database of data contributed by church members and others, with the data they have collected on individuals. International Genealogical Index™ consists of an international personal name database of birth, christening, and marriage information about persons now deceased. To understand the use of these and the other finding aids, visit a Family History Center. The volunteers there are very helpful.

Tree Tips
Look in the White Pages of the telephone directory of larger cities under Church of Jesus Christ of Latter-day Saints for listings of local Family History Centers.

One of the most useful segments of FamilySearch is the Family History Library Catalog. Through this you will learn of the extensive microfilm holdings of the Family History Library. You can borrow most of these microfilm rolls for a nominal fee through a Family History Center. You will find microfilmed deeds, probate records, many vital records, and much more.

The Magnificent Allen County Collection

The Allen County [Indiana] Public Library at Ft. Wayne has one of the largest collections of genealogy material in the United States. For years, they have systematically added to their collection, which is considered one of the finest in the country. They have a strong collection of periodicals and, as a result, have developed the PERSI index previously described. They have many thousands of genealogy books of all descriptions. You can access their catalog on the Internet through their World Wide Web site, http://www.acpl.lib.in.us/Genealogy/genealogy.html.

Other major collections can be found at The New England Historic Genealogical Society Library in Boston, Massachusetts; The New York Public Library in New York City; The State Historical Society of Wisconsin in Madison, Wisconsin; and others. You will be surprised, as your search progresses, to learn the extensiveness of available genealogical collections. And, as interest escalates, these collections grow.

Religious and Ethnic Libraries

Some churches and ethnic groups maintain libraries and archives. In many cases the hours they are open are limited, so inquire ahead of time if you plan to visit. Looking for the records of the Baptist Church in Virginia? Or the Lutheran Church of Pennsylvania? They maintain archives, as do many others. Some even have their early minutes and registers available on microfilm. Check with your reference librarian for guides that will lead to the location of many church archives. Also examine Elizabeth Petty Bentley's *The Genealogist's Address Book,* pages 457–477.

Lineage Society Libraries

The best known and most extensive library in this category is the Daughters of the American Revolution Library in Washington, D.C. Members of the D.A.R. can use the library at no charge; others pay a daily fee. Besides their book holdings, they have considerable material, such as Bible records and other items, that has been submitted in support of applications.

Tree Tips
Most lineage societies are by membership only. If you have an interest in joining and qualify, an existing member can sponsor your membership.

Besides the well-known D.A.R. Library, there are others. Examine the listings in Bentley's *The Genealogist's Address Book,* pp. 479–488, and also Ancestry's *The Source*, rev. ed., pp. 692–707 for the addresses of lineage societies. Not all maintain libraries. A letter to them should elicit a description of their holdings. (Be sure to enclose an *SASE.*) Many have also published either their lineage books or other pertinent materials.

The Library of Congress

The Library of Congress has a genealogy department, but don't stop with that collection. There are numerous books in other departments that will be of assistance. Among them are the rare books, the newspaper finding aids, photographs, and the map section; all will be important in your search. Consult James C. Neagles', *The Library of Congress: A Guide to Genealogical and Historical Research,* for an understanding of the vast facilities.

Relative Resources

Bentley, Elizabeth Petty. *The Genealogist's Address Book.* Third ed. Baltimore, MD: Genealogical Publishing Co., 1995.

Black, Henry Campbell. *Black's Law Dictionary.* Sixth ed. St. Paul, MN.: West Publ. Co., 1990.

Genealogical Periodical Annual Index. Bowie, MD.: Heritage Books. Various compilers since its inception in 1962.

Greenwood, Val D. *The Researcher's Guide to American Genealogy.* 2nd ed. Baltimore, MD: Genealogical Publishing Co., 1990.

Neagles, James C. *The Library of Congress: A Guide to Genealogical and Historical Research.* Salt Lake City, UT: Ancestry Publ., 1990.

PERSI (Periodical Source Index). Fort Wayne, Ind.: Allen County Library Foundation. 16 vol.

PERSI (Periodical Source Index). Fort Wayne, Ind.: Allen County Library Foundation. Annual supplement. 1986–

Genealogical Research: Methods and Sources. Rubincam, Milton, Editor. American Society of Genealogists, 1960.

Smallwood, Grahame Thomas, Jr. "Tracking Through Hereditary and Lineage Organizations." In Loretto Dennis Szucs and Sandra Hargreaves Luebking, *The Source: A Guidebook of American Genealogy.* Revised ed. Salt Lake City: Ancestry Publ., 1997. pp. 457–477.

Addresses

Family History Library, 55 North West Temple St., Salt Lake City, UT 84150. [Write to them for a listing of Family History Centers in your state.]

National Genealogical Society (NGS). 4527 17th Street, North, Arlington, VA 22207-2399. [Maintains lending library for members.]

National Society, Daughters of the American Revolution (D.A.R.), 1776 D Street, N.W., Washington, DC 20006-5392. [Extensive library. Small fee for nonmembers.]

The New England Historic Genealogical Society. Book Loan Department, 99-101 Newbury Street, Boston, MA 02116-3087. [Maintains lending library for members.]

The Least You Need to Know

- Genealogical collections and repositories vary drastically in size.
- Many families have "family histories" published on their family.
- There are many different types of libraries that will assist in the search.
- Some especially notable genealogical collections hold voluminous helpful material.

Chapter 8

Your Family's Hometown

In This Chapter

- Using the public library to find relatives
- Learning to recognize the records your family left
- How other county records can assist in the search
- Some of the treasures in the museum

You may be one of the fortunate persons who lives in the same county where your family has resided for more than one or two generations. If so, you may be surprised that within your family's own county, there are a number of repositories to assist in your search. You will familiarize yourself with the records your family could have generated in the county in which they lived. If your family did not live in the same area in which you now reside, consider making a trip to where your parents and grandparents lived most of their lives.

Chapter 12 tells you how to prepare for the trip to your ancestors' hometowns, and Chapter 13 explains the materials available in the courthouses there. This chapter concentrates on what is available in the libraries and museums of your ancestors' hometowns.

Go to the public library where your immediate family lived. Ask if there is a genealogy section, and a "local" history section. Both will be useful to your search. The genealogy section will include "family histories," books devoted specifically to the genealogy of a family, and many other published and manuscript aids related to lineages. The local history section consists of books, pamphlets, scrapbooks, and other items devoted

Tree Tips
Ask at the library for the name of the official county or city historian. They too can assist by pointing you to local collections.

specifically to the county. Find out too if there is a genealogical society in the area. They may meet in the public library but often have their own headquarters and library. You are seeking any records mentioning your relatives while they lived in the county.

Some of your family's records will be in their original form in the courthouse. Some, however, have been abstracted and published—those you will find in the library. Also in the library might be items that are originals—scrapbooks, photographs, and others.

Getting Started in the Public Library

Take with you the names, dates, and locations of your family members who resided in the county. Your goal is to find their birth dates, marriage dates, spouses, and death dates as starters. This helps in documenting the line, in establishing that you have the correct lineage. Stay alert for records that mention the churches they attended or their religion. (Knowing that, you can later determine if the church had records naming them.) A record showing where they were buried can later supply you with further leads. Each of the major events in their lives may have associated records that can help identify to whom they were related and reveal something of their lives.

Your purpose is to find everything there that could bear on your family. Nothing is too insignificant to note. Be sure to write down fully in your notes the day of your library trip, the name and address of the one visited, and in which book or file you found the information. You want to be able to find it again. In the variety of records that the library holds, you might learn:

- Birth date and birthplace
- Name of parents
- Death date and town or township
- Marriage date, place, and spouse
- Biography, possibly with photograph or pen sketch
- Military service
- Names and addresses of relatives
- When they moved into the county
- When they left the county
- Occupation
- Acreage owned

It will take some digging, but you may initially be unable to locate something specific. Stick with it. As you learn more about the records, your success will increase. And with each success, your enthusiasm for the search will increase, too.

Shelves of Possibilities

Once you start browsing the library shelves, you will be amazed at the resources available. Books and finding aids of every description exist. Look for such things as:

- Old Settlers' files
- Obituaries/necrology/funeral records
- Tombstone surveys
- Vertical family files
- County histories and indexes
- Published vital records
- Published deeds, probate and court records
- Scrapbooks
- Gazetteers
- Voting registers
- City directories
- School records
- Artifacts and photographs

Old Settlers Remembered

Many counties have projects to preserve information on their earliest settlers in what is commonly called "Old Settlers' files." These may consist of recollections of descendants, biographies, or even taped interviews. Examine them for entries for any of the surnames of your family who resided in the county. Note also the name and address of the persons who submitted the information; they may be alive or might have family still living. Contact with them could yield some wonderful memorabilia.

Often the information in Old Settlers' projects was not documented. Though the data will be helpful, don't accept it as "fact" until you have verified it with other records.

> **Genie Jargon**
> **Necrology** is a list of persons who died within a certain time frame, or a collection of obituaries. You may find the collection so titled in the library.

Death Records

Many local libraries have indexed their early obituaries or established a *necrology* file. The content of the obituaries varies. Normally, those in smaller towns were more extensive than in larger cities. Check this file for members of your family. (See Chapter 15, "More than News in the Newspaper.")

Genie Jargon

A **vertical file** is a collection of resource materials, usually pamphlets, letters, clippings, and others. It is normally arranged in manila folders and filed in alphabetical sequence by subject or name.

Vertical Files: Just Waiting to "Talk"!

As interest in genealogy has escalated, libraries receive letters from all over the country inquiring about their early residents. To preserve these, they often create *"vertical files,"* a set of folders stored in a filing cabinet. Typically, all the inquiries are in one folder, or if warranted, the library establishes individual folders by surname or subject. Included may be letters, clippings, Bible records, photographs, research notes, charts, and other beneficial items. These can yield many new clues, and also the names of others seeking the family.

County Histories: The "Mug" Books

Almost every county in the United States has had at least one county history published, and some have several. They vary in content. Those published in the late 1800s or early 1900s typically consisted of histories of each of their townships or towns, churches, lodges, medical profession, schools, newspapers, county government, notorious happenings, and even those who served in the military from the county. They may include the name and place of origin of the early pioneers of the area—who established the first grist mill, the first physician, town officers, and other similarly valuable information.

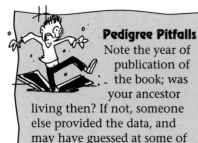

Pedigree Pitfalls

Note the year of publication of the book; was your ancestor living then? If not, someone else provided the data, and may have guessed at some of the facts.

The county histories are sometimes referred to as "mug books" because often they included biographies with photographs (or pen sketches) of the early citizens. The lack of a biography was no reflection on a person's standing in the community, however. The books were mostly on a subscription basis; those who paid were included; others were not. To subscribe or not depended upon the frugality and monetary priorities of the individual. The histories published in the late 1800s were supplied by people far closer to the time of the events and should be (but aren't always) more accurate than recollections of present day descendants.

Tree Tips

Consult P. William Filby's *Bibliography of American County Histories,* which is useful. Look also in your library for Town Histories. Though these are not listed in Filby, many have been published.

View the mug books with caution. If the biography includes several earlier generations, there can be multiple errors caused by loss of memory or lack of knowledge of the family background. (Or even, occasionally, by a desire to elevate their standing in the community or in order to obscure details of a less than desirable past.) It was the rare biographer who knew the details of his family intimately for several generations unless the family left careful written records. All facts must be confirmed. Nonetheless, the biographies are unique and provide an insight often lacking in any other source. You will learn of your ancestor's schooling, jobs, purchase of the farm, the church he attended, when he "found" religion, and other fascinating facts.

A common problem with published county histories is the absence of an index. Usually only the name of the subject in the biographies was listed; the other names within the sketch weren't indexed. And rarely were the names in the town and historical sections indexed. It can be a tedious process to locate your ancestor's name among the pages. Fortunately, as the use of computers has increased, many individuals or groups have initiated projects to remedy this shortcoming. Inquire at your local library: Even if an index has not been published, there may be a card index created locally.

Tree Tips
If you can establish the name of the community in which your family lived, you can first search those sections in the unindexed book. The location will give you a starting place.

Vital Records: The Facts of Life

Vital Records—births, marriages, and deaths—are among the richest of documents that help build the family tree. Searching them may take some effort, because it often requires going to a variety of locations. They can be scattered among the shelves of the courthouse, city hall, county health department, local historical society, and even church and state archives. First, check at your library to see if anyone has compiled or published any of the local vital records. Although you don't want to rely upon the published version (because of possible omissions and errors in transcriptions), it will assist in initiating the search. The preface of the book of vital records might explain where the various records are housed and which, if any, have been destroyed.

Local Records

If you are fortunate, your county may be one of those for which abstracts of other early records have been published. These can include a variety of land records: deed abstracts, surveys, land entries, and others. Though you should also examine the originals in the courthouse, the published records have the advantage of an all-name index to the book. The courthouse will only index the main parties. Estate records are another favorite among compilers. They include decedents, as well as estates involving minors and incompetents.

Lineage Lessons

Decedents' estates are those involving deceased persons. In addition, there are estates for minors who may have property to be guarded by court appointed guardians, or estates handled by guardians or conservators for those who are not able to handle their own affairs.

A multitude of other published abstracts might be found: court minutes, order books, inventories, and others. Look for mention of members of your family and clues to relationships. Later you will make your first trip to the courthouse and experience the excitement of using the original records. For now the published books in the library can aid you in understanding the variety of available records.

Local Scrapbooks

Preparing scrapbooks of local events was a pastime for some townspeople. It gave them a sense of community. Reading them, you will get a sense of life in the community as it grew. Seldom have these been indexed, but a few hours in the library can reward you with an article involving your ancestor. If he was robbed, or elected mayor, or celebrated an anniversary, the report might be among those pages. If not, you will still be left with a flavor of the area in early days.

Gazetteers and Atlases

The county gazetteer (a geographic dictionary) or atlas published in the late nineteenth or early twentieth century is a treasure. The pen sketches of the homes and farms are priceless. The wagons and farm implements in the yard, the crops growing—these reflect a way of life. Also included are township maps, many showing the name of the property owners on their section of land. Nearby cemeteries may be noted. These are of value, not only in establishing the family's residence, but in indicating an area to search for a family cemetery. Acreage, occupation, and even their place of nativity may be included. The names of the neighbors can also be helpful.

The Historical Atlas Map of Santa Clara County, California, published by Thompson & West of San Francisco in 1876, includes a Business Directory. Businessmen are listed by name, address, occupation, nativity, the year they entered the state, when they came to the county, their post office, and the number of acres owned. You learn that Sheriff J. H. Adams came in 1849 from Illinois during the gold rush, and that Dr. Benjamin Cory of Ohio came even earlier, in 1847. These wonderful atlases are not to be overlooked. Some pen sketches measure 12" × 14" while others are 8" × 12" or other sizes. They are unique in design and historical significance. Some of the commercial companies, such as Thompson

& West, Lewis Publishing, and others specialized in such histories, preparing them for many counties and states. The originals are collector's items.

The office and residence of one of San Jose, California's early physicians.

If you can find a pen sketch of your family's home or farm in an early atlas, a good reproduction of it will be wonderful for framing. The preceding figure shows the office and residence of G. W. Breyfogle, M.D., at the corner of Third and St. James Streets in San Jose, California. This reproduction from *The Historical Atlas Map of Santa Clara County, California*, provides a wonderful sense of a bygone era.

Tree Tips
When seeking a gazetteer or atlas, try to find the original publication. In recent years, many have been reprinted, but cost cutting measures have forced the reduction in the size of the pages, often losing detail and readability.

He Voted with Pride

Some areas have voting registers, and may even have published their early registers. In California, the published voting registers of many counties before 1900 can be found in libraries. They include data not easily obtainable from other sources. The *Great Register for Santa Clara County* for 1892 includes age; physical description (height, complexion, color of eyes, color of hair); visible marks or scars, if any, and their location; occupation; country of nativity (usually shown as the state); place of residence; post office address; date when naturalized; place where naturalized and by which court; date of registration; and whether sworn.

A marvelous sense of the man—what he looked like, how he made his living, if he was an immigrant—are all revealed. John Cotler, a farmer, was age 58 and born in Ireland. He was naturalized 17 August 1855 in the U. S. District Court in Boston. His descendants now know where to find his naturalization papers. Charles Cranz, age 74, was born in Germany and naturalized on 10 April 1840 in Canton, Ohio; you learn too that he was 5' $7\frac{3}{4}$" tall, with a light complexion, blue eyes, and brown hair, and a farmer by occupation. Though not all states have such detailed registers, determine what is available for the county of your search.

City Directories: Home Sweet Home

The availability of city directories will vary. Larger cities, such as Philadelphia, Boston, Baltimore, and New York have directories extant from the early or mid-1800s and some even earlier. Small towns may at first be included in the directories of their neighboring large cities but probably had their own in later years. Very rural and sparsely settled areas might have all the towns in the county in one volume.

> **Tree Tips**
> If you are unable to learn about voting records at the library, check with the county registrar of voters for information on the earlier records.

It is unlikely that within a county, the city directories are all housed in the same repository. In mid- and large-sized communities, each has its own library and maintains a set of its own directories. Once you have established where in the county your family lived, determine if the town has its own collection. These directories will not only place your ancestors in the county or town at specific times, but may lead you to the old home, perhaps still standing.

Additionally, watch for:

- Others of the surname listed at the same address because they are relatives
- Widow's listing, giving her deceased husband's name and occupation
- Individual's first listing in the town (to indicate arrival)
- Individual's last listing in the town (to indicate departure from the area or death)

If the directory has a reverse listing by street address (called a householder's index), you can check for neighbors. Some may be married daughters (families often lived in close proximity in earlier times). After you learn his occupation, you can follow your ancestor from job to job. Even the date of death might be pinpointed within a year or two if the husband and wife are listed in one directory, and in subsequent directories only one appears as a widow or widower. If the whole family disappears from the directory entirely and does not reappear in subsequent issues, they probably moved from the area.

Another useful section in the city directories is that of businesses. If your ancestor was a tailor, examine the business listings of tailor shops. Also examine the advertisements. They are charming, and you may be rewarded with your ancestor's ad entreating the public to purchase the finery he offers.

Lineage Lessons

Do not assume that the spouse died in the same year that the surviving spouse is first listed as a widow or widower. It may take a year or two for the directory listings to reflect such events. If a husband is shown in several editions with his wife, and then shown alone, he is likely widowed. Watch for subsequent issues that might reveal a new wife.

Learning with School Records

If you know what school your family attended, and it is still in existence, contact them for school records. They may be reluctant to furnish records from their files but often will if sufficient time has elapsed. If the school is no longer standing, try the department of education of the county. If you do not know which school they attended, examine the city directory for the appropriate time period and determine which schools are listed on nearby streets.

Tree Tips
In trying to locate schools that may have existed in your family's neighborhood, obtain a detailed street map of the town and use it together with the city directory and telephone book.

She Grew Roses; He Went to Lodge

Clubs, lodges, and fraternal organizations may still hold records of your family. Some have national headquarters and will answer inquiries if an SASE is included. The published county history, previously discussed, may give some information on the organizations that existed when your ancestors first lived in the area. Determine if any are still in existence.

If your ancestor was a member of the Chamber of Commerce or other civic organization, get in touch with them. Even if they don't maintain records of past members, they may remember him and offer some recollections. They may have retained newsletters of their organization, or minutes, which can add flavor to the life history you are building.

The women might have joined garden clubs, knitting circles, and church affiliated groups. Try to find them. It will give you a glimpse of their personalities to know their interests and hobbies.

Artifacts and Memorabilia

Museums can show vividly how your ancestors lived. Relics from the early times of the community, photographs, sketches, portraits—all assist in portraying your ancestors in the community. If there was musical talent in your family, you will enjoy seeing the old instruments they played. If Great-Grandpa was a druggist, some of his paraphernalia might be included in the museum's display.

Be sure to inquire about indexes to manuscripts or photographs or other holdings of the museum. They may hold many original records and family memorabilia. If your ancestor was a collector of anything—postcards, thimbles, or fans—see if the collection was donated to the museum. Such collections are often annotated with intriguing bits of information about the donor; you may learn something of your ancestors' travels, interests, and talents. When the Arizona State Historical Society wrote to inquire about a quilt in their collection donated by a descendant of the town's jailer (related to my husband), they were able to supply a fascinating tradition of the quilt being stitched by the girls at the Bird Cage Saloon in Tombstone, Arizona. It was said to be their gift to the jailer's baby daughter.

Photographs: A Peek into the Past

Perhaps one of the most treasured finds in local museums are the photographs. Families who long despaired of ever finding a photograph of their great-grandfather may find his class photograph framed and displayed in a case. Museums normally have indexes to their photograph collection and can assist you in locating those.

If you find a photograph in the museum's collection that you would like to have reproduced, usually museums are cooperative. Expect to pay for the negative and prints, and consider an additional donation for their assistance.

Relative Resources

Filby, P. William. *A Bibliography of American County Histories*. Baltimore, MD: Genealogical Publishing Co., 1987.

The Least You Need to Know

- The library in your ancestors' hometown has numerous manuscript and published records to assist in tracing your ancestors.
- If your family lived in your own town, you will find vital records, court records, funeral records, and much more in your own backyard.
- Additional records for search can include such diverse sources as school, city directories, and voting registers.

Part 3
Following the Trail

It's time to start searching for your family in the census, and through it follow them in their journeys north, south, east, and west as they migrated. The thrill of finally finding your family on the census, and realizing that probably at least one of them was there at the very time the census taker was writing down the information, will make you feel very close.

You may be like many others: You hate to write letters. How to start? What to ask? This will be easier with the guidance you read here. You will find some tips to increase the power of your letters, making the most of every one of them.

Chapter 9

Census Research: Have You Done Your Homework?

In This Chapter

- What is the census and why is it important?
- Preparing for the first records research
- Understanding the Soundex code
- Coding your surnames

Most genealogists start their records' research with the U.S. federal population *census*, a count taken every ten years since 1790 to determine the number of congress members for each state. Our forefathers didn't know that they were laying the foundation for one of the most fundamental research documents for genealogy.

Census Importance

Why are the censuses so important to your quest for information on your ancestors, and why are they among the first records to search? Widely available, they place your ancestors in a specific place at a specific time, and the related information on them leads you to other locations and records.

The objective of the census is to account for every individual living in the United States on a designated day. The chances are good that your ancestors were enumerated if they resided in the U.S. on the day the census was taken. Later chapters give suggestions to help you find them if they seem to be missing.

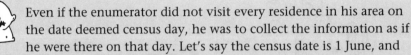

Lineage Lessons

Even if the enumerator did not visit every residence in his area on the date deemed census day, he was to collect the information as if he were there on that day. Let's say the census date is 1 June, and the enumerator doesn't get to a household until 13 June. The baby born 2 June should not be listed on the census because he was not in the household on the census date. Similarly, if an individual died 2 June, he should be listed on the census because he was alive on 1 June, the designated date.

What can you learn from the census? At various times the census questions pertain to military service, citizenship, marital status, and other topics. Some responses will surprise you. Thinking the family 100 percent Southern, you may be amazed to find Great-Grandpa was a Union vet from the Civil War. Or if you presume everyone in your family had been in the United States for generations, it will be interesting to know that Great-Grandma Barbara was born in Germany. If family tradition says that your 3rd great-grandfather was born in Ireland, but the census information says he and his father were both born in Virginia, you have a discrepancy to check.

Genie Jargon

A **census** is an official population count that often includes related information used for government planning.

The census may be the first place you find your ancestors in their family groupings. Maybe Grandma is older than you thought, or your mother has an older brother no one mentions.

Preparation Saves Frustration

Before you head out to a repository to search the census records for your family, do your homework. Your research is easier and more efficient if you are systematic.

Make a list of the likely heads of households (person in charge of the family unit, such as husband/father, grown son, or widow) for whom you have gathered some information from talking to your relatives and going through all the material you found at home. Be sure to include any variant spellings of the surnames.

For each individual on your list, add a time period (the estimated dates of their life spans based on what you already know) and a probable state and county of residence. For example, take a look at the following sample of a census search:

Abraham Gant	1920	Morgan Co., Ky.
	1910	Estill Co., Ky.
	1900	Estill Co., Ky.
	1880	Orange Co., Va.
Joseph Jaspers	1920	Monroe Co., N.Y.
	1910	Monroe or Erie Co., N.Y.
	1900	Erie Co., N.Y.
	1880	too young

The approximate birth dates of the individuals on your list will indicate a starting point for the census search. (The 1890 census is omitted from the list because it is virtually nonexistent.) Which ones would likely be on the 1920 census? Which on the 1910 census? If your parents were children in 1920, they will be enumerated with whomever they were living with at that time: parents, grandparents, aunts and uncles, orphanages, or other.

Unless you suspect otherwise, when you begin, assume any ancestor under ages 18–21 were living with their parents, and start your research with them. Group your list of individuals by the areas where you expect they were living.

Where Did They Live?

The county is the division of government where you begin to look for your ancestors in official records, so first determine in which counties your ancestors' towns belong. If, like so many old towns, their town has disappeared from current maps, look up the town in a gazetteer. There may be several towns of the same name; be sure to get the one in the area where your ancestors lived.

The closer you can locate the residence for your ancestors, whether street address, township, or ward, the more quickly your search is likely to go. But don't be discouraged if those are the very things you are hoping to uncover by searching the census. You will be successful; it will just take a little longer. If you are unable to zero in on a county, the search is not hopeless. Examine the state census indexes carefully for your ancestors' names. You can often determine the county from those indexes.

Tree Tips
Review the material you already have on your ancestors. You may find the county of residence amongst the family papers, on death certificates, in obituaries, or in city directories.

Which Census to Search First?

Because of privacy laws, the latest census available for research is the 1920 census. Generally, you will start your research with the most recent censuses, 1920, 1910, or 1900, and track the individuals back through each census taken during their lifetimes. The objective is to conduct a complete census search for each individual on your list. You may wonder why you need to keep getting additional censuses when you found them in one census listing. There are three main reasons: You want to compare the data you find, the composition of the household may change, and each census has different information that can lead you to other records.

Last Touches for Your List

Your research list should now be a list of individuals with some indication of the census years in which you may find them listed, the probable counties and states in which they lived during those years, and the most recent available census on which you might expect to find them. At this point, to prepare for your search for the actual census listings, you will need a code for each individual on your list that you will be searching for in 1920, 1910, 1900, and 1880. (The 1890 population census is virtually nonexistent, nearly all of it having been destroyed by a fire, January 21, 1921, in the Commerce Department building.)

Genie Jargon

Soundex is an indexing system based on the phonetic sound of the consonants in the surname. Each name is assigned a letter and three numbers. The letter is always the first letter of the surname. The **Miracode** for the 1910 census uses the same sound system but arranges the resulting lists by the visitation number assigned by the enumerator, rather than page numbers of the census schedule as in the Soundex.

Cracking the Code

Federal indexing for the 1880, 1900, 1910, and 1920 censuses is based on a phonetic system called the *Soundex* (or a similar one called *Miracode*). It was devised to overcome the vagaries of spelling by grouping together surnames that sound alike, but are spelled differently. In the Soundex, Bream, Breem, or Briem will be found in indexes under B650; Wier, Weer, Wiere, and Ware would be W600.

The 1880 census was Soundexed only for households having children under the age of ten. (These children were the first to become eligible for old age benefits in 1935.) This does not mean that other households were not enumerated. It does mean that if your ancestor was not in a household with children under the age of ten, he will not be on the Soundex indexes.

Those 1880 Children Retiring

With the passing of the Social Security Act in 1935, the government had to determine who was eligible for benefits. Those eligible needed to prove their ages. If they had no birth record, they could help substantiate the birth by a census record. The government, realizing that the first group of applicants were born before there was statewide registration of births, needed an efficient way to locate individuals on the census for verification of the birth. The only ones in the household that were important to the government in this initial Soundex were those who were under ten in 1880. It was that group that would be applying for Social Security.

Lineage Lessons

Only the Soundex for 1880 has the limitation of including only the households with children under ten in the home. The 1900 through 1920 censuses include in the Soundex all heads of households. In 1910, only 21 states had a Soundex or Miracode; the rest of the 1910 census must be searched using other methods, discussed in Chapter 10.

Learning the Soundex System

Applying the Soundex code to the surnames on your list before you go to the repository will speed up your census research when you get there. Table 9.1 explains the code.

Table 9.1 Soundex Coding Key

Number	Letter Equivalent
1	B P F V
2	C S K G J Q X Z
3	D T
4	L
5	M N
6	R

The letters A, E, I, O, U, W, Y, and H are disregarded. To apply the Soundex to your surnames, follow these steps:

1. Use the first letter of the surname to begin the code.
2. Cross out all the vowels and the letters *W*, *Y*, and *H* in the surname.
3. Using the table, assign an equivalent number to the first three letters left in the surname.
4. Disregard any remaining letters in the surname.

If the surname has less than three letters left, assign zeros to those places.

Further refinements:

- Double letters are treated as one and coded with one number; thus 2 *Ls* will be 4, not 44.
- Two or more letters with the same code number that appear in sequence in a surname are assigned one number; thus *CK* in Dickson is coded as 2, not 22, Szalay is S400.

- A name that yields no letters is assigned 3 zeros, thus *Chu* becomes C000.
- Code names with prefixes, such as Van, Von, De, Le, with and without the prefix. You may find it either way in the Soundex.

Examples using these rules are shown in Table 9.2:

Table 9.2 Soundex Examples

Name	As Soundexed
Aguilar	A246
Mendelsohn	M534
Beebe	B100
Li, Lee, Law	L000
Flick	F420
Von Kemp	V525 or K510

Let's have some practice. Try coding these names:

INGALLS (ING~~A~~L~~L~~~~S~~)

As Soundexed: I524

- First letter, I, is the initial letter the code uses for filing.
- N = 5
- G = 2
- Eliminate A (ignore all vowels).
- Treat the double L as one letter = 4.
- Disregard the S (because the code has only 3 numbers).

STADT (ST~~A~~DT)

As Soundexed: S330

- First letter, S, is the initial letter the code uses for filing.
- T = 3.
- Eliminate A (ignore all vowels).
- Treat the D and the T as one letter = 3.
- The code must have three numbers; add a zero.

Indexes Before the Soundex

There are various published indexes for the 1790 through 1870 census before the first Soundex of 1880. With the help of CD-ROM technology, more consolidated, comprehensive indexes for all years and all states are being created. Watch for them.

While most indexes cover an entire state, others are regional. Occasionally, an individual or a genealogical society prepares an index or a transcription of a census for one county. Copies of these indexes and transcriptions may not be widely distributed. Nonetheless, check for indexes at all the libraries and repositories where you look for other sources.

No matter how good the index, some mistakes are made. If you don't find your family on a particular index, do not assume they are not on the census. They may have been missed in the indexing, alphabetized incorrectly, or you may be looking in the wrong geographic location.

Tree Tips
Many genealogy programs will give you the Soundex codes for every surname in your database.

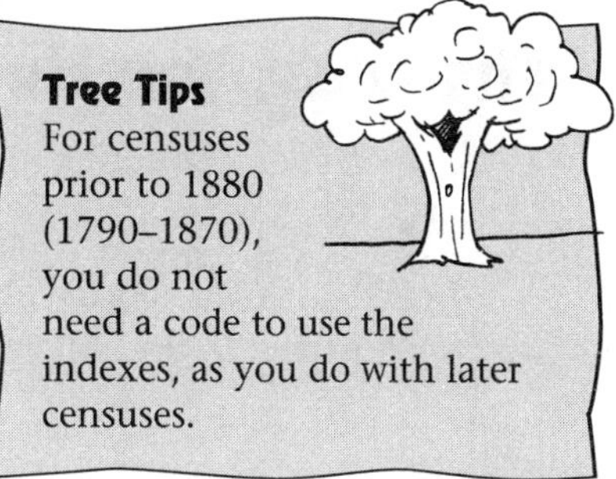

Tree Tips
For censuses prior to 1880 (1790–1870), you do not need a code to use the indexes, as you do with later censuses.

Locating a Copy of the Census

Once you have your list of individuals with their states and counties of residence, their names Soundexed for 1880–1920, and a list of censuses you expect them to be on, you need to know where you can find the census microfilm and any pre-1880 indexes that may be available.

Microfilmed copies of the federal census are widely available. The National Archives and its regional branches have a full set from 1790 through 1920, with many (though not all) existing indexes. Large libraries and repositories often have complete sets, although some have only the series for your state. Your local library might have selected censuses for your county. The Family History Library has a complete collection, and their copies may be borrowed and viewed at their Family History Centers. Other copies are available through rental services.

Is It True?

Keep in mind that census information needs to be corroborated with other records for reasons that are discussed in Chapter 10. Don't be misled by accepting the census information as completely accurate.

You will return to the census again and again as you discover new individuals, or new information calls for a reevaluation of your earlier work. Each time you discover a new surname, conduct a complete census search on that family.

Lineage Lessons

Even when information on the census is accurate, it can be misleading. On the 1870 census, Lewis Dunn's birthplace is listed as West Virginia, but the 1860 census shows Virginia as his birthplace. Which is correct? As it turns out, both are correct. The actual place of his birth is in an area that was once a part of Virginia, but became part of West Virginia when that state was admitted to the Union in 1863.

The Least You Need to Know

- List and Soundex the surnames you are researching.
- Determine the probable states and counties where your ancestors lived.
- Start your census research with the most recently available census, where you can expect to find the families you are researching.

Chapter 10

Making Sense of the Census

In This Chapter

- The search path for locating the census record you need
- Variations in the federal population schedules
- Using the census for clues
- Deaths and Civil War veterans from the census

Your ancestor's family is sitting around the kitchen table at their farmhouse, talking to the census taker. The baby is crying in the background, while two-year old Hannah is chasing the cat under the table. When was little Jake born? Where was Grandmother born? How old is Mattie? I often imagine these scenes, and wonder how long it took the census taker to elicit all the information he needed on the large family of parents, 12 children, and assorted farm hands and helpers. What the census taker wrote down forms the basis of the federal population schedules—one of the most frequently used sources in genealogy for both beginners and experienced searchers.

Counting All Those People

The federal census from 1790 through 1920, taken every ten years, is available for public perusal. The original schedules are normally not available for study but have been microfilmed. Though some states had significant losses of early census records, the only serious loss for a whole census year was the 1890 population list, lost in a fire in 1921. Only a very small portion was saved, and it is filmed on National Archives' Micropublication M407.

Lineage Lessons

Because of privacy laws restricting access to the census for 72 years, the census of 1930 won't be available for general use until the year 2002. If you need information on your own listing or you are related to a deceased person, you can submit a request to the Census Bureau. They will provide, for a fee, some very limited information on an individual. (The full household listing cannot be obtained until the census is released for public use.)

Index Information

Except for a few instances when the census taker recopied the lists alphabetically, the census lists in early years were written in order of visitation. This made them time-consuming to use; a researcher had to conduct a page-by-page search in the county's listings to find a particular family. Various commercial companies and individuals in the past few years have remedied this situation by creating indexes. These are available in book form at libraries, and many are now on CD-ROM.

In the census indexes, normally only the head of household is indexed, not each individual family member. From 1790 through 1840 the head of the household was the only one listed in the census by the census taker; it therefore would not have been possible for the indexer to include others in the dwelling. The censuses of 1850 and later did include all individuals living in the dwelling, but most of the indexers only picked up the head of the household to index. If your ancestor was a child during the 1790 census, you won't find the child by name but will have to search for the head of a household in which he may have lived.

Pedigree Pitfalls

Many of the indexes were entered into a computer and then sorted. If the name was typed incorrectly, it will be sorted incorrectly. Andrew Williams, mistyped "Willaims" or John Smith, mistyped "Simth" will not appear in their proper places in the index. Consider all possibilities.

You will have to be creative. Not only do variations abound in spelling, but you must contend with errors the indexer made. The name of the head of the household could have been mistyped in preparing the index in the 20th century, or the indexer may have misunderstood it. Even the original census taker could have erred. Remember that many inhabitants were unable to read or write. The census takers spelled the names the way they sounded. This problem was compounded by the heavy accents of immigrants. Check all variations of the name. (See Chapter 6 for naming problems encountered.)

The head of household is not necessarily the father. It could be a widowed mother, relative, guardian, or other person. Occasionally there was a separation, and you will find both the father and the mother as heads of household.

Though indexes for the pre-Soundex years vary, the index will probably show the name, county, township, district or ward, and a page number.

The Search Path

If you understand the steps in locating a census, you will find it is a simple process. Let's integrate that process into a search path, in order to understand the steps needed to find a census listing. The search path differs depending on whether you are searching the Soundex years (1880–1920) (see Chapter 9) or the earlier census (1790–1870).

Search Path 1880 Through 1920 Census

Step One (using Soundex):

- Code the surname (Chapter 9).
- Determine at least the state and, if possible, the county.
- Use a catalog to determine the appropriate Soundex microfilm and roll number depending on coded name.
- Find the entry on the Soundex microfilm.
- Copy all the data shown, particularly the county, E.D. (Enumeration District), and page (sheet) number.

Step Two:

- With the numbers you found on the Soundex, return to the microfilm catalog. Look for state and county (and E.D. if the county is on more than one roll) to find the proper roll on which to obtain the full listing.
- Using the microfilm roll, find the family's full listing on the microfilm.
- Copy all the data shown.

Search Path 1790 Through 1870 Census

- Determine the state and, if possible, the county.
- Locate published indexes; find the head of household noting the state, county, township, and page number it lists.

- Using the information you found in the index, check the microfilm catalog for the appropriate microfilm and roll number.
- Using the page number and township or ward from the index, find the family's listing on the roll of microfilm.
- Copy all the data shown.

Soundex (Index) Microfilm 1880 Through 1920

You already have the Soundex code for the surname from reading Chapter 9. You need that code to find the indexed listing. The Soundex microfilm is arranged:

- First by state
- Second by code
- Then by first name

Since the Soundex brings together all similar sounding surnames, there will be many different surnames listed within that code. Once you find the code on the microfilm, you will find that within the code it is sub-indexed by the given name of the head of household. That cuts the search time considerably. For example, you code your surname and search the Soundex for that code. Once there, you observe that to find the surname with the first name of Thomas, you can roll the film to the first names starting with T, and quickly locate any Thomas.

Let's Practice

At the repository, ask to see the microfilm catalog. You coded the surname Carlson as C-642; you want to find Charles Carlson who lived in North Dakota. The catalog shown on the following page indicates the 1920 North Dakota Soundex is Micropublication M1580, and that the code C-642 is on Rolls 8 and 9. Since you are searching for Charles Carlson, you will examine Roll 8 because it includes Code C-642 through the first name of Katherine. (If you were searching for Martin Carlson, you would examine Roll 9. That roll starts with Code C-642, first name of Lars, and continues through the rest of C-642 codes and on to the next numerical codes.)

Using the same example, you now find microfilm M1580 of the Soundex in the cabinet and take Roll 8. When you put it on the microfilm reader, you will notice in examining the roll that there are "title cards" at the beginning of each of the codes, so you know when the code changes. Proceed to Code C-642. Once you are in C-642, start watching the alphabetized first names. You want Charles Carlson, so proceed to the first name of Charles. You are there…but wait. Do you have the right listing? Recheck the surname! Remember that all the surnames sounding alike will be together; there could be a number of surnames coded as C-642 that show a Charles as a given name. But not all will be for Carlson. If you do not find Charles Carlson, don't give up yet. Was his full name Charles

William Carlson? Since this is in strict alphabetical order by the given name, you have several alternatives: C. W., Chas., Charles W., Charles William, and even Chuck or another nickname.

NORTH DAKOTA M1580

1. A-000 Irak—A-536 Bunt O.
2. A-536 C.—B-200 Isebell
3. B-200 J.B.—B-356 William
4. B-360 A.J.—B-531 Thomas L.
5. B-532 (N.R.)—B-625 William O.
6. B-626 (N.R.)—B-653 Willie
7. B-654 Agathe—C-462 Winnie
8. C-465 Adelade—C-642 Katherine
9. C-642 Lars—D-400 Iva
10. D-400 J.C.—E-200 Tonnes

First ten rolls of North Dakota Soundex from the catalog.

What Will It Show?

There are four different census cards that appear in the various Soundex: the Family Card; the Continuation Card (when the family doesn't fit on one card); the Individual Card (for those who lived in a home in which the head of household bore a different surname); and the Institution Card. Certain items from the full listings were extracted and entered onto these cards to form this Soundex index. You will be particularly interested in the Family Cards (illustrated below) and the Individual Cards. If your ancestor, Jonathan Carlson, was living with his grandfather Jackson Martensen, Jonathan would be listed on an Individual Card. That card would include the name of Jackson Martensen and the reference numbers of the Martensen household so that you could then obtain that listing.

(HEAD OF FAMILY) VOL. ______ E.D. ______
SHEET ______ LINE ______

(COLOR) (AGE) (BIRTHPLACE) (CITIZENSHIP)

(COUNTY)

(CITY) (STREET) (HOUSE NO.)

OTHER MEMBERS OF FAMILY

NAME	RELATIONSHIP	AGE	BIRTHPLACE	CITIZEN-SHIP

Sample Family Card from the 1920 Soundex.

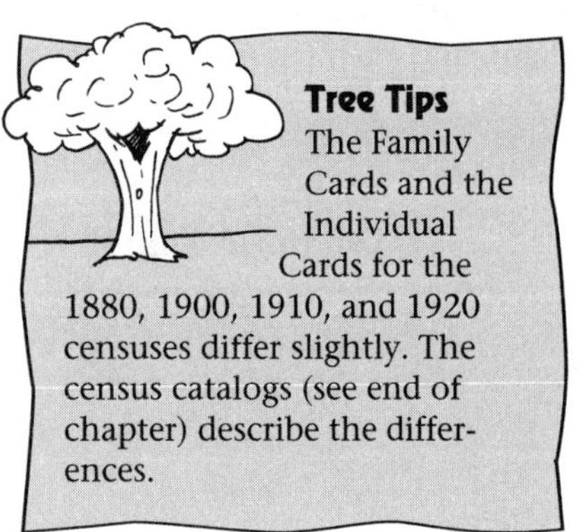

Tree Tips
The Family Cards and the Individual Cards for the 1880, 1900, 1910, and 1920 censuses differ slightly. The census catalogs (see end of chapter) describe the differences.

The head of the household is listed, with his or her age, birthplace, and citizenship. This is followed by the city, street, and house number. Then those living in the same home are listed, along with their relationship to the head of household, age, birthplace, and whether they are citizens. But most important to you right now is the upper right hand corner, where you will find Vol. [Volume], E.D. [Enumeration District] number, Sheet [Page] number, and Line. You particularly need the E.D. number and Sheet number to find the whole listing. Remember, the Soundex is only an index; it does not contain everything that is available in the full listing. It is important to copy those references; you will need them to obtain the full listing on another set of microfilm.

Use the Microfilm Catalog

You used one set of microfilm to access the Soundex and to get the needed reference numbers. Specifically, you now know from the Soundex the state, county, Enumeration District number, and page number. Go to the microfilm catalog again. This time check the section in the catalog that is for the full 1920 Federal Census (not the Soundex). Determine the Micropublication Number and the roll you will need. If there is more than one roll for the county, watch for the roll with the Enumeration District number you found on the Soundex. In the example of North Dakota, you will find that the 1920 census is Micropublication T265, and that the rolls with the North Dakota counties are #1330 through #1343, as shown in the following figure. Since you now have the county from the Soundex, check to see on which roll that county is listed. If the repository does not have the census microfilm catalogs issued by the National Archives, they will have their own catalogs available to assist you in determining which microfilm roll you need.

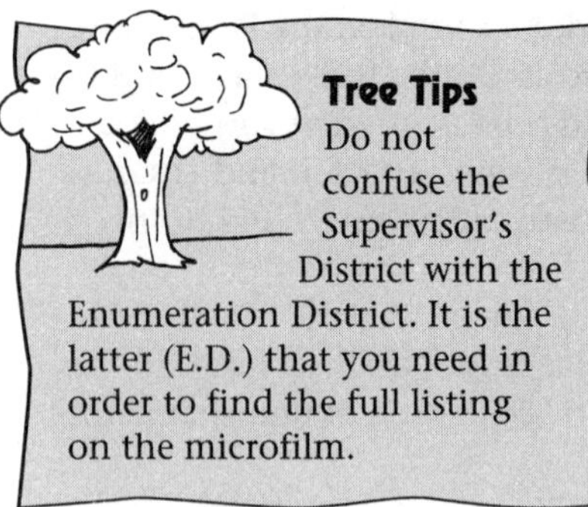

Tree Tips
Do not confuse the Supervisor's District with the Enumeration District. It is the latter (E.D.) that you need in order to find the full listing on the microfilm.

NORTH DAKOTA

1330. Adams Co. (EDs 1-11), Barnes Co. (EDs 1-19), Benson Co. (EDs 20-35), Billings Co. (EDs 12-20), and Bowman Co. (EDs 21-31).
1331. Bottineau Co. (EDs 36-56), Burke Co. (EDs 32-41), Burleigh Co. (EDs 57-69, 267, and 70-76), and Divide Co. (EDs 42-49).
1332. Cass Co. (EDs 1-2, 12-21, 5-11, and 22-26) and Dickey Co. (EDs 77, 257, 78, 260, 79, 259, 80-82, 258, 83, 84, 262, 85, 256, 86, and 87).
1333. Cavalier Co. (EDs 27-42), Dunn Co. (EDs 50-59), Eddy Co. (EDs 88-95, 266, and 96), Emmons Co. (EDs 97-113), and Griggs Co. (EDs 121-128).
1334. Foster Co. (EDs 114-120), Golden Valley Co. (EDs 60-68), Grand Forks Co. (EDs 54-65, 43-53, and 66-72), and Grant Co. (EDs 69-81).
1335. Hettinger Co. (EDs 82-89), Kidder Co. (EDs 129-134, 261, and 135-140), Logan Co. (EDs 155-162, 263, and 268), La Moure Co. (EDs 141-154), and McKenzie Co. (EDs 90-106).
1336. McHenry Co. (EDs 163-178, 264, and 179-182), McIntosh Co. (EDs 183-191), McLean Co. (EDs 107-124), and Mercer Co. (EDs 125-133).
1337. Morton Co. (EDs 134-152), Oliver Co. (EDs 167-172), Mountrail Co. (EDs 153-166), and Nelson Co. (EDs 73-83).
1338. Pembina Co. (EDs 84-101), Pierce Co. (EDs 192-201), Ramsey Co. (EDs 102-117), and Renville Co. (EDs 173-181).
1339. Ramson Co. (EDs 118-128), Stark Co. (EDs 197-210), Richland Co. (EDs 129-148), and Sioux Co. (EDs 182-187).
1340. Rolette Co. (EDs 202-211), Sargent Co. (EDs 149-158), Slope Co. (EDs 188-196), Sheridan Co. (EDs 212-220), Steele Co. (EDs 159-163, 211, and 164-167), and Towner Co. (EDs 168-175, 212, 176, and 177).
1341. Stutsman Co. (EDs 221-226, 269, and 227-243), Traill Co. (EDs 178-189), and Wells Co. (EDs 244-247, 265, 248, and 255).
1342. Walsh Co. (EDs 190-210), Williams Co. (EDs 239-256), and Ward Co. (EDs 211-217).
1343. Ward Co. (EDs 218-238).

From the 1920 Federal Population Census Catalog.

There They Are!

You now have the roll of microfilm in hand. Finally, you can locate the full family listing. Proceed to the county you need on the film. Look for the Enumeration District (E.D.) number you obtained from the Soundex. The E.D.'s will be arranged numerically, usually in the upper right hand of the census page. Then proceed to the page (sheet) number you found, and look for the listing.

One of your most exciting moments will be in locating your first census record. There they are—the whole family, Grandpa, Grandma, and all the children, including your mother when she was four. It's fun to imagine your grandpa and grandma trying to remember their former homes so they could give the birthplace of each child, along with answering the census taker's other questions.

Once the listing is found, hand copy it in its entirety. Census forms like those shown in Appendix E will be

Tree Tips
Even if you know there is an error in the listing, copy it exactly as it appears. Be sure to include everyone listed in the home, such as boarders, servants, and so on. You may later realize that there was a relationship.

of use. Copy the entries exactly as you see them. If it shows Jas. don't write James. If it shows William don't write Wm. If it shows John Charley Harvey, don't take it as John C. Harvey. If it shows Mary A. and you have proof that she is Mary Ann, don't expand the A. to Ann. Write Mary A., as it is entered. If you do wish to add a note, add it in brackets so it is clear that this was an addition. Be sure to include the sex. You may think it is obvious that John is a male and Ann is a female. But what about Willie? Later you may wonder if that was a daughter named Wilhelmina or a son named William. Nothing will be too minor and can later be helpful. If there is a microfilm reader/printer, you can make a microcopy.

Using the Pre-1880 Schedules

Indexes for censuses from 1790 through 1870 are not available in Soundex. They have been indexed by a variety of indexers, however, and are available in published books. The repositories that carry the microfilm normally have a large number of these indexes. Though indexes vary, they usually show the name, county, township, district or ward, and a page number.

Tree Tips

Often there is a stamped page number, as well as one or two handwritten page numbers. Some indexers used the stamped page numbers, others used those that were hand written. If you cannot find the listing, you may be using the wrong set of page numbers. This is particularly true in the earlier census.

Once you have the indexed entry, determine from the catalog which roll you need. The rolls will be arranged first by state, and then by county. For the pre-1880 census, you will not need to determine an Enumeration District; it is indexed by the page number (and township), which will lead you to the listing. In a few minutes, you'll find that long sought listing.

An understanding of the variations among the census records will assist in assessing the usefulness of what you find. Once you realize the diversity of the questions asked, you will be amazed at the picture they can provide of your ancestors. Though the early census years (1790 through 1840) named only the head of household by name, nonetheless, important information is ascertained. Beginning in 1850, each person in the home was listed, making this resource of major importance in genealogy.

The First in 1790

Marshals were required to list the number of inhabitants within their districts. They were to omit those Indians not taxed (those who did not live within the towns and cities) and list those who were taxed. They listed free persons (including *indentured servants*) in categories of age and sex. The rest were counted as "all others," that is, slaves.

Broad Categories and No Names

Free white males in the 1790 census were listed by two age groups, those of 16 years and upwards, and those under that age. The total free white females were listed with no age distinction at all. Only the head of the household was listed by name. John Jackson, who was age 40 and who had a son, age 18; a son, age 12; a wife, age 38; and two daughters, ages 8 and 10 would be listed as two males 16 or over, one male under 16, and three females.

In 1908, the federal government transcribed and printed the 1790 census for all available states: Connecticut, Maine, Maryland, Massachusetts, New Hampshire, New York, North Carolina, Pennsylvania, Rhode Island, South Carolina, Vermont, and the reconstructed census of Virginia. The 1790 census for Delaware, Georgia, Kentucky, New Jersey, Tennessee, and Virginia were lost or destroyed. (Because of the importance of Virginia, a substitute for that state was prepared by using tax lists of the 1780s.) The printed 1790 census is available in most large libraries. A reprint edition by Genealogical Publishing Company in 1952 made the set widely available.

> **Genie Jargon**
> An **indentured servant** is one who entered into a contract binding himself or herself into the service of another for a specified term, usually in exchange for passage. The number of years could vary; usually it was four to seven years.

> **Tree Tips**
> When the census schedules show age brackets such as males 10 to 16, males 16 to 26, and so on, the ages included within the category are actually one year under the next category. For example, males 10 to 16 includes males through age 15; males 16 to 26 includes males through the age of 25.

Creatively Using Sparse Information

With the broad categories in the 1790 census, you may wonder what value it could be in your search. Understandably, it will not be as much help as later census records that were more detailed. Nonetheless, the 1790 census will place your family in a specific location. If the name is not too common and you can establish an approximate birth from other records, you may even be able to backtrack to the 1790 census to get ideas of possible parentage.

Creatively Using Even Sparser Information

Let's say you are tracing Jonathan Calavary who was born, according to a Bible record, on 3 March 1783. You find him in census records in 1830, '40, and '50 as head of household. But who is his father? He was only about seven when the 1790 census was taken. He should therefore be listed as a male under 16 in his father's home in 1790. Search the 1790 federal census for the state for the name Calavary. You may find a family with a male listed aged under 16. With that unusual surname, there won't be many, and it will be a starting place for the search.

Lineage Lessons

Since only the head of household is actually named in the censuses of 1790 through 1840, it isn't possible to determine with certainty which are family members. Some of the others listed by age may not be part of the immediate family. Another relative or a helper could have been living in the home.

1800 and 1810 Census

The 1800 and 1810 censuses were more expansive. The head of the family was listed; the free white males and free white females were listed by age: under 10, 10 to 16, 16 to 26, 26 to 45, and 45 or older. It also included the number of other free persons in the household (except Indians not taxed), the number of slaves, and the place of residence.

In some early censuses, the lists were copied and rearranged alphabetically by the census taker. This loses the advantage of listing the family with neighbors. But most often the lists are in the order that the families were contacted by the census taker.

1820 Adds Males 16 to 18

The 1820 census asked the same questions as in 1810. It also added a category for males 16 to 18, while retaining the 16 to 26 category. Other questions included the number of those not naturalized; the number engaged in agriculture, commerce, or manufacturing; the number of "colored" persons; and the number of other persons, with the exception of Indians.

1830 and 1840 Censuses Narrow Age

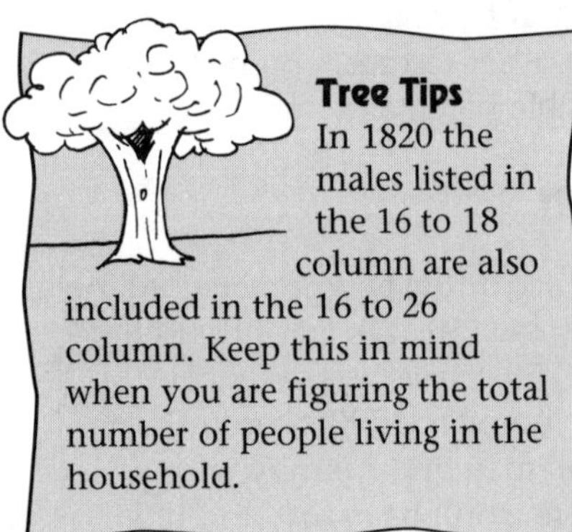

Tree Tips

In 1820 the males listed in the 16 to 18 column are also included in the 16 to 26 column. Keep this in mind when you are figuring the total number of people living in the household.

In 1830, the age categories were narrowed, enabling researchers to establish ages with more precision. The categories for male and female were: under 5; 5 to 10, 10 to 15, 15 to 20, 20 to 30, 30 to 40, 40 to 50, 50 to 60, 60 to 70, 70 to 80, 80 to 90, 90 to 100, and over 100. The number of those who were "deaf, dumb, and blind" and the number of aliens were listed. In addition, the number of slaves and free "colored" persons were included by age categories.

The 1840 census contained the same columns as 1830, with an addition important to genealogical research. A column was added for the ages of military war pensioners (usually for Revolutionary War service). Also added were columns to count those engaged in agriculture; mining; commerce; manufacturing and trade; navigation of the ocean; navigation of canals, lakes, and rivers; learned professions and engineers; number in school; number in family over age of 21 who could not read and write; and the number of "insane."

The value of knowing the age of pensioners in the 1840 census is immense. The pensioner might have been the soldier, or the widow, or other entitled person. You will find that Mary Conklin at age 97 was living with Mary Montanya in Haverstraw, Rockland County, New York. John Jones of Metal, Franklin County, Pennsylvania was living at the remarkable age of 110. This listing of pensioners was extracted and published by the federal government in 1841, with a reprint by Southern Book Company in 1954 and subsequent reprints with an added index by the Genealogical Publishing Company.

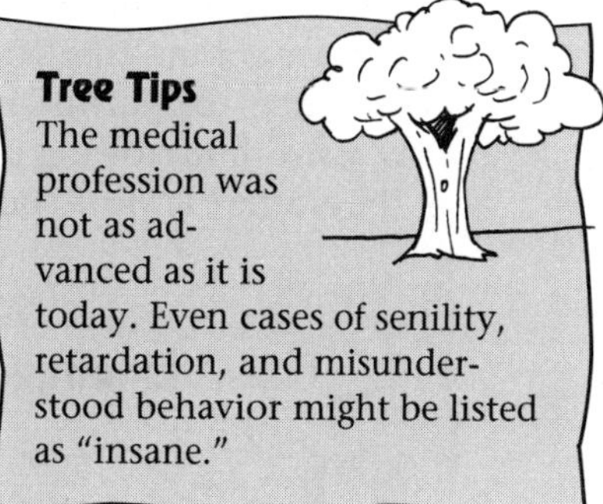

Tree Tips
The medical profession was not as advanced as it is today. Even cases of senility, retardation, and misunderstood behavior might be listed as "insane."

Everyone Has a Name in 1850

The 1850 Federal Census was the first to require the name and age of *everyone* in the household. Its value to genealogists increased dramatically as a result. A dwelling number and family number was assigned to each listing in the order of visitation. Questions included name, age, sex, color, occupation, value of real estate, birthplace, whether married within the year, attended school within the year, and whether they could read or write (if over the age of 20). Additionally, whether any were deaf-mute, blind, insane, "idiotic," or convict.

Tree Tips
Take down all the details from the listing. Any item in the census can later prove useful in identifying family members. The page number and household number will also assist in locating the listing again.

The census is useful for clues in naming patterns, in identifying the household as of a certain date, occupation, and migration. The value of real estate gives some idea of the worth of the family and is an additional clue that there could be land records available in the county.

Those Others Living with the Family

Those living with the family should be carefully noted because they might be relatives—a mother-in-law or a married sister. And very important, the families listed a few listings before and after the family should be noted because they too may be related. If not, they may still assist the search because families usually did not move in isolation. When migrating from one area to another, they were often accompanied by family or friends. That information can lead you to a prior residence.

Let's say you are tracing a family listed in the 1850 census of Montgomery County, Tennessee and note the older members of the family were all born in North Carolina. You know they moved between 1844 and 1846, because a child was born in Tennessee in 1846. The surname is common. Where in North Carolina to look? Check the neighbors. You notice that some of them were also born in North Carolina and, judging from the birthplaces of the children, seem to have moved around the same time. Look in the 1840 census index of North Carolina for the surname, *and the surname of the neighbors.* This may assist in narrowing the search when you find similar names grouped together in one of the North Carolina counties.

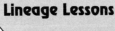

Lineage Lessons

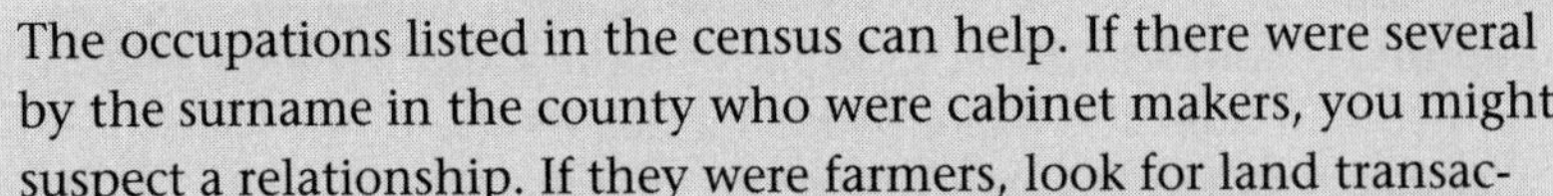

The occupations listed in the census can help. If there were several by the surname in the county who were cabinet makers, you might suspect a relationship. If they were farmers, look for land transactions. If your ancestor was a doctor, perhaps the medical school he attended has data. The census can even point you to military records when it shows "sailor" or "Col., U.S. Army" as the "occupation."

Slaveholders and Slaves

There were separate slave schedules taken with the 1850 census. The name of the slave owner was given, the number of slaves he owned, and the number of former slaves now freed. The slaves, however, were not listed by name. These schedules have been microfilmed.

Leads and More Leads

The clues that result from the use of a census listing are many. Your family was listed in 1850 Pennsylvania and part of the information shown was:

Name	Age	Sex	Birthplace	Occupation	Real Estate
SMITH, Jonathan	39	m	Virginia	Farmer	$100
Mary	37	f	Virginia	keeping house	
Barnabus	11	m	Virginia		
Catharine	9	f	Maryland		
Joseph	7	m	Pennsylvania		
Martha	3	f	Pennsylvania		
Jessie	1	f	Pennsylvania		
JORDAN, Barnabus	65	m	Virginia	retired	

How does this help? You now know that Jonathan Smith was born ca. (about) 1811 in Virginia, and that his wife was born ca. 1813 in Virginia. Their son Barnabus was born ca. 1839 in Virginia. Catharine's birthplace indicates that they moved to Maryland between about 1839 and 1841. But soon thereafter they moved to Pennsylvania, in time for the birth of Joseph about 1843, followed by Martha and Jessie. You now have an idea of the migratory pattern of this family. In addition, since Jonathan Smith was a farmer and had real estate valued at $100.00, you can check for a deed on the farm. Even the township is helpful. Using that, county histories can be consulted for early inhabitants.

Lineage Lessons

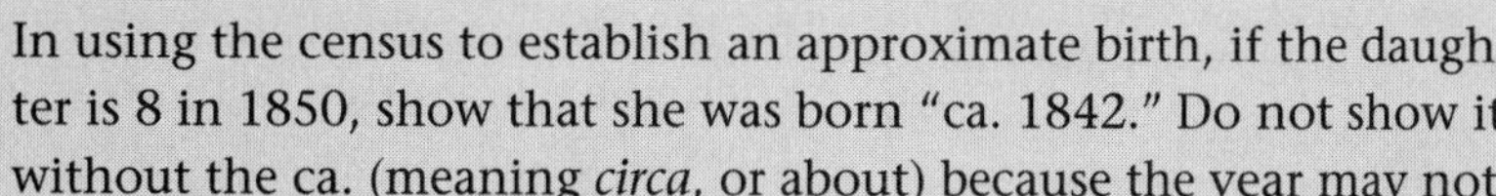

In using the census to establish an approximate birth, if the daughter is 8 in 1850, show that she was born "ca. 1842." Do not show it without the ca. (meaning *circa*, or about) because the year may not be correct. In 1850, the census year was measured from June 1, 1849 through May 31, 1850. The actual month of birth affects the calculation of the age. Aside from that, there are many errors in ages. When asked the age of my own four children, I need to stop and calculate it and can err. If you use ca. this will caution others that it is not firm. If you later find the exact birth from a Bible or other record, you can then enter the full date and remove the *ca*.

What about Barnabus Jordan, aged 65, living with the family? You note that he was born in Virginia (as was Mary Smith, Jonathan's probable wife), and that Jonathan and Mary Smith named a son Barnabus. Possibly Barnabus Jordan is Mary's father. Though this census does not give the required proof, it is another "lead" to follow.

Do you stop here? No. Check the listings before and after Jonathan Smith. Two listings before is Martin Smith, age 69, born in Virginia, and Mary Smith, age 67, born in Virginia. Could they be Jonathan's parents? Three listings after Jonathan is Thomas Gordon, 40, and Matilda Gordon, 35, both born in Virginia. Among their children is a son, *Barnabus* Gordon. Perhaps Matilda is a sister of Mary. The name similarity of the child Barnabus, together with the ages of Mary, 37, and Matilda, 35, both born in Virginia, would suggest that they might be sisters. Although it will need further investigation, you have another clue.

The 1860 and 1870 Censuses

The 1860 federal census contains information similar to that of the 1850 census, but adds a column for the value of personal property and a column for those who were paupers. There were also separate slave schedules, as in 1850.

In 1870, a column was added for Father Foreign Born and another for Mother Foreign Born. (If marked, this can lead to a search of naturalization records and ship passenger lists.) Also, if an individual was born or married within the year, the month of the event was to be recorded.

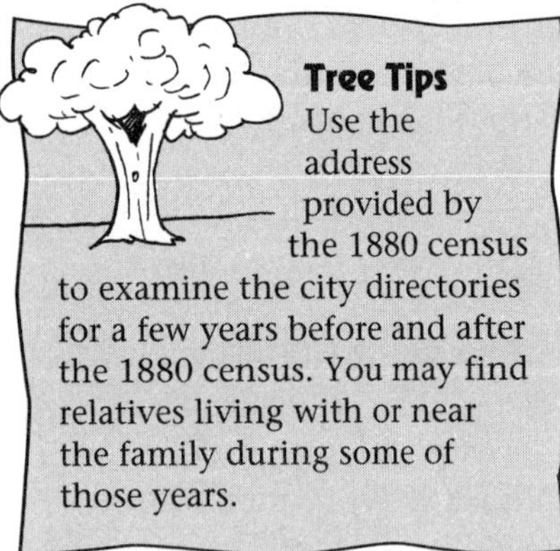

Tree Tips
Use the address provided by the 1880 census to examine the city directories for a few years before and after the 1880 census. You may find relatives living with or near the family during some of those years.

1880, 1885, and 1890 Censuses

The 1880 census adds the birthplace of the father and the mother (state and country only) in the population schedules. This has created an important resource, but it must be used with caution. Often the person did not know where his or her father or mother were born, and so only guessed. The 1880 census added another entry important in your search: the relationship of the person listed to the head of household, such as "wife," "brother," "mother-in-law," "boarder," and so on. Whether they were single, married, widowed, or divorced was noted. Another helpful addition is the address of those who lived in cities or urban areas.

Special 1885 Federal Census

Five states and territories conducted an 1885 census partly funded by the federal government: Colorado, Florida, Nebraska, Dakota territory, and New Mexico territory. These are at the National Archives in Washington, D.C.; only those for Colorado and Nebraska have been microfilmed.

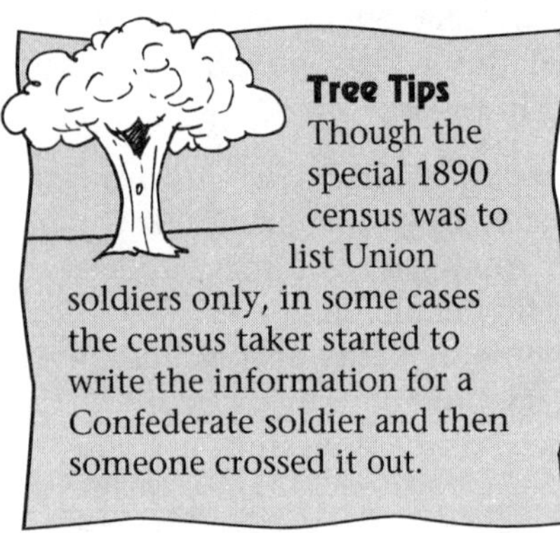

Tree Tips
Though the special 1890 census was to list Union soldiers only, in some cases the census taker started to write the information for a Confederate soldier and then someone crossed it out.

Special 1890 Civil War Census

With a few minor exceptions, most of the 1890 federal population census was burned. A special census taken that year for Union soldiers, however, was only partially destroyed. It is missing states and territories from A through Kansas and part of Kentucky, but the rest survives and includes the soldier's rank, company, regiment or vessel, enlistment, discharge, length of service, post office address, and some other remarks. This is available on microfilm in the National Archives.

Changes in the 1900, 1910, and 1920 Censuses

The 1900 census has the month and year of birth in addition to age and the number of years married. The mother was required to list how many children she had borne and how many were still living. For immigrants, the year of entry, the number of years in the United States, and whether naturalized were noted. Various other questions were also included.

In 1910, refinements were made. One of the most important additions was the question of whether the males were Union or Confederate veterans. This can lead you to military records.

Lineage Lessons

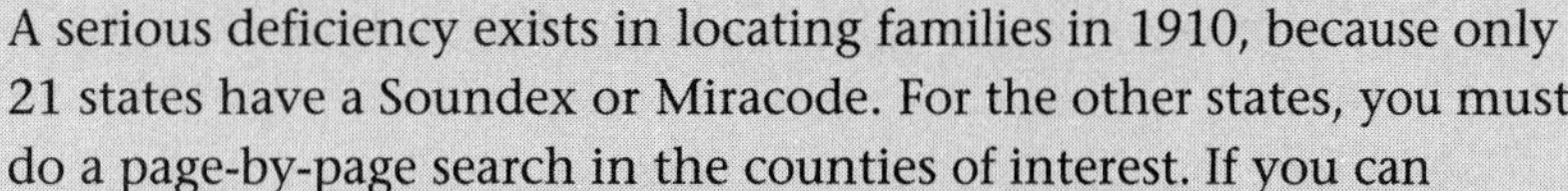

A serious deficiency exists in locating families in 1910, because only 21 states have a Soundex or Miracode. For the other states, you must do a page-by-page search in the counties of interest. If you can establish the address, your search can be shortened by narrowing it to an Enumeration District. Consult the National Archives Micropublication T1224, Census Enumeration District Descriptions. Also available on microfiche at the National Archives branches and many libraries is a 1910 city street finding aid.

In addition to names, ages, and so on, the 1920 census adds the year of immigration, whether naturalized, and the year of naturalization, as well as other important information.

Mortality Schedules

Starting in 1850, a listing was made by the census taker of those who died during the previous 12 months (June 1, 1849 to May 31, 1850). This mortality schedule is an important search record. It includes the name of the deceased, sex, age, color, whether widowed, place of birth, the month in which the death occurred, their profession (or occupation or trade), the cause of death or the disease, and the number of days ill. The originals of these are not centrally located. In addition to the 1850 mortality schedules, the 1860, 1870, and 1880 census included similar lists with a few changes. In 1870 the place of birth of the parents of the deceased was included. Mortality schedules were also taken with the special 1885 federal census. Greenwood's *Researcher's Guide to American Genealogy* has a listing of mortality schedules and the physical location of these important records.

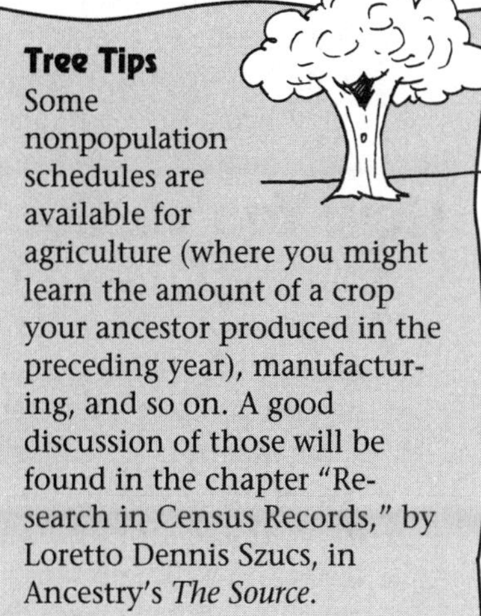

Tree Tips

Some nonpopulation schedules are available for agriculture (where you might learn the amount of a crop your ancestor produced in the preceding year), manufacturing, and so on. A good discussion of those will be found in the chapter "Research in Census Records," by Loretto Dennis Szucs, in Ancestry's *The Source*.

The Family History Library has some of the mortality schedules on microfilm, and a microfiche listing of those available in other locations. Look also for the index to the 1850 through 1880 mortality schedules by Accelerated Indexing Systems.

Lineage Lessons

In addition to federal census records, a number of states conducted a state census. These are not centrally located. The best source for information on these records is Ann S. Lainhart's *State Census Records,* widely available in libraries. It explains the differences between the state and federal census, questions asked, and the location of these records.

Can I Trust These Old Records?

You might be perplexed when you find that the census listings you obtained from 1850, 1860, 1870, and 1880 all conflict. "How can that be," you wonder. The problem is that you do not know who supplied the answers. Perhaps the father did not remember the exact ages of the children. Perhaps the mother was shy and illiterate and became confused. Perhaps one of the children supplied the answers and did not know the correct answer. Add the possibility that the census taker made an error or that he entered the data incorrectly. Also, some problems exist on individual rolls because of pages skipped when microfilming or poor quality of microfilming when the project was started.

If these weren't problems enough, some of the census returns had two additional handwritten copies made from the original. Upon completion, one went to the Bureau of Census, one to the state government, and one to the county government. Now the chance of error was multiplied. The person writing the copies could have skipped an entry, erred on reading a name, or made any number of other errors.

Now You've Got Something to Work With

Obtaining census records starts to lay the foundation for the documentation you will build on your family. By comparing the listings in the various census years, you can reconstruct a fairly accurate list of the family members and the places in which they lived. You can even determine something about their background through questions on naturalization or military service. You will get further insight as to their worth, those in the family with afflictions, and other details. Always get all the available census records for your ancestors, not just one or two. Every listing is a potential source of important leads and will help build that solid, documented line for you. For additional reading, consult *Guide to Genealogical Research in the National Archives,* Chapter 1.

Relative Resources

Census of Pensioners for Revolutionary or Military Services Under the Act for Taking the Sixth Census. Washington, D.C.: Blair and Rives, 1841. reprint 1954, Baltimore, MD: Southern Book Co.

Greenwood, Val D. *The Researcher's Guide to American Genealogy*. 2nd ed. Baltimore, MD: Genealogical Publishing Co., 1990.

Guide to Genealogical Research in the National Archives. Washington, D.C.: National Archives, 1982, Chapter 1, pp. 11–38.

Lainhart, Ann S. *State Census Records*. Baltimore, MD: Genealogical Publishing Co., 1992.

Szucs, Loretto Dennis. "Research in Census Records." Loretto Dennis Szucs and Sandra Hargreaves Luebking. *The Source*. Revised ed. (Salt Lake City, UT: Ancestry, 1997.) Chapter 5, pp. 104–146.

Catalogs of Census Microfilm

The 1790–1890 Federal Population Censuses: Catalog of National Archives Microfilm. Washington, D.C.: National Archives, 1991.

The 1900 Federal Population Census: A Catalog of Microfilm Copies of the Schedules. Washington, D.C.: National Archives, 1978.

The 1910 Federal Population Census: A Catalog of Microfilm Copies of the Schedules. Washington, D.C.: National Archives, 1982.

The 1920 Federal Population Census: Catalog of National Archives Microfilm. Washington, D.C.: National Archives, 1991.

Addresses

American Genealogical Lending Library, P.O. Box 244, Bountiful, UT 84011-0244. [For microfilm rental.]

Bureau of Census, P.O. Box 1545, Jefferson, IN 47131. [To Order "Application for Search of Census Records" for 1930.]

National Archives Microfilm Rental Program, P.O. Box 30, Annapolis Junction, MD 20701-0030. [For microfilm rental.]

The Least You Need to Know

- The 1790 through 1840 censuses only list by name the head of household.
- From 1850 on each person in the household is named.
- In 1880 the birthplace (state and country) of the parents is listed, and the relationships to the head of the household.
- Census records have many errors created by faulty memories or lack of knowledge by those who supplied the information.

Chapter 11

Corresponding Effectively

In This Chapter

- ➤ The importance of knowing where to write
- ➤ The letter that will bring a response
- ➤ Samples of concise letters
- ➤ Some cost cutting ideas

Writing letters will substantially aid your search. You can do it from your home with amazing results. In this chapter are some ways to increase the effectiveness of the letters and some cost cutting measures to help the tight budget.

Keep in mind your goal and the goal of the responder. You want some data. The responder wants to supply the data with the least effort and time as possible. Your letter will be more effective if you remember certain basics. Clearly state what you want to achieve with the letter, send it to the right place, and make a good impression so it will be taken seriously.

Other considerations:

- ➤ Use full-size (8.5 × 11) paper
- ➤ Eye appeal (wide margins, space between paragraphs, no smudges)
- ➤ Include your name and address on the letter

- Be concise
- Enclose an LSASE (long self-addressed stamped envelope)
- Address the right facility
- Know dates of state vital statistics
- Know the holdings of the repository
- Offer to pay
- Don't unnecessarily limit your request
- Offer variant spellings for the family name

The Mechanics of Correspondence

Before we get into what to say in a letter requesting information, let's talk about some basics that should be a part of every letter.

Make It Look Neat

Use standard letter size paper when writing. If the recipient files the letters, standard size paper makes it easier, especially if they use a two-hole punch at the top. Smaller size paper tends to get lost in the stacks or slip down among larger papers.

Make your letter attractive. A letter that is crowded on the page has no eye appeal and leaves the impression that reading it will be a chore. Leave sufficient margins on the sides, as well as the top and bottom. And leave a blank line between paragraphs to set them off. If you do not have a typewriter or computer, take care to write legibly and neatly.

In this electronic age, many letterheads are prepared on the computer. Be sure to use a large enough typeface. Those with poor eyesight may mistake the 1 in your letterhead for a 7 if it is too small. Avoid some of the script or other fancy typefaces if the numbers are not easily distinguished.

Include How to Contact You

Be sure to include your name and address on the letter. It is easy for a letter to be separated from an envelope. Without an address, the letter you spent so much time composing may never get a response. Position the address at the top of the first page, not at the end of the letter. When it is answered or filed, the responder can immediately identify the sender without having to shuffle through the whole letter. Small courtesies that assist responders lighten their load and put you in a more favorable position for a reply.

Tree Tips
Keep a copy of the letters you send, at least until you get an answer.

Invest in a rubber stamp with your name and address. You will use this often. When you write to someone and include enclosures, rubber stamp the enclosures on the front so the recipient knows at a glance how to reach you. If the recipient photocopies your enclosures and sends them to someone else, that person also needs to know who supplied the data.

Spell It Correctly; ZIP It Right

When you send a letter, you are eager for a response. It is disappointing to have the letter returned in a few weeks because you misspelled the street name or inserted the wrong street address. Recheck the address. If in doubt, your library may have a telephone book with the address to which you're writing so you can verify it. You can also check one of the CD-ROMs that show addresses for residences and businesses, or even a mailing list on one of the on-line computer services that provides addresses.

Tree Tips
If you are a user of the Internet, look for the Postal Service's ZIP plus four directory available on-line at http://www.usps.gov/ncsc/lookups/lookup_ZIP+4.html.

The post office has assigned four additional numbers to ZIP codes to assist in getting the mail to its destination. Though it's not required that you use those additional digits on first class mail, it's a good habit. Always show them in your return address, too.

An SASE for Reply

Many repositories and individuals will not answer letters unless you enclose an SASE. While you are at it, make it an LSASE. The responder may have important data to send you that will not fit into a smaller envelope. If you are to receive the information, the responder is forced to prepare a long envelope, put postage on it, and hope for some other use for the smaller stamped envelope you sent. Meanwhile, your request might be set aside and forgotten. Or, the responder may opt to send you a brief reply that fits the smaller envelope and decide not to include copies that could have been easily slipped into a larger envelope.

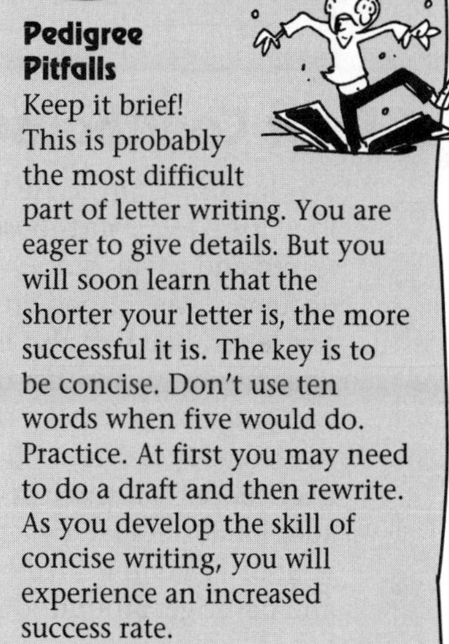
Pedigree Pitfalls
Keep it brief! This is probably the most difficult part of letter writing. You are eager to give details. But you will soon learn that the shorter your letter is, the more successful it is. The key is to be concise. Don't use ten words when five would do. Practice. At first you may need to do a draft and then rewrite. As you develop the skill of concise writing, you will experience an increased success rate.

What Should I Say?

When you are seeking information about your ancestor, be specific. A "please send me everything you have" letter, whether to a repository or to a relative, will probably remain unanswered.

To assist in developing the technique for writing an effective letter to a business or repository, consider the goal of the letter. What is it you want? Information about the parents? The names of the children? Each of these is approached in a different manner. State clearly what you want in your letter. Different records need to be examined, depending on your goal. If you are searching for Ezekiel Madison's parents, you might check the obituary, death certificate, birth record, marriage record, and various others. To find Ezekiel Madison's children, his obituary could help, but his death certificate, birth record, or marriage record would not disclose that information. Each request involves different search techniques. Responses will be more on target if the responder knows your goal. Before you write, decide on one or two things that you are hoping to find. Then, ask for exactly what you want.

Lineage Lessons

Do you want to prove that two persons were married? Or to prove they married in a specific county? There is a difference! A number of records might prove the couple were married: deeds naming them as husband and wife, receipt of a wife's inheritance signed for by her husband, and more. But the question as to whether they were married is different from determining in which county they were married. The latter requires you to look at records that disclose the location: the recorded marriage record, the family Bible, the pension application in a war pension file, and others. These subtle differences become second nature as you learn about the records and their use in your research.

"Dear Courthouse"

Writing to a courthouse is somewhat different from writing to an individual or a library. In writing to a courthouse, keep your requests separate. That is, if you need a marriage record and a will, write two separate letters. This is not the time to save postage. If those documents are in two different departments, you will slow the process by writing only one letter. You will also be depending on a clerk to fulfill your order and then transfer your request to another department. A glitch can develop. If, however, you are ordering two of the same type of document, such as two marriage records, include both requests in the same letter; they will be handled by the same clerk. Always limit any request; if you need more than three or four documents, even if they are of the same type, order the additional ones later. Otherwise, a busy clerk will process simpler requests first, setting your more complicated one aside. The clerk could then forget or misplace your request and never get around to responding.

Alternate Spellings

The clerk of the courthouse will not know that the surname you seek can be spelled in a variety of ways. They will look only for the name you request. If you write for the will of John Critchfield, show it in your letter of request as "John Critchfield (Scritchfield, Crutchfield)" and any other spellings you have encountered. Otherwise, they may miss the record.

Write to the Right Place

> **Tree Tips**
> Don't know the exact title of the department you want? Write on the envelope: "Probate Department" (for estates) or "Marriage Record Department" or "Deed Department." It will reach the appropriate clerk.

You want to obtain a deed from Groton, Connecticut. Should you send your request to the registrar of deeds at the county courthouse? You need a will from Lynchburg, Virginia; on the map it appears to be in Campbell County. Send them a letter? In both of these instances, your letter would have been unsuccessful. Each would have cost you two stamps (for your letter, and for the return envelope you enclosed). You might even assume that they didn't have the information when you don't get a response. All the while, the records could be on their shelves.

What went wrong? Connecticut does not have county courthouses; they have town halls where the deeds are recorded. You wrote to a nonexistent facility. And Lynchburg is one of almost 30 independent cities in Virginia. They have their own courthouse and are not a part of the adjacent county. The use of a guidebook to determine the appropriate addressee is essential.

Several books will assist you in these determinations: Everton's *Handy Book for Genealogists, Ancestry's Redbook,* and Marcia Wiswall Lindberg's *Genealogist's Handbook for New England Research,* 2nd ed.

In writing to local governments, keep these points in mind.

- In some New England states, the document you want may be in the Town Hall.
- It may be in a probate district office (encompassing several towns).
- It may be in a county courthouse.
- In Virginia, it may be in the courthouse of an independent city.
- The county may have more than one courthouse.

To find the addresses of other places to write, use the many directories available in your library; there are directories of funeral homes, newspapers, libraries, and others. *Directories in Print,* 14th ed., will amaze you with the listings it includes. Also helpful is Bentley's *The Genealogist's Address Book*. Use these resources to determine the correct address; you want the letter to get there on the first try.

State Registration of Vital Statistics

All states eventually provided for registration of vital statistics on the state level. The beginning dates varied from state to state, but generally are in the first part of the 20th century. Before that time, counties maintained their own registers, but the starting dates of those also varied. You need to know the beginning date of state registration for vital statistics. Without that, you will be unsure whether to write to the State Department of Health or to the courthouse. One particularly good source is Thomas Kemp's *International Vital Records Handbook*. The starting dates of state registrations, fees, addresses, and a copy of the forms on which to order the documents are included. The forms can be freely photocopied; they are not restricted. Another source that is helpful, though it does not include a copy of the forms, is "Where to Write for Vital Records" in Ancestry's *The Source*.

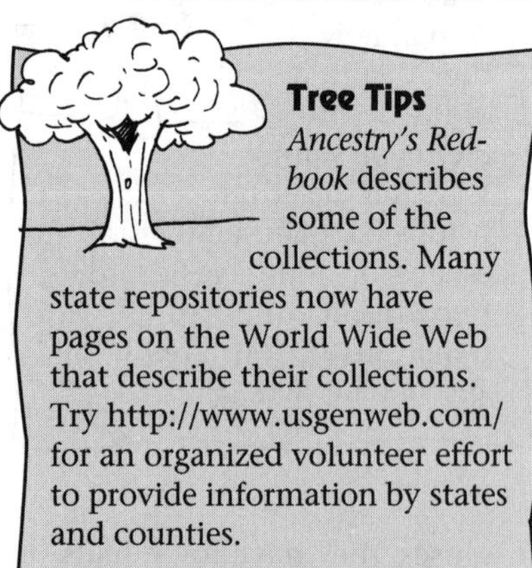

Tree Tips

Ancestry's Redbook describes some of the collections. Many state repositories now have pages on the World Wide Web that describe their collections. Try http://www.usgenweb.com/ for an organized volunteer effort to provide information by states and counties.

What's on the Shelves?

When writing to a repository, knowing its holdings will increase your success rate. Which of the state repositories has the best newspaper collection for an obituary? Which is more likely to have the military muster rolls of the state? Look for published guides, which might be available in your library.

What's It Going to Cost?

It is normally a good practice to inquire about the cost of a document or service in advance of placing an order. If you don't, you may be surprised with a fee higher than you had expected. For mail order requests, some New York counties, for instance, charge $25.00 to search a record under 25 years old, and $70.00 for records over 25 years old. Their photocopy charges by mail can be as high as $3.00 per page. When you write, first explain what you need, and then add "please quote for a copy of these records before proceeding." The alternative is to send a limited "blank" check, (or a small check for $5.00), with the notation, "if it is higher, please let me know before proceeding."

Tree Tips

Some repositories accept credit cards. If you are in a hurry for the information, you can call to inquire.

Offer to Pay Promptly

When writing for a record for which payment will be required, you have options.

- Enclose a check with the exact fee.
- Offer to pay upon being advised of the charges.

- ➤ Send a check for a small amount and ask them to advise you if more payment is required.
- ➤ Send a check without the figure inserted but with a limitation clearly marked.

If you are ordering a birth or death record, or some other record with a standard fee, the guide books may provide the amount of the fee. If so, enclose a check or money order with your request.

If you do not know the amount, you can insert a clause "I will pay the cost immediately upon knowing the charge." This may delay fulfillment of your request because the responder then has two options:

1. To send you the information with the bill.
2. To write to let you know the amount.

An alternative is to send a check for a small amount, for instance $5.00, and to request that any overpayment be refunded or that you be notified if the charge is higher than the amount of your check.

"Not Over $..."

An optional method is to send a signed check with a limitation, as shown in the following figure. But *never, never* send a signed check with an unlimited blank amount. The proper way to send such a check is to date it, *always write in the name of the payee,* sign it, and then, under the line where the amount is to be filled in, in block letters write "NOT OVER $5.00" or some other amount. Draw attention in your letter to the blank amount that needs to be completed. "I am unsure of the cost so I enclose a check marked 'Not over $5.00.' Please fill in the correct amount. If it is more, please let me know." If you do not put in a limiting amount, any amount can be inserted in the check. Be very cautious. There are several advantages to enclosing a check if you observe the precautions. Your request will not be delayed, and the responder will spend less time fulfilling your request. You both will be "winners."

Date: *[fill in appropriate date]*

Pay to the order of *Clerk of the Court of Juniper Co.* $________

______________________________________Dollars

[NOT OVER FIVE DOLLARS]

[Your signature here]

Example of a check with a clear limitation and with the payee filled in.

Never send cash. You may feel it is such a small amount that if it should get lost, it isn't a problem. But this creates an awkward situation; the recipient may feel that you will question his or her honesty if the funds happen to be lost.

Sample Letters

Letter writing is a skill that can be mastered. When you see the high success rate that can be accomplished by observing a few "rules," it will excite you to see what can be accomplished by mail. The following examples of letters demonstrate the technique of keeping requests simple but to the point. Develop a few letters of your own and save them as templates to use when you write future requests.

Trying to Find a Will

In the first example, you are writing to get some information from an estate. You are hoping that your great-grandfather left a will. But don't limit yourself to requesting the will. If he died without a will and had sufficient property, there still could be an *administration*. Depending upon the reply to the letter shown below, you can follow up with a request for additional documents.

[Your name and address]

December 5, 2001

Probate Office
[address here]

Dear Probate Office:

I would like to obtain a photocopy of the will of:

John W. Jorgensen died 3 March 1842

If he did not leave a will, I would like to obtain a photocopy of the petition for administration and the administration bond.

Please let me know the cost for photocopies, and I will send the fee immediately. Enclosed is an SASE.

Thank you for your assistance.

Sincerely,

Lineage Lessons

An **administration** is normally an estate in which there was no will. The administrator was appointed by the court to handle the estate. Some counties will have a document, called a **petition for administration**, setting out the name of the heirs and possibly their addresses. It depends on the state and the time period. The administrator's bond is more widely available. This was required as security for the performance of administrator duties in handling the estate. Though the genealogical information on it is less than you will find on a petition, it provides clues.

As you dig deeper, you will find that there are many additional papers involving estates that can help. For now, writing for a will or administration will get you started. See Chapter 13, "Courthouses: Gateway to the Past."

The Obituary

Obituaries are of tremendous value to your search, but obtaining them seems to be a stumbling block. First, determine not only the county but, if possible, the town or township within the county in which the family lived. The county may have had more than one newspaper; if so, you want to find the one that covered their home area. Then, write to the local library where they lived or the public library of the county seat to see if they have copies or films of the newspapers that they can check.

Suzy Que
1111 Apple Blossom Court
Anywhere, MO 12345-6789

Public Library
[address here]

Dear Library:

I am seeking a photocopy of the obituary of:

Joseph H. Johnson, died 14 April 1892 in the town of Sunshine

I enclose a check marked "Not Over Five Dollars." Please fill out the proper amount for a copy. If it is more, please let me know.

Thank you for your assistance.

Sincerely,

Ordering a Vital Record

If you are writing to the county for records created before state registrations were required, try the example shown below. Don't unnecessarily limit the date when requesting a marriage record. Judge what it might be from the birth dates of children but allow enough leeway, perhaps 5 to 10 years.

> [Your name and address}
>
> December 5, 2001
>
> Register of Marriages
> [Courthouse Address here]
>
> Dear Marriage Registrar:
>
> I would like to order a photocopy of the marriage license and certificate for:
>
> Joseph Cruse (or Kruse) to Virginia Malley about 1860–1867
>
> I enclose an SASE for reply, and thank you for your assistance.
>
> Sincerely,

Dear Cousin...

If you are writing to a relative for the first time, introduce yourself. Let them know your purpose and what it is you are seeking. You could include a family group sheet with the letter shown in the following figure, which may pique interest, but don't flood the cousin with data at this point of the contact.

> [Your name and address]
>
> [date]
>
> [His or her name and address]
>
> Dear [ ],
>
> I have been working on the family history for two years, and just found out from a relative that you and I are related as second cousins. We both are great-grandchildren of George Milliken and his wife Susan Masters. My family is through their daughter Jane, who married Jesse Cooper. My mother told me that she lost track of your

family after your parents moved—about 30 years ago. I am delighted to now be in touch.

I was told your grandparents passed away many years ago. Can you tell me when and where they died, and where they are buried?

I have also been hoping to find someone with a photo of our great-grandparents, George and Susan. Do you have one that can be copied, or do you know of anyone in the family who does?

I would be so glad to hear from you and to exchange information about our families.

Your cousin,

A Penny Saved...

The cost of letter writing has escalated. Not only do you pay more for postage, but also for paper, envelopes, and supplies. You want to make those letters count. If they do not achieve your goal on the first try, the cost of producing the letters again, and the time expended, must be considered. Be sure you know the current postal rates not only for the first ounce, but for additional ounces.

Invest in a postage scale. The small scales go to one pound, or, for a slightly higher cost, you can get a two-pound meter. It will not take long for you to recoup your investment. Without a meter, you probably often guess at the weight, adding additional postage "just to be sure."

Tree Tips
Keep the Post Office 800 number close by, and use it to inquire about rates when you are in doubt. Request the basic leaflet on postal rates from your local post office so you can refer to it as needed.

Relative Resources

Bentley, Elizabeth Petty. *The Genealogist's Address Book.* 3rd ed. Baltimore, MD: Genealogical Publishing Co., 1995.

Directories in Print: A Descriptive Guide to Print and Non-Print Directories, Buyer's Guides, Rosters and Other Address Lists of All Kinds. 14th ed. NY, Toronto, London: Gale Research, 1996. 2 vol.

Eicholz, Alice, Ph.D. *Ancestry's Redbook.* Salt Lake City, UT: Ancestry, 1992.

Kemp, Thomas Jay. *International Vital Records Handbook*. 3rd ed. Baltimore, MD: Genealogical Publishing Co., 1994.

Lindberg, Marcia Wiswall. *Genealogist's Handbook for New England Research.* 2nd ed. Boston, MA: New England Historic Genealogical Society, 1985. Reprint from 1980, New England Library Association.

Szucs, Loretto Dennis, and Sandra Hargreaves Luebking. *The Source: A Guidebook to American Genealogy*. Revised ed. (Salt Lake City, UT: Ancestry, 1997). Appendix F "Where to Write for Vital Records," pp. 736–756.

The Least You Need to Know

- The concise letter will bring more results.
- Don't combine a variety of different requests in the same letter.
- Keep the letter appealing to the eye.
- Addressing the letter properly will ensure that it gets to the right place.
- Knowing the proper rates and weight will reduce postage costs.

Part 4
In Your Ancestors' Footsteps

Grab your suitcase, we're going on the road! In Part 4 you'll visit the areas where the family lived. You'll walk the same ground they walked so many years ago. You'll learn to use the courthouse records, to visit the cemetery and glean new clues, and to search the fascinating newspapers while there. You'll also learn of the marvelous military records that await you on the trip to the National Archives or its branches. Excitement beckons—start packing!

Even if you don't plan a personal trip in the near future, the advice and techniques in this section will assist your research.

Chapter 12

A Little Traveling Music, Please

In This Chapter

- Planning a research trip
- What to take
- What to do before you leave
- What to do when you get there

You've read some genealogy guide books, researched a number of census records, corresponded with relatives and repositories, and developed a familiarity with the kinds of records that will advance your knowledge of the family. Soon you will be eager to travel to certain counties for a firsthand look at the records created by and for your ancestors. Some of the most exhilarating experiences in genealogy result from delving into original records (rather than published or filmed ones) and from walking the roads trod by your ancestors.

Decide which counties are likely to produce the most information on the most people. Review the information you've accumulated and narrow the possibilities for the first trip. Your decision will be influenced by many things: time, distance, and cost of travel; priorities, such as a family reunion or an elderly relative in poor health; a burning curiosity about one ancestor in particular; and other personal issues.

Counties Have Ancestors, Too

Before you go too far in planning your trip, be sure you are headed for the right county. Counties are the political subdivisions of states. Their current boundaries are not necessarily the ones they've always had. New counties were carved out of one or more old ones, or counties were absorbed by adjacent counties. Disputes and/or new surveys redrew the lines between counties. Why should you care? Because the records of your ancestors are in the counties as they were when they lived there.

Genie Jargon

The **parent county** is the county from which a present day county was formed.

Some states have forms of government other than counties. Some New England states are organized around towns, rather than counties. In Virginia there are numerous independent cities, completely autonomous from the counties they adjoin. Louisiana counties are called parishes. Read up on the political divisions of the state as you start your research there. Skipping lightly over the preparation can lead to many disappointments, not the least of which is to find you are in the wrong county.

Genie Jargon

County seat is the town that is the administrative center for a county. Don't assume it is the largest town in the county. A few counties even have two courthouses.

Your ancestor may have spent his entire life on the same piece of land yet have resided in two or more counties due to boundary changes. If you don't know about the *parent county,* you can miss all the valuable records he left there. To know where to look, you must find the dates the counties were organized and the names of the parent counties.

If you are looking for 1905 records in the present day Wyoming County of Teton, you need to know that the county was formed in 1921 from Lincoln County and the records you want may be in the parent county of Lincoln.

To find parent counties, consult Everton's *Handy Book for Genealogists* or *Ancestry's Redbook.* For boundary changes, see William Thorndale and William Dollarhide's *Map Guide to the U.S. Federal Censuses, 1790–1920.*

While you are zeroing in on the county, also find the *county seat;* that's usually where the county records are kept.

Do Not Pack Lightly

The old admonitions about packing lightly for travel do not apply to genealogy. At the minimum you need these reference materials to make your research trip effective:

- Pedigree charts
- Family group sheets
- Research calendar

- Your notes
- Genealogical society membership cards
- Listing of county formations and parent counties
- Maps of state and county roads
- Prioritized checklists
- Lists of facilities' addresses, phone numbers, and hours
- Names of possible contacts

Tree Tips
If you belong to a genealogical society, pack your membership cards. Some states require membership in a genealogical society in order to use certain records.

Also useful are travel guides, such as those from the American Automobile Association and state genealogical guides. Excellent genealogical guides have been published for many states. All slightly different, they usually provide historical background, overviews of the state's court systems and laws, and sections on each county covering repositories and records. Read them for background information before your trip. Take them with you to consult when you find a new avenue to pursue.

Prepare a Packet and Checklists

For each surname you are researching on this trip, prepare a packet or notebook that includes the pedigree charts, family group sheets, research calendars, and your notes. Review this material looking for the gaps in your information, and start some lists of what you want to know.

Put in your packet the checklists covering what you are missing and the priority of the information you need. Are you trying to locate the deeds you think must exist because on the 1860 census Grandma is listed as having $1,000 worth of real estate? Are you missing a marriage date? Are you trying to prove a death date? Missing a wife's maiden name?

Pedigree Pitfalls
Never take original documents in your travel packet. They can be lost or destroyed. Instead, take *copies* of anything that you think will be helpful.

Decide which of these you want to tackle first and what records you need to see. Are you most interested in deeds? Estate records? Marriage records? Perhaps you are trying to locate a hard-to-find family history, or you want to search for obituaries in the local newspaper. It's a rare genealogist who has time to exhaust all the possibilities on the first onsite research trip, so decide ahead of time what is most important to you. Go through the list again and add an "if time allows" list.

Have alternate names or ideas, because your original plan may be thwarted when you get to the courthouse. At a courthouse to search the 1870 tax records stored in the attic and inaccessible without an escort, I arrived to learn that the escort's mother had died the previous night. The office was shorthanded due to vacations and no one else could help. The trip would have been wasted if I hadn't had a secondary set of objectives.

Mapping Your Strategy

Become familiar with the county you're interested in and its surrounding counties by studying several kinds of maps before your trip. You need present-day highway maps to find your way around and to give you an overview of the local scene. But even if your ancestor's town still exists on present-day maps, try to find maps contemporary with his life.

Try to determine where your ancestors lived in relation to the county seat. Then remember the conditions they faced in trying to get to the courthouse to conduct official business such as recording a deed or getting a marriage license. If they had to navigate some rugged terrain, they may have opted to delay recording the deed. If they lived near the border of another county or state, they may have records in the other location. This can be crucial to your finding the records. Mystified as to why there was no marriage record for a couple I was sure must have married in a particular county, I expressed my puzzlement to the clerk. I learned that couples sometimes took the train eighteen miles to a town in the next state to marry because there was no waiting period and the age limit was lower.

The Lay of the Land

Topographic maps are another helpful aid to secure before you travel. These maps will delight you with their detail. Farm roads, cemeteries on private lands, and churches are all usually marked on these maps prepared by the U.S. Geological Survey. Done on scales such that it takes several maps to cover one county, they are more useful for research purposes than the usual county maps of today.

Genie Jargon

A **topographical map** is a detailed, precise description of a place or region. It will graphically represent the surface features, such as elevation and creeks.

You will enjoy poring over the maps, locating the creeks and ridges and comparing the features with the deeds you find at the courthouse to determine the location of your ancestor's land. When the deed reads "under and on the great mountains on the branches of Rockey Creek," you'll know where to look.

The maps, also called quadrangle maps, are available for a nominal fee from the U.S. Geological Survey Map Distribution Center. Ordering them is a two-step process. Write first for the index and catalog booklets for the states your are researching. Then use the descriptions to order the maps you need.

In the following section of the topographic map, from the Baldwinsville Quadrangle, New York, note the cemeteries shown.

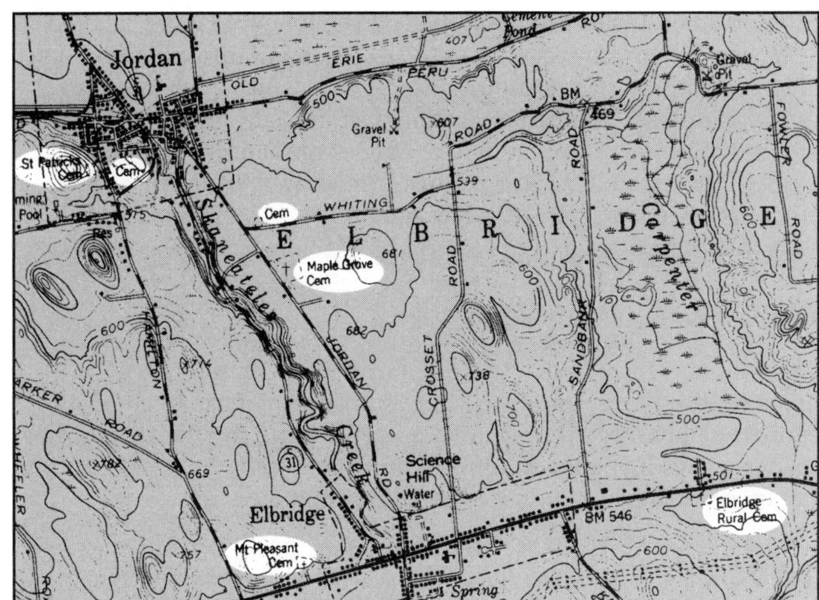

From a topographic map in New York.

Contingency Plans

Another map for your travel packet is a simple outline map of the state with only the counties and their county seats marked, such as is found in *Ancestry's Redbook* or in a computer program such as AniMap. You may need to refer to such a map for ideas of other counties in which your ancestor's records might be found. If you are researching in Noble County, Indiana, and you find a deed that says your ancestor was "of LaGrange County, Indiana," you'll want to look at your map to see where that is and consider the possibility of going there while you are on this trip.

Call Ahead

This cannot be over-emphasized. Make a list of all the places in the county that you want to visit; you can get ideas from state guides, comprehensive guides dealing with all states, and directories that list museums and historical societies. Try to determine what special collections of materials may be in the county. Call each and ask their hours and whether the records are open to researchers during those hours. Be sure to ask if there are holidays, special events, or unusual circumstances that will interfere with your access.

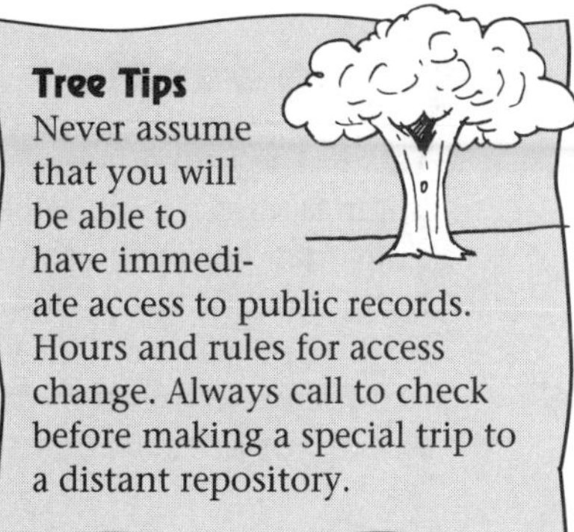

Tree Tips
Never assume that you will be able to have immediate access to public records. Hours and rules for access change. Always call to check before making a special trip to a distant repository.

Imagine my surprise to find a handwritten sign on the courthouse door saying "Closed Monday for Deer Day Holiday." This rural county closed government offices and schools on the first Monday of the hunting season! Another time, I called ahead but didn't ask the right questions. The courthouse was open on Columbus Day, but I did not ask if I would be able to research that day. Unfortunately, the small room housing the old records I needed was closed for research because county officials were counting absentee ballots in there. Another time, records I particularly wanted to see were inaccessible because they were being microfilmed.

Pack for Research

Pack comfortable shoes. You may have to do much of your research standing. Old courthouses have limited research space and high counters. You may have to climb a ladder to reach the earliest volumes stored near the ceiling. Clothing should be "business casual." You'll have better service if you are not in sweatshirt and jeans. Take clothes that won't show the dirt; old records are dusty and stored in areas that are rarely cleaned.

Now You've Arrived

You always have a tight schedule on a research trip, so use your checklists and the information in Chapters 8, 13, and 14 to make a tentative work plan for each day. Courthouses usually open and close early, but libraries often have evening hours. Small museums and historical societies may have very limited hours; if you want to visit them, you will have to plan around their schedules.

Tree Tips
Take rolls of quarters and dimes to use for copy machines, parking meters, vending machines, and telephones.

Most research facilities are closed on Sundays. Use that day to visit the cemeteries, attend the church services at your ancestors' churches, find the old home place of your ancestors, and visit with distant relatives you may find. Reflect on your feelings as you gaze at the same mountains your ancestors saw; walk the creek bank where they fished; or sit in the church pews they once occupied.

Engaging People

Talk to the individuals providing services for you: staff members at the courthouse, the libraries, and the Chamber of Commerce; the volunteers at the museum; and tour guides. They may know of a source, record, or individuals that you would not find on your own. In one courthouse a clerk produced an interim report of the survey of the county's historic properties. This working document with its detailed maps, photographs, and historic background of the county's communities was an outstanding research aid, one I would not have found in the normal course of quiet research.

Old-Timers Can Tell It All

Often, there are individuals in town who knew your ancestors. They were their neighbors or their fathers were in business with them. Their mothers were in the same church groups. These old-timers are delighted to reminisce with someone who has not heard their stories dozens of times. They may also tell you things the family won't: "Your grandpa was quite handsome, and he got around some."

The old-timers may have photographs of your family. Ask if you may get them copied while you are in town.

Small towns and rural communities may have an unofficial historian—someone who seems to know all the old stories about the area. That individual may be eager to show you where the old tavern stood or tell you that your aunts and uncles and other children from the farms were picked up in a covered wagon and driven into town for school.

Tree Tips
Remember that the details of your family history usually interest only you and your relatives. Simply mention the purpose of your trip and ask if there is anything you've overlooked.

While You're in Town

Buy the local newspaper. You may get an idea for another source of information from something you see in the paper. Perhaps there is a farm auction or an estate sale; old books, such as county histories, and old photographs often turn up at these sales. It may be worth your while to inquire.

Check the bulletin boards at the library. Local genealogical societies often have no office; to reach them you must know the officers. Meeting announcements or flyers about their services are often posted in public places. Even if you don't contact them now, you may want to engage someone from the society to follow up on something when you get home.

Pick up any brochures on local historic sights. The information in them will give flavor to your family history, making your ancestors more "real" to you.

Tree Tips
Check the telephone books for surnames you are researching. There may be descendants still living in the area. If you can't contact them on this trip, you may be able to reach them when you return home.

Getting Religion

If you have determined your ancestors' religion, try to locate their meeting place. Your ancestors usually did not venture too far for church services. Check city directories and old maps to help locate the churches closest to your ancestor's residence.

Investigate the possibility that the church is still active in the local area. Call the church offices to locate the old church records. There may be membership lists, participants in church ceremonies, or a church history mentioning your ancestor as a founding member. More often, the church is gone and the archives, if they survive, have been transferred to the library or a central church repository.

Be a Tourist

Absorb the atmosphere. Read the historic plaques. Buildings your ancestors saw every day will help you to visualize their times. When was the courthouse built? Your ancestors may have walked up these very steps to get their marriage license. Take a walking tour of town. Look for monuments inscribed with names; your ancestors' names may be on a war memorial.

Drive the country roads. Imagine the days of times long gone, preserved in such serene scenes as the one pictured below. Visit the old home place if it still exists. There may be a McDonald's on the spot now, but let your imagination replace that with the pictures you saw at the museum. Visit the cemeteries. Information and ambiance await you there. Chapter 14 details how to make the most of this part of your trip.

A wonderful scene from History of Oneida County, New York.

Before taking off on this trip, immerse yourself in the names of your ancestors and their associates. You want the names of associates in your subconscious so that they jump out at you if they are mentioned—they may lead you to your ancestors. You don't know what you will find when you get to the county, so anything you have tucked away in a corner of your mind may be useful.

Relative Resources

Eicholz, Alice, Ph.D. *Ancestry's Redbook.* Revised ed. Salt Lake City, UT: Ancestry, 1991.

Handy Book for Genealogists, The. 8th ed. Logan, UT: Everton Publ., 1991.

Szucs, Loretto Dennis, and Sandra Hargreaves Luebking. *The Source: A Guidebook of American Genealogy.* Revised ed. Salt Lake City, UT: Ancestry Publ., 1997.

Thorndale, William, and William Dollarhide. *Map Guide to the U.S. Federal Censuses, 1790–1920.* Baltimore, MD: Genealogical Publishing Co., Inc, 1987.

Computer Map Program

AniMap, The Gold Bug, P. O. Box 588, Alamo, CA 94507.

Topographic Maps

Map Distribution Center, U.S. Geological Survey, Box 25286, Federal Center, Denver, CO 80225.

The Least You Need to Know

- Advance planning is the key to making the most of your time and money on a research trip.
- Maps are some of the best investments for your research trip.
- List what you want to know, and learn where the answers are likely to be.
- Call ahead to check the hours of the places you want to visit.

Chapter 13

Courthouses: Gateway to the Past

In This Chapter

- ➤ Using the indexes to find documents
- ➤ Letting documents tell the tale
- ➤ What to look for in the documents

I always feel a thrill when entering a courthouse. It never diminishes. There is excited expectation of what might be on the shelves or stored in a dusty attic. Walking up the stairs, worn with the steps of those who have entered for 150 years, I am swept with a sense of history. Visions of those family members who might have climbed the same stairs as they came to pay their taxes or to settle their grandfather's estate come to mind. I wonder if I will find a forgotten record stuffed in one of the metal boxes in the clerk's office that will solve a long-standing genealogical problem.

I never turn down an opportunity to poke around in the records. Several years ago when we were traveling through Arkansas, my husband announced that he needed to stop and do some minor motor repair. Not about to overlook an opportunity, I replied, "How about doing it in front of the courthouse?" So he did the repair, while I happily explored the records, even though I had no one to research in that county!

Pedigree Pitfalls

Women should be particularly careful to wear flat shoes. Men should wear loafers or athletic shoes, not dress shoes. Floors are often uneven, and stairs can be narrow. Sometimes you'll even have to climb a ladder. Many of the early records have been copied from the originals into very large (and heavy) bound books. If you are unable to climb stairs or handle the books, bring someone with you who can. The clerks are busy and, except in an isolated case or two, cannot take the time get books down for those who come to use the records.

What to Expect

Some courthouses have made an effort to carefully preserve their records. They have flattened the original papers and now store them in file folders. Some have even laminated the registers. Others, due to lack of interest or lack of funds, have done little. The records may be in deplorable condition. Be prepared for anything.

Another problem is the burned courthouse. Many were destroyed during the Civil War, or the old structure caught fire in some other manner. The clerk tells you, "The courthouse burned in 1865." Don't become discouraged. I've found that a few additional questions may have surprising results. The first is, "Which records were destroyed?" followed by, "Which were saved, and where are they stored?" It is amazing how often certain records were saved, but the clerk may not offer that information. Ask the right questions!

Typical courthouse shelves, with heavy books and metal boxes.

Checking Your Wish List

In the previous chapter you developed prioritized lists. You have a clear understanding of what you hope to find. Is it the marriage license of your grandparents? The will of a great-grandfather or perhaps the deed to the old farm? Be sure to take with you the names of the people you are seeking and an idea of the time period.

The History of the Farm

Perhaps at the top of your priority list you noted your desire to examine the deed to the old family farm. If so, your first step is to locate the office that holds the land records. There are a variety of offices in the courthouse: the County Clerk's office, Circuit Court Clerk's office, County Recorder's office, and others. Each has a principal clerk (often elected) and other clerks who assist. If you are searching for a land record and did not determine ahead of time which office holds the deeds, ask one of the courthouse employees or check the directory that is usually posted near the front door.

Deeds have almost always been indexed. Land was important. A way to keep track of who owned it was essential. A deed was signed by the seller, who gave it to the buyer as proof of the sale. The buyer usually then took it to the courthouse, where either the seller or the witnesses came in to court to verify that the grantor signed it. This created a notation in the court minutes (a book recording a day by day account of what happened in court) that it was acknowledged, and the court ordered the transfer of property to be recorded. Usually, the original deed remained with the clerk of the court for several days, or even weeks, until he had a chance to transcribe it into one of the deed books. The original deed was then returned to the new owner.

Tree Tips

Land transfers were not always recorded. The land may have been inherited rather than transferred by deed, or deeds among family members may not have been taken to the courthouse in order to save the recording fee. Diligent searching, however, should produce something, perhaps even years after the original purchase, when the land was sold out of the family.

Lineage Lessons

Sometimes the buyer never came back into the courthouse to get the now recorded copy of the deed. The original deed of your ancestor's property may be in that old box marked "original deeds" or "deeds not picked up" on the top shelf.

The Approach to the Clerk

Genie Jargon

The record books are normally stored in **vaults**—fireproofed rooms designed to help prevent destruction of the books in case of a fire.

When you enter the deed office, a clerk will offer to assist you. Do not go into the details of your family's history. The clerk is probably busy with the day's current work and does not have time to get involved. Instead, because you know what you want and the time period, ask simply, "May I see the deed indexes for 1800 through 1875" (or whatever records and time period you are seeking). The clerk might take you into the *vault* and show you where to find the indexes, or just point you to the vault and let you proceed on your own.

Indexes Can Trip You Up!

Enter and look around for the index books. Deeds are always indexed under both seller and buyer. There might be separate indexes: one for grantor (seller), sometimes called a Direct index, and one for grantee (buyer), sometimes called an Indirect index. Alternatively, the grantors and grantees may be listed together in one book called a General Index. If so, the grantors may be in the front part of the book, and the grantees in the back. In other variations of a combined index, the left page could be the grantor index, and the right page the grantee index. Each index book covers a period of time. Index Book No. 1 may be for 1802–1840, Index Book 2 for 1841–1890, and so forth.

For example, if the clerk transcribed the original deed into Deed Book A, page 121, he would then index the deed under the name of the seller and the buyer, and show the book and page reference in the index. Let us say John Mathews is the seller, and George Graham is the buyer. If there was more than one seller or more than one buyer (perhaps the property was owned jointly by John Mathews and his brother-in-law David Donaldson, and sold to George Graham and his wife Martha Graham), the deed was then usually indexed in each of the sellers' and buyers' names. There are exceptions.

Lineage Lessons

A court clerk might suggest that you need only look at the grantee index, and not the grantor index. The theory is that if there is no record that a particular person bought land, then there could be no record of his selling it. Don't listen! There can be a variety of reasons why the purchase was not entered in the grantee index, although later the sale appears in the grantor index. The first deed may have been a patent or grant from the state or federal government, inherited, overlooked when the index was prepared, or just not recorded. Always check both indexes.

Sometimes the record was indexed only under the name of the first grantor (seller) or the first grantee (buyer) listed on the document, with the notation *et al* (and other persons) or *et ux.* (and wife) following. If it only shows "John Mathews, *et al*" or "George Graham, *et ux.*," be sure to follow through and locate the actual deed. It will reveal the names of the rest of those involved (referred to as the *parties* in legal documents). Any record in which there are multiple parties should be carefully examined; often it is a transaction between family members.

Making Sense of the Index

Open the index book, and see if it is a standard index and easily understood. There are many variations to indexes. Each has its own name, and many are still in use. There are Russell indexes, Cott indexes, and others. Look inside the front cover. There should be a diagram or chart and an explanation of the indexing system used in that county. Read it carefully. If, after a few minutes, you are still unsure, ask the clerk to explain the system.

In the following figure, using the so-called Russell system of indexing, go to the index book with the initial letter of the surname you are tracing. Then determine the first key letter as listed at the top of the figure (*l, m, n, r,* or *t*), to find where in the deed books the surname is indexed. For example, if the surname is Martin, you are searching in the *M* index. Ignoring now the initial letter of the surname (you are already in the *M* book), search for the first key letter. The next letter is *a*, not one of the key letters (*l, m, n, r,* and *t*), so it is ignored. The next letter, *r*, in Martin, is the first key letter of that name. Looking at the columns, you note that Martin is therefore indexed on pages 14, 24, 34, 44, 54, and 64.

TO LOCATE NAMES IN INDEX

Determine first key-letter following initial letter in Family Name. Find section number in the column headed by said key-letter, opposite given name initial desired. Names not containing a key-letter will be located under "Misc." Corporations, etc., will be located under the first key-letter following the initial letter in the first word of the name, or if no key-letter, under "Misc." Always omit the article "The."

Given Name Initials	Key Letters and Section Numbers					
	l	m	n	r	t	Misc.
ABCD	11	12	13	14	15	16
EFGHI	21	22	23	24	25	26
JKL	31	32	33	34	35	36
MNOPQR	41	42	43	44	45	46
STUVWXYZ	51	52	53	54	55	56
Corps., etc.	61	62	63	64	65	66

Sample of the Russell index, arranged by certain key letters.

In the left column of the same figure, the letters ABCD, EFGHI, and so on represent the initials of the given name. If you are searching for Abraham Martin, go to page 14 of the index. If you are searching for Mary Martin, proceed to page 44 of the index.

If you are searching a name such as Rowse in the Russell system of indexing, since there are no key letters (*l, m, n, r,* or *t*) following the initial letter of *R*, you would use the Miscellaneous column. (Anything not falling within the key letters is considered miscellaneous.) Abraham Rowse would be on page 16, while Mary Rowse would be on page 46. The Russell index, though prevalent (and still in use), is only one of numerous types of indexes.

What Should You Note?

After you determine how to use the index, look for entries that involve your family. The indexed entry will include the name of the grantor and grantee along with the date of the document, date recorded, type of document, book and page where it is recorded, and perhaps a very short property description showing the township, lot number, waterway, or other brief designation.

While you search the index, note the column that designates the type of deed. Typical designations might be warranty deed, deed of trust, gift deed, power of attorney, partition, or others. Each is a specific way of conveying land or rights. You will, in the course of your research, become familiar with all these terms and understand the value of each. Chapter 8 in Ancestry's *The Source* gives detailed information, as does Chapter 17 of Val D. Greenwood's *The Researcher's Guide to American Genealogy.*

Be sure to note the reference given in the index: the book or volume number and the page number. You will need this to find the document. Note too the type of document.

Lineage Lessons

When you find the book and page reference, take note of any abbreviations that appear immediately before the volume number. There may be separate volumes for specialized records. For example, "PA" (Power of Attorney), "DT" (Deed of Trust), or some other designation might precede the volume number. PA 3 p. 2 would indicate Power of Attorney, Book 3, page 2 (instead of a Deed Book). Those volumes should also be on the shelves.

Search Strategies in Deeds

While you are working with the deeds, take some time to copy all the index entries for your surnames of interest in the appropriate time period. Even if you don't have time to look at each on this trip, you will have the list for later reference. If, after you return home, you find you need another deed, you can order it by mail, citing the book and page number. (Or, you may be able to order microfilm of the records from the Family History Library.)

Be particularly alert to indexed entries that appear to involve several persons. They could be family members. The words *et al* (*et alii*, and other persons) can be a tip-off to such transactions. If the document is designated Power of Attorney, Gift Deed, Partition (involving divisions), or if an estate is mentioned, you should take the time to examine it. These types of documents often show family connections. You are not only interested in the property, but in proving relationships. Ideally, you will look at all the documents involving your family, but time limitations will force you to make choices.

Is He Augustus W. Redman, A. W. Redman, or Gus?

When using the indexes, consider possible alternate versions of the first or given name. This will include initials, first and middle name reversed, and even nicknames. George Washington Smith may be found as George, as Washington, G. W., George W., Washington G., W. G., G. Washington, and Wash. It will be important to know all the variations. If you don't know that Patsy was a nickname for Martha; Nabby for Abigail; Jane and Jennie for Virginia; Peter for Patrick; Polly for Mary; Nancy for Ann; and others, you may miss the listing you are seeking. Rose's *Nicknames Past and Present* contains hundreds of nicknames, all cross-indexed.

It's There Somewhere

You searched the index and noted a deed to what appears to be the old family farm, listed as Book B, page 510. Look around and see if you can find some books that are marked on their spines with the word "Deeds." Watch for Books A, B, C, and so on. The numbering system varied from area to area.

It is permissible for you to remove a deed book from the shelf and put it on the counter for examination, but be sure to put it back (in the same spot) when you are finished. The counters on which you will be working are usually high and slanted. Other researchers (perhaps title searchers from the local land title companies, attorneys, or other genealogists) will be working there also.

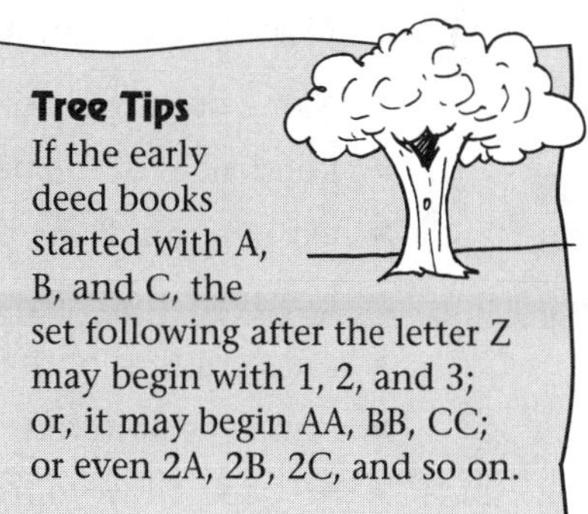

Tree Tips
If the early deed books started with A, B, and C, the set following after the letter Z may begin with 1, 2, and 3; or, it may begin AA, BB, CC; or even 2A, 2B, 2C, and so on.

Use as little counter space as possible. If you have a coat, hat, umbrella, or briefcase, find a spot off the counter to place them; counter space is generally limited.

Finally...It Is in Hand

Once you find the Deed book you seek, turn to the page you noted from the index. The document you want should start on the indexed page. Follow it through to the end, which may be several pages later. In Chapter 3 you learned about transcribing and abstracting. Use those techniques to get the information, or if you wish to have a copy of the entire document, ask the clerk about photocopying costs and procedures. The clerks may prefer to do the photocopying themselves, or they may point you to the photocopier and have you make the copy. The fees vary but usually are nominal.

Lineage Lessons

Though it may at first seem easier to make photocopies, the expense can mount quickly. Good abstracting techniques enable you to keep your photocopying costs to a minimum. Another disadvantage of relying on photocopies without making an abstract is that you (or the clerk) may inadvertently cut off some words from the side or bottom of the copy or a key date in the binding edge may be blurred. Abstract it while you have the whole record in front of you. If you find later that the photocopy is incomplete or even unreadable in spots, you'll know you have the data in your abstract.

Success at Last!

You are now looking at the deed. It is two pages long. What to do? First, you need to read through the document. Until you become familiar with old handwriting and terminology, this will be a slow process. But it is through such readings that experience develops. You are seeking certain items from the deed:

- Name of the parties (grantors and grantees)
- Residences of the parties
- Occupation of the parties
- Consideration "paid"
- A description of the property being sold
- Names of adjoining property owners mentioned
- Any special wording that might help in identification of the parties or the property
- Signatures or marks exactly as they appeared
- Names of witnesses exactly as they appeared
- Date and place the deed was acknowledged in court

- Who acknowledged the deed
- Date of the deed, and date the deed was recorded

Copy names exactly as they appear (Chas., Rebeckah, and so on). Residences are important; they may even include mention of a former or later location: "John Gott, formerly of Lebanon, Connecticut" or "Richard Smith, now of Marion County, Indiana." Occupations are not only of personal interest, but can be used to segregate the records of two people with the same name.

Tree Tips
Always carry a magnifying glass with you to the courthouse. On the difficult to read writing, the glass can help tremendously.

The "consideration," (that is, what was given by the buyer to the seller to obtain the property), may be monetary. It might also be something else of value such as "love and affection" (plus a token amount of 5 shillings or $1.00), or five horses, or anything else that the parties agreed upon.

The property description in the document will help you locate the land. Additionally, it can provide clues through proximity. If someone of the same surname lived on the adjoining farm (mentioned in the property description within the deed), note it. Even if they did not have the same surname, neighbors might have been related, or they might have been former neighbors who moved with the family from another area.

Lineage Lessons

The signatures in the transcribed deed books are not the original signatures of your ancestors. The clerk copied them and often tried to duplicate the appearance. If the seller signed with an *X* (or other mark), the clerk tried to duplicate that, too. This can be important. Two men with the same name who left records in the same area can be distinguished by their signatures or marks. One might be able to sign his name, while the other always signed with an *X*. This will enable you to segregate their records.

I Saw It Myself

All deeds had to be acknowledged or proved in court, either personally by the seller or by the witnesses who testified that they saw the seller sign the deed. If the seller moved and personally acknowledged the deed in another county or state, you have clues to a possible new residence.

The date of the deed is important, as well as the date it was recorded. Often a deed is not recorded until years later. The delay can have special significance. Perhaps the father died and his widow received her *dower third,* with the remainder to go to the children. She continued to live on the property, undisturbed, and after her death ten years later, the children sold the property. A document's recordation date many years after the date on the document should alert you to a possible change in the family status: the death of the mother, a parent's remarriage, or the children coming of age. Watch too for special clauses in the deed that might help with relationships: "I give and convey… the land I inherited from my father Joseph Masters…" Important relationship clauses such as this are best quoted in your abstract, so there are no misinterpretations.

Lineage Lessons

The law usually allowed the widow a **dower third** (or some other portion, depending upon state, time period, and other factors) in the land. She not only received a dower third upon the death of her husband (he could not will it away from her), but if, during his life, he sold property, she had to sign a release of her dower interest. If she was unable to travel to the county seat, court appointed representatives visited and questioned her, asking her whether the property was sold with her consent.

Moving On

Work with the land records for as long as your time allows. They are one of the most valuable of genealogical records, often showing relationships and yielding clues. If you don't have time to finish, you will at least have the information from the deed index. You may find that the Family History Library has microfilmed some of the records you need. Though they do not film all the records in the courthouse, the ones you seek may be available.

Those Departed Relatives

Genie Jargon

To reach the **age of majority** is to become of legal age. This usually was 21 for a male, and 18 or 16 for a female, but the age differed from state to state and in different time periods.

Once you've tracked the deeds of your family in the courthouse, you'll want to do some research with *estates.* Estates are the whole of one's possessions, especially the property and debts left by a person at the time of death. They are another valuable source of clues. Relationships are often specified. Normally, those you first encounter will involve estates of decedents, (that is, persons who died).

There are other types of estates. Perhaps a minor inherited some property and the court appointed a guardian to manage his or her estate until the *age of majority,* or, you might find the estate of an incompetent who was in need of a guardian.

More of Those Indexes

Sometimes the clerks have created a consolidated index of the early estates, which includes a variety of estate documents. There may also be individual indexes for wills, administrations, bonds, and other records. Sometimes the only indexes available are those in each individual book. Will Book A has its own index, Will Book B its own, and so on.

Died With or Without

Basically, you are seeking two kinds of decedents' estates: testate and intestate. When a person died leaving a will, he is referred to as dying testate; when he died without one, he died intestate. If he died leaving *real* or *personal property* that needed to be settled, an estate proceeding was filed in the county of residence. Some people, however, did not have sufficient property (determined by the state laws) to necessitate a court proceeding, so you may never find an actual record.

> **Genie Jargon**
> **Real property** is immovable property: land and, generally, what is erected or affixed to the land. **Personal property** is generally money, slaves, or goods: those items that are movable and tangible. Animals, furniture, and merchandise are personal property.

Taking Charge

If your ancestor left a will, he usually named within the will an *executor* to handle his affairs. This created a *probate* proceeding. If he died without a will, the court appointed an *administrator* to handle the estate; the process referred to as the administration. There are many variations: The court may appoint an administrator to handle a will if the executor named did not want to serve, or if the executor died or moved to another state. You will learn these important refinements as you use the records.

The Probate Process

Probate, the action to prove and admit a will, was initiated (usually by a relative or creditor) after the death of the testator. Notice was given by the clerk of the court that the will would be heard on a particular day; anyone contesting it could appear. At the time of the hearing, the court required proof, by testimony of the witnesses, that the will was signed by the deceased and was signed of his own free will. If the court approved the probate, the will was transcribed by the clerk into a Will Book in much the same manner that a deed was transcribed into a Deed Book. The will was assigned a book and page number and was indexed

> **Genie Jargon**
> **Probate** is a process of legally establishing the validity of a will. An **executor** is a person designated by the person making the will to handle his or her estate, as set out by the will, after the death of the **testator** (the person who made the will). An **administrator** is appointed by the court to handle the estate of a deceased person who has not left a will.

under the name of the deceased. The original will also remained in the courthouse records; it was not returned to the family, as was an original deed. That original will, and other loose documents that would be created in the following months, in many states created a "probate packet," which is hopefully still in the courthouse. If so, the index should have a column for *File Number* so that the packet can be located.

> **Tree Tips**
> It may be worthwhile to have the complete probate packet photocopied. Sometimes items from the packet are lost, or even the entire packet can be lost or misfiled.

The original loose papers in the probate packet should always be examined, if they do exist. Here you will find the original will (important to your search if the clerk's transcribed copy in the Will Book has an error). If your ancestor could write, the original packet might reward you with his or her original signature. The heirs may have signed receipts for their portions of the estate, providing additional signatures. If an heir was a married woman, the receipts often give the name of her husband, because he signed "in right of his wife" because he controlled the couple's assets. Other valuable documents are also included.

But He Didn't Leave a Will...

If the person died intestate (that is, without a will), the first record was usually when a relative (or creditor) came into court and requested permission to administer the estate. A variety of records could be generated from such actions, but these were not always indexed. To find them, you might have to do a page-by-page search of the record books. Search also for an administration packet, similar to the probate packets already mentioned. The index should have a file number to these records.

Checking the Estate Records

In the beginning, the various estate records appear overwhelming. As you use the records and study the guide books, you will become more knowledgeable. Keep in mind that you are seeking one of two types of records: a testate estate (with a will), or an intestate estate (often called an administration), without a will.

Each generates a variety of additional records. You may find a petition to initiate the estate process; bonds for the executor or administrator in case they don't fulfill their duties; inventories of the decedent's estate; accounts listing all that was owed and due to the estate; petitions for the sale of the real estate of the deceased; estate sales when the property of the estate was sold at public auction; distribution of the estate; receipts of the heirs for their portion; and others. Each one of these can provide wonderful leads, and a rare insight into the lives of your ancestors. The inventory may, by the tools listed, give clues to the trade of your ancestor; you'll be provided a glimpse into their education by the books they owned; and you'll find other intriguing bits of information.

Let the Published Indexes Assist

The classic in published estate indexes is Clayton Torrence's *Virginia Wills and Administrations 1632–1800*, (Baltimore: Genealogical Publishing Co., 1965), published as an index to the early estates of Virginia. Others have created indexes to some other states: the wills of North Carolina, the estates of Ohio, and so on. These indexes are valuable to your search; often their compilers consulted not only the county records, but those documents that were transferred to the state. Use these books at your library, copy the references, and then use the reference to locate the original records.

I Do Take Thee As My Lawful...

Find out which office holds the marriage records. Often it is the same office in which the deeds or estates are located, although larger courthouses might have a separate office of vital records. Ask to see the marriage indexes. In most cases, they will be open for inspection, although some states do not allow access to the actual records. There may be a separate index for grooms and brides, or there may be an index only to males.

Once you locate the book and page reference in the index, check to see if the marriage books are available for use. When you find the record you seek, take down all the pertinent information, including the names of the bride and groom, residences, ages, occupations, date of the license, date of the marriage, who performed the marriage, witnesses, consent if either was a minor, and so on.

Nothing on the record is too insignificant; the smallest detail can lead to further records or identification of the individuals. The witnesses may be related to the bride or groom. If either the bride or the groom was a minor, a parent's or guardian's consent will be valuable. Finally, the name of the person officiating might help identify a church and lead to further sources.

Marriages generate a variety of documents: marriage bonds, licenses, applications, consents for the marriage of a minor, and certificates or "returns" showing that the marriage took place. Sometimes these are in separate books with separate indexes, or they might be combined into the same record. What is available depends on the time period, laws, and local customs.

In addition to the bound marriage books, in which the clerk entered the details of the marriage, you may find original, loose marriage bonds. In earlier times, a bond was given by the intended groom. If he changed his mind and did not marry the intended bride, his securities on the bond had to pay the amount of the bond. As an option to taking out a bond, he may have had the *banns of marriage* announced.

Tree Tips
If there is only a groom index, check to see if the marriages of the county were published. If so, the published book should provide an index to brides.

Lineage Lessons

The **banns of marriage** was an announcement, usually in church, of an intended marriage. Normally, it was announced successively for three weeks. In some areas this was the prevailing custom. A marriage bond necessitated paying a fee to the clerk of the court, so the alternate method of "publishing" the banns of marriage was an attractive substitute. The banns of marriage may be noted in church minutes but are not recorded in the county record books.

Entering and Leaving this World

Also look for records of births and deaths. The laws vary as to the beginning date when registrations were required by each state. Prior to state registration, the counties normally maintained their own birth and death registers. The starting date of these county registers varies widely. The information may be minimal compared to present day records, but if they exist, they will be enormously helpful.

The Tip of the Iceberg

On each subsequent trip to a courthouse, you will find records you did not think to examine the first time. Always look at a document with a view towards deciding if there could be other documents connected with the same action. If so, pursue those, too. They may have the answer to the relationship you have been pursuing.

Pedigree Pitfalls

As states institute more restrictions, it is becoming increasingly difficult to access birth and death records. In some cases, viewing the older records is allowed, although access to current records is curtailed.

There is no substitute for "hands on" use of the records. In the office of deeds, there can be survey books, plat books, mortgages, oil leases, power of attorney books, tax books, and a variety of other related records.

In the probate office you will find court minutes, court order books, inventory books, bond books, account books, settlement books, estate packets, and others. If they have been preserved, you may also find the packets of the originals of the court documents.

In the civil records office there will be papers involving small and large claims: citations, debts, attachments, levies, summons, divorces, notices required to be published in the newspaper, and depositions, just to name a few.

Each trip you make to the courthouses will bring new memories and experiences. You may be offered coffee, or you may be ignored. Either way, remain courteous and friendly, and thank the clerks when you leave. The impression you leave will influence treatment of the next genealogist who arrives. You will remember each experience; the strawberry festival in the courthouse parking lot, going down three sub-basements and through three locked doors to work in the old deeds, or finding another visitor there working on the same family. You may stop and consider, in awe, that you are actually holding in your hands a document that was written during the Revolutionary War, or a document signed by your ancestor dividing his few possessions in 1720. He was holding the very same paper you now have in your hand.

Tree Tips

As you read the suggestions in this chapter, go to your own local courthouse and practice. Even if you don't have ancestors in your own county, pick one of your surnames. Look up the records. It is an excellent way to become familiar with the record books.

I'll bet that you, too, will become addicted!

Relative Resources

Black, Henry Campbell. *Black's Law Dictionary.* Sixth Ed. St. Paul, MN.: West Publ. Co., 1990.

Greenwood, Val D. *The Researcher's Guide to American Genealogy.* 2nd ed. Baltimore, MD: Genealogical Publishing Co., 1990.

Szucs, Loretto Dennis, and Sandra Hargreaves Luebking. *The Source.* Revised ed. Salt Lake City, UT: Ancestry, 1997. Chapter 8 pp. 242–287.

Rose, Christine. *Nicknames Past and Present.* 2nd ed. revised. San Jose, CA.: priv. publ., 1995.

The Least You Need to Know

- The books in the courthouse are large and heavy; bring someone to help if you cannot lift them.
- Have an idea of which records you would like to access and the time period.
- Start your search with the indexes.
- Carefully abstract the records you find. Be alert for any clues to relationships.

Chapter 14

A Picnic in the Cemetery

In This Chapter

- Cemeteries for research
- Finding the records
- Locating the cemeteries
- Recording the information

Cemeteries are quiet, peaceful places for contemplation and remembrance. They are also an excellent source of genealogical information. Plot placement, tombstone inscriptions, and records can fill in blanks, lead you in new directions, or add insight to your knowledge of your ancestors as people.

Why should you visit the cemetery if you already have a death date? Because you never know what you will find. Here are two children who died in infancy that you never knew about. Grandma's tombstone has an inscription that moves you to tears. Grandpa's marker is engraved with a Masonic symbol suggesting other records to check.

The Chicken or the Egg?

Tree Tips
The names of those two children who died in infancy may hold the clues to family relationships, if they were given family names.

Cemetery research has two goals: to find the cemetery and to find the records created by the ending of life. Whether you look first for the cemetery or the records is like the chicken and egg problem. Without knowing the cemetery, you'll have trouble locating the records; if you haven't found the records, you may not know which cemetery or where in the cemetery the grave is located. Different circumstances require different approaches. You need to decide the best approach based on the information you have.

The Usual Preparation

On your trip to the area where your ancestors resided, allow time to search for burial records and for the cemeteries. You are already prepared with the background information you need on the surnames and any variants, and the approximate dates of death, as well as names associated with your family. You may have the name of a cemetery from a death certificate, an obituary, or interviews with family members. Your library research may have turned up cemetery surveys that list your ancestors, or you may have clues from a county history.

Pedigree Pitfalls
Confirm the accuracy of published cemetery tombstone surveys. Mistakes can be made in the original survey and in the copying of the survey notes to the typewriter or computer.

Courthouse research on the trip will turn up deeds so you can locate your ancestors' residences. Where your ancestors lived in the area often influenced where they were buried. Travel was limited, and people were usually buried close to the home place. In many cases, they were buried on the home place.

Once you locate your ancestors, look at your county and topographic maps to find possible cemeteries. Numerous cemeteries can be found within small geographic areas.

Kinds of Cemeteries

Both the cemetery and its records are important to your research, and they may not be in the same place. There are several kinds of cemeteries: public, private, family, religious, and fraternal. Everything about their records varies: the information, the location, the accessibility. Cemeteries change hands; a commercial venture goes bankrupt and a municipality takes over, or, conversely, the county can't afford the upkeep and sells the cemetery to a business enterprise. Cemeteries are abandoned when all descendants in the family are gone, and the property moves out of the family. Or the town is down to 200 residents who no longer bury their dead in the town cemetery and have no wish to keep it up.

Public cemeteries are owned and maintained with taxpayer money by a governmental jurisdiction (county or town). Their records may be at the courthouse, city hall, or in an office on the cemetery grounds. Their records, occasionally difficult to locate, are open to the public.

Private cemeteries, or memorial parks, are for-profit businesses. Although their records are private, most are willing to help researchers.

Family cemeteries range from a few gravestones in a corner of the pasture to larger cemeteries where not only the extended family was buried, but others from the community who had close ties to the family. These records, if they exist, are usually more difficult to find; they may have been deposited at the library or historical society, or they may have been handed down through the family to someone who left the area. In some cases, the deed to the property made a provision to preserve the family burying ground.

Tree Tips

Large cemeteries may have ethnic sections established by tradition, covenants, or discrimination. They might have a "Potter's Field" where the poor or unknown are buried; often no records are kept on the individuals buried in this section.

Church cemeteries may adjoin the church or may be located some distance away. Church burial registers may take some digging to find. They may be at the church, but in many cases they moved with a minister or are archived at another location such as a regional church archive or a university collection.

Fraternal organizations, such as the International Order of Odd Fellows (I.O.O.F), also maintain cemeteries, sometimes adjoining another cemetery. A fraternal organization may also have a special section within a cemetery.

When the Cemetery Moves

Public works projects, such as dams and highways, sometimes make it necessary to move cemeteries, or the government may decide to consolidate several military cemeteries. In these cases, attempts are made to identify all the burials and move the remains to another location, but the original relationship of the graves to each other may be lost in the move. Occasionally, developers are unaware of, or disregard, the small cemetery on a property, and all records, both paper and stone, are obliterated.

Burial space in the churchyard may become full, forcing the church to start a new cemetery. You may need to search both. Sometimes churches remodel and build over an old unused cemetery. Churches merge or split; this, too, affects the cemeteries and their records.

Sexton's Records

Both public and private cemeteries have *sexton's* records. These are the records you want to see. Some cemeteries have a small sign at the entrance with instructions on how to reach the sexton. For others, call the listing in the telephone book. In very small towns or rural areas, there may be no telephone listing. Ask local people for the name of the custodian of the records. The records of cemeteries no longer in use or abandoned are somewhat harder to find. Check the libraries and historical societies for leads.

In a small cemetery the sexton may do everything: dig the graves, cut the grass, maintain the records, sell the plots. The records may be in his home. He can be a valuable resource if he has lived in the community a long time.

Large cemeteries usually have an office where the records are maintained and a maintenance staff that does the actual work of opening and closing the graves. This does not always hold true, however. At one large cemetery I visited, the sexton maintains his records in card files at his florist shop across the street from the cemetery gates.

Genie Jargon
A **sexton** is a caretaker responsible for burials and maintenance of the cemetery.

Sexton's records vary, but may include burial registers, plats, plot records, and deed records for the plots. You may also find records of grave openings, indicating an ordinary burial, that a body was exhumed and shipped elsewhere, or that someone else is buried in the same grave. Don't expect to find complete records; it is unusual, especially for long-existing cemeteries.

Burial Registers

These will be in chronological order by the date of burial and may be indexed. If not, you will have to search through the lists based on the estimated date of death. The burial register may have only the name, burial date, and plot. Others are more extensive, listing age, birthplace, marital status, death date and place, and cause of death.

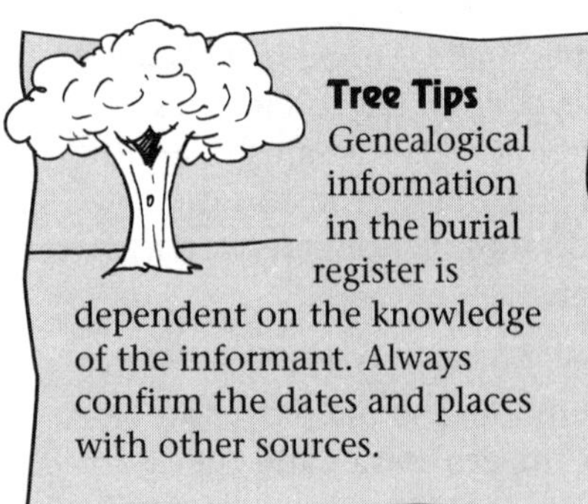

Tree Tips
Genealogical information in the burial register is dependent on the knowledge of the informant. Always confirm the dates and places with other sources.

Plats

The plat maps of the cemetery show grave locations and plot ownership. Active cemeteries keep these up to date in order to know which plots are for sale. Usually, there are no dates, and if the plot owner's name is different from the surname you are researching, these may not help you. However, the plats can help you figure out where in the cemetery the graves of interest to you are located.

Plot Records

These are usually card files with the name of the plot owner, date of purchase, and names and dates of burials in the plot. If the plot is in perpetual care, which requires a yearly maintenance fee, you might be fortunate enough to find a present-day descendant on the records. You can usually assume that everyone buried in the plot is related. However, assumptions can set back your research. When my husband and I visited the cemetery where his grandparents are buried, we saw a marker for someone no one in the family had mentioned. Suspecting a scandal of some sort, we asked my mother-in-law. She replied that Grandma was a kindly soul and when a stranger in town dropped dead and no one knew his kin, she had him buried in the family plot.

Tree Tips
The plot records may give you the married name of a daughter who purchased the plot. They might also list individuals buried in the plot who have no markers.

As with other land transactions, the cemetery plot owner receives a deed. It is recorded in the cemetery records by the sexton, and in some areas, is also recorded in a special county deed book.

Do I Need to Visit?

Yes, do visit! The sexton's records do not describe the monuments, nor do they tell you who is buried in proximity to your ancestors.

There is no substitute for strolling through the cemetery. Your ancestors walked this very ground. Grandma wept as she buried her third child during the smallpox epidemic. Grandpa chose to lay his parents to rest at the top of the hill overlooking the lake. Sons and daughters planted trees in loving memory—those same giant trees with roots now threatening to topple the monuments.

Locating the Cemetery

The libraries and historical societies in the counties of your ancestors may offer finding aids for the cemeteries. These aids vary tremendously, from a simple map showing the major cemeteries in the county to printed abstracts of one cemetery's records. In a tiny one-room historical society in Illinois, there are dozens of binders for the cemeteries in three contiguous counties. Each binder has a short history of the cemetery, a map to locate the cemetery, photographs, and an indexed list of all the tombstone inscriptions found there. Similar records can be found elsewhere.

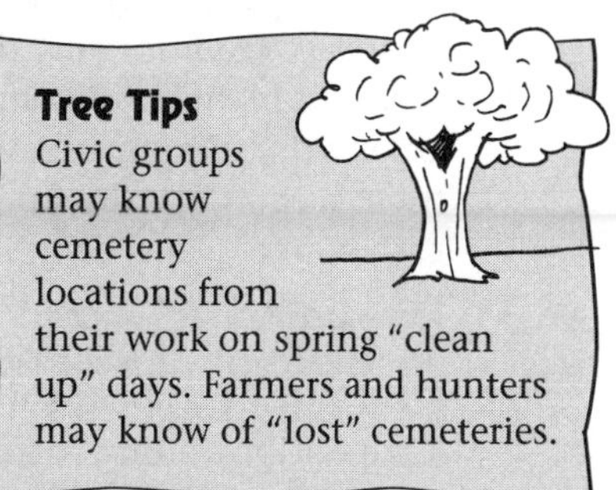

Tree Tips
Civic groups may know cemetery locations from their work on spring "clean up" days. Farmers and hunters may know of "lost" cemeteries.

Follow the Money

Who paid the bill for the funeral? Funeral homes and morticians can be your biggest allies in finding the cemeteries and their records. They keep records, and they work enthusiastically with you to find information.

Families traditionally return to the same morticians for all funerals, so the funeral directors are often well acquainted with many family members and may be able to refer you to relatives still in the area. They also know all, or most, of the cemeteries in their county and many in adjoining counties.

In more modern times the funeral director collects the information for the death certificate and the obituary. These records can give you birth dates and places, siblings, and children, as well as occupations and other personal information. Remember, though, that the information was given by someone other than the deceased, so it may not be accurate.

> **Pedigree Pitfalls**
> When you are actually ready to visit the cemetery, it is prudent to take someone with you. Cemeteries are often in isolated spots; use some caution. Your companion can help you hunt for names on the markers if you do not have a map of the cemetery.

Even if the death took place before death certificates were required, the funeral records are worth pursuing. For listings of morticians and funeral directors, consult *The Yellow Book of Funeral Directors* or the *National Directory of Morticians*. If you can't find these in your library, try your local funeral home.

If a funeral home is no longer in business, contact other funeral homes in the area. They often know where the records are and may even have the records themselves. Conscious of the value of the records, many funeral directors make it a point to preserve old records whenever possible.

Procession to the Cemetery

The absolute best time to visit a cemetery is on Memorial Day, formerly known as Decoration Day. Traditionally, this is the day when all the family gathers to spruce up the burial grounds, plant shrubs, and put out fresh flowers and flags. Cousins play hide and seek among the monuments while the old folks reminisce about days gone by. I remember these gatherings well from my childhood, with my father trimming the grass around his grandparents' and baby sister's graves and my mother tending to her great-grandmother's plot. Then it was off to another cemetery where other greats were buried, with time out for a picnic or, if the weather was bad, an indoor gathering. My grandmother counted it a good year when her peonies bloomed in time for Decoration Day; there was a subtle competition among friends and relatives for the best looking bouquets in the Mason jars set on the graves.

All family cemeteries are different, from the imposing monument in the cemetery in the following figure of the Hon. Joseph Bush family in *History of Chenango and Madison*

Counties, New York (Syracuse: D. Mason & Co., 1880) to a cemetery full of mostly field stone markers surrounded by a barbed wire fence. No matter the kind of cemetery or whether you go on Memorial Day or some other day, there are a few steps to success:

- ➤ Dress appropriately.
- ➤ Take pencil, paper, and camera with plenty of film.
- ➤ Plan your route to take in several cemeteries.

The Bush family cemetery.

No Fashion Statements

The well-dressed cemetery researcher wears long pants, long sleeves, and old shoes or, preferably, boots. Cemeteries are well-known for their abundant flora and fauna, especially chiggers, gnats, ticks, snakes, and small rodents. The grasses may be high and full of burrs, the ground uneven and full of small depressions. Don't let these things deter you, but do be aware of the hazards.

Tree Tips
Liberal use of bug spray may keep you from being distracted by flying creatures while you try to record the information throughout the cemetery.

A Picture Is Worth a Thousand Words

Whether you are a skilled photographer or strictly amateur, photograph the cemetery. Try to get a few panoramic shots, then focus on plots, then the markers. Write a complete description of the cemetery: name, location (explicit enough so you can find it again), and overall condition. Sketch the plots that are meaningful to your research and tell where they are: "between the first two lanes to the east of the entrance, middle row, large double granite marker facing west with the name Harcourt. Nearby are Waggoners and

Ballards." If you have the plot description from the records, use it. It will be something like Section A, Block 6, Lot 2.

Mark Your Maps

You have a limited amount of time; make the most of it. Plan an efficient route so you don't waste time zigzagging back and forth throughout the county. If the cemeteries are on private property, get permission before opening the gate and crossing the field.

Engraved in Stone

The highlight of cemetery visits is reading the tombstones. The variety is astounding. From huge monuments to simple wood plaques, all were placed in loving memory of individuals who had strengths and weaknesses, as do we. They are teeming with information about our ancestors if we will only read them.

The inscription may be only a name and range of dates or it may be akin to a family group sheet in marble with information on the parents on the front of the marker and all the children and their birth dates on the back. Relationships are engraved on the stones: "wife of John A. Davis," "son," "beloved husband." One of the most important finds may be the inscription on a woman's tombstone that says "Daughter of" and names her parents. This may be the only record you will find of her maiden name.

The stone you find may be only a chiseled stone as in the following figure (from a gravestone in the small family cemetery at *Bellevette* in Nelson County, Virginia).

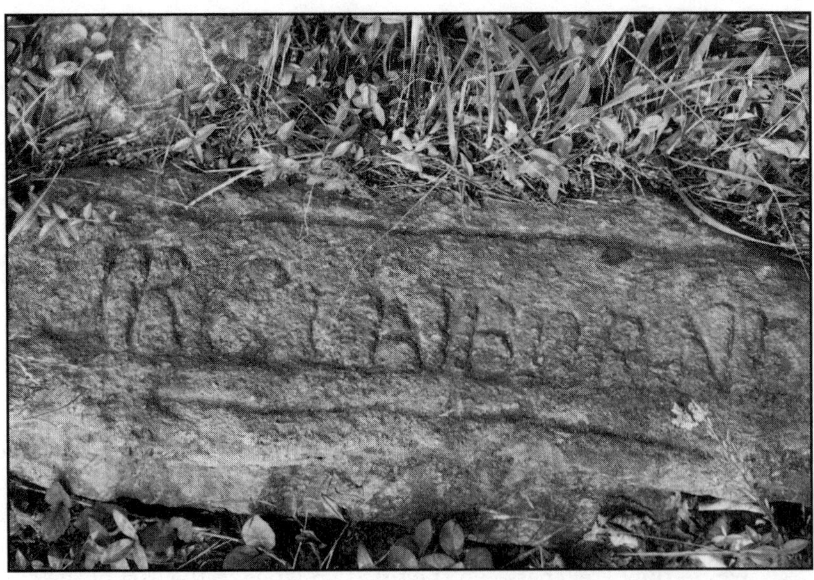

A chiseled stone in a family graveyard.

Perhaps you'll find some sentiment.

Dear Mother, in Earth's Thorny Paths

How long thy feet have trod

To find at last this Peaceful rest

Safe in the arms of God

There may be a reference to a Bible passage, or the entire inscription may be in another language. Look carefully at any symbols or emblems on the tombstone; they can be valuable clues to membership in organizations that have records regarding your ancestors. They represent membership in fraternal, patriotic, civic, religious, and veterans groups. Learn to recognize the more common ones, and sketch unfamiliar ones to research.

Pedigree Pitfalls
Be aware that some monuments are placed in memory of someone who is buried elsewhere. Monuments might also have been placed many years after a death, when the family was finally able to afford the cost. You may find family members or interested associations replacing crumbled markers with new plaques. In all of these cases of stones erected later, there is more chance of error in the information.

Reading the Markers Can Be Difficult

Sometimes, the bottom part of the marker has sunk into the ground or the words are eroded. Weeds and tall grasses may completely obscure the marker. Dirt cakes in the letters; lichen creeps over the symbols.

For cases like these, it is useful to have with you a few tools: a trowel, grass clippers, stiff brush (*never* a wire brush), rags, and clear water. With these you may be able to clear away enough debris to make out the information.

Pedigree Pitfalls
Never use harsh chemicals or abrasives on tombstones. Their damage is irreparable. Attempt only gentle cleaning.

In the recent past, genealogists were encouraged to take rubbings of the tombstones, but that practice is now out of favor. Tombstones are now an endangered species needing protection from the elements and genealogists.

Sometimes You Are Disappointed

Age, environment, neglect, and vandals all take their toll on cemeteries. Many tombstones were made of sandstone and they are crumbling to dust. Years of freezing and thawing cracks the stones, and pieces are missing. Weather erodes the inscriptions. Vandals may have tipped over the markers. In one cemetery, dozens of stones were in a pile at the base of a tree. I could have cried as I realized there was no way I was going to know whether my ancestor's stone was in that big pile.

Lineage Lessons

The impermanence of tombstones means the record you make today may someday be the only evidence that this marker ever existed. Take photographs, but also make it a habit to record the information carefully and completely. Don't depend on the photographs alone. Cameras malfunction at the worst possible times; photographs fade. Sometimes what you thought you captured on film does not show up.

Don't Leave Yet

Look carefully at the tombstones in close proximity to your ancestor's burial place. Relatives were often buried in clusters, and you might recognize some names.

The tombstones tell of great sorrow as you find a family burying babies year after year. Look at the dates on tombstones throughout the cemetery. You may find many families burying children on the same days. Suspect an epidemic such as diphtheria or influenza. In 1918 "Spanish flu" decimated whole families.

A clue to the cause of death of women is often found on the tombstones: "Mary Smith, died 6 October 1878, age 22." Next to her is "Sarah, infant dau. of J. A. and Mary Smith, 7 October 1878." Mary no doubt died in childbirth.

Last, spend a little time communing with your ancestors. They want to be remembered. You are their ticket to immortality.

Relative Resources

National Yellow Book of Funeral Directors. Youngstown, OH: Nomis Publications. Annually.

National Directory of Morticians. Youngstown, OH: National Directory of Morticians. Annually.

The Least You Need to Know

- Search both the cemetery and the records to get a more complete picture of your ancestors.
- Information in the records and on the tombstones is from an informant and subject to error.
- Take a companion to the cemetery with you.

Chapter 15

More than News in the Newspaper

In This Chapter

- The differences among newspapers
- The variety of notices they carry
- The finding aids: indexes and inventories
- The value of the notices

In 1855 your ancestor left the hometown to join a wagon train to Oregon, noted in the local newspaper. Another wrote home in 1862 after a major battle of the Civil War and made the local news when he related details. In 1920 an old-timer wrote his lengthy reminiscences of the history of the town he helped settle in 1885. Newspapers are crammed with fascinating items. You will be enthralled when reading the news and the quaint notices in the early newspapers.

Dailies, Weeklies, and More

Not all newspapers are the same. They differed then and differ now in frequency of publication and in their focus. There are

- Daily newspapers: published in larger communities
- Weekly newspapers: small town newspapers or a local competition to the daily

- Ethnic newspapers in native languages
- Religious newspapers

Seldom will you be accessing the original newspapers. Because of their size, the fragile newsprint, and the scarcity of copies of early issues, access to the originals is usually restricted. Libraries across the country have microfilmed many of their holdings; these are often available on inter-library loan.

Newspapers in the Area

Many issues of early newspapers have not survived; those that have are often incomplete series. Look for published inventories that tell you which newspapers were published in the area and which issues are now available. Many newspapers have undergone numerous ownership changes. Others are no longer published, but their back issues might be available. Try *Gale Directory of Publications and Broadcasting Media* (formerly *Ayer Directory of Publications*). It will lead you to newspapers still in existence and give you background information on their predecessors. If the newspaper you seek has gone out of business, it will not be listed in *Gale* but could be in a former *Ayer Directory* if the paper was in business during the years when *Ayer* was published.

Some state libraries with extensive newspaper collections have compiled special lists of available newspapers by county and by town. *Illinois Libraries* devoted an issue to "Newspapers in the Illinois State Historical Library." It lists those available in that repository, by town or city, name, and issues available, as well as a cross-index. The Ohio Historical Society published *Guide to Ohio Newspapers 1793–1973,* covering issues available throughout Ohio libraries. Look for others.

Checking for an Index

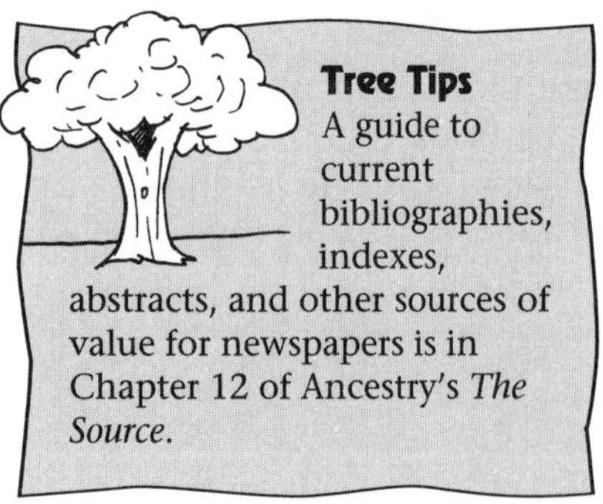

Tree Tips
A guide to current bibliographies, indexes, abstracts, and other sources of value for newspapers is in Chapter 12 of Ancestry's *The Source.*

A surprising number of 19th-century newspapers have been indexed in recent years. Not every name, but certain subjects and the principal names are indexed. If the newspaper was indexed for genealogical purposes, the items indexed were primarily those involving births, marriages, and deaths. If the purpose was other than genealogical, the items indexed probably covered the regular news stories. Determine whether there is an index for the newspapers in your area of search.

Even if an index has not been published, the genealogical society or library may have created an unpublished manuscript or card index available locally.

Accessing the Newspaper

Once you determine which newspapers were published in the area of your search and whether they are indexed, you need to find out which repository has the newspapers and whether you can borrow their microfilm of the issues on inter-library loan. Ask your reference librarian.

Reading Every Word?

Nineteenth-century newspapers are difficult to read; they often combined all types of local items into one long column. It is hard to immediately locate the item you are seeking, unless you are fortunate enough to be working with a newspaper that headed its columns "Births," "Marriages," or "Deaths." There are some shortcuts to finding notices when indexes are lacking. Determine the name of the community in which your family lived. That leads you to the local columns in the newspaper.

Columns headed by the name of the township or community included diverse items all mingled together. Residents who took trips, visitors from out of town, those who were ill, deaths, social events, and other items were listed one after the other without break. The item in one that "Mart Drolling was here Friday to attend the funeral of his brother" is the only shred of information that has been ascertained on this death. The community notices can be particularly valuable when listing visiting relatives from out of town or noting the trips residents made to other localities to visit their kin.

Also observe the format. Where were the obituaries generally placed? Did the newspaper have a special column in the classified ads? Were deaths usually placed on a specific page? Once you have determined whether the newspaper had a routine position for the notices, look for that section in each issue. If you still can't find the notice, you'll need to carefully examine the whole issues, page by page, to determine if a notice was published.

Topics to Target

Many articles and notices from the newspaper can be of assistance in genealogy, regardless of whether they are 19th- or 20th-century newspapers. You may find:

- Obituaries and death listings
- Family thank yous after a funeral
- Birth announcements
- Marriages and anniversaries
- Church news involving members (particularly births, marriages, and deaths)
- Sales of property
- Summons and citations
- Estate notices

- "Left my bed and board"
- Went west
- Advertisements
- Unclaimed mail at the post office
- Letters to the editor
- Visiting family and community events

He Died on the Fifteenth of June

Notices of death can vary greatly, whether in current newspapers or those published 200 years ago. They may be listed briefly in a column of deaths (usually called "Death Listings"). There might also be a full obituary including age and place of residence, a summary of the deceased's life, and other important details. Always, without exception, these should be sought. The name of the parents, where the deceased was born (providing the prior location of the family), when born, when and where died, and the places the deceased had lived—all might appear. This information can point the way to other locations for you to search. The notice might also include the marriages of the deceased and the names of survivors: brothers, sisters, children, and others. The church where the funeral was held and the cemetery point you to more sources. Occupation, professional career, war service, special skills (weaving, making quilts), town offices held, and other such gems may appear.

Tree Tips
When you are trying to get information from a county in which the courthouse burned, the newspaper can help fill some gaps.

Check Several Papers

Do not limit yourself to one newspaper. Determine which newspapers were in the area, and examine them all. In the weekly publications, check at least three to four weeks after the date of death. Examine daily issues for at least a week later. Occasionally, the notice was not published for a significant time beyond the date of death. It is impractical, on a routine basis, to examine the newspapers for an extended period, but if it is important to your search and you have not been able to locate the notice, take the time.

Once you have located the notice, do not stop. Look at the next two or three issues. In its rush to publish, the newspaper might at first have scanty details and enlarge upon them the following day. I have found this to be true often enough to warrant the search for at least a few days beyond. If the newspaper is a weekly, check the issue for the following week. In the issue of 6 December 1905 of the *St. Lawrence Republican,* a Nicholville, New York newspaper, the obituary starts: "Hiram M. Rose whose death was mentioned *in last week's issue...*" (italics added). The subsequent notice tells that he was born in Vermont, came to New York as a boy, and gave his various residences during his life as well as where his mother and father died. It includes his three marriages, the year and to whom, and the children born of each. If you had stopped with the first notice, you would have missed this.

If the deceased died on 4 August 1871, do not assume that the newspaper of the same date would be too early. If you start searching with the following day, you may miss the notice. The newspapers were more flexible than present-day newspapers in their ability to add last-minute items, or that issue may have been late going to press.

Even a brief notice, such as the one that appeared in the *New York Herald* of Saturday June 26, 1852, can provide valuable details. The death of William E. Rose was reported, "after a short but severe illness," aged 27 years, 1 month, and 7 days. Relatives and friends of the family and members of Hook and Ladder Company No. 1 were invited to the funeral to take place from his late residence at 33 Forsythe Street. This brief notice provides an age at death from which a birth can be calculated; a residence address, so city directories can be checked for others of the surname at that address; possible land records if he owned the residence; and even the occupation, which can lead to union or guild records in connection with his work.

Other Unexpected Rewards in Obituaries

An immense value of obituaries is locating relatives who moved elsewhere. The list of survivors can include the brother who went west and the uncle who still lives in Boston. Others who traveled a distance (and might be related) may also be listed.

When you find the notice, try to get a photocopy (or a microprint if it is on microfilm). Note the date of issue, full name of the newspaper, and the page and column of the notice.

Urban versus Small Town Newspapers

Normally the small town newspaper was more expansive in its notices than the larger urban newspapers. Tight-knit communities wanted details. They knew the family intimately and could provide interesting bits of data. The sheer volume of people in populated areas mandated that only selected obituaries could be included: usually prominent individuals or long-time residents. This holds true even in the present day. It can be especially important to check for death listings in a city newspaper, because they publish so few fuller obituaries.

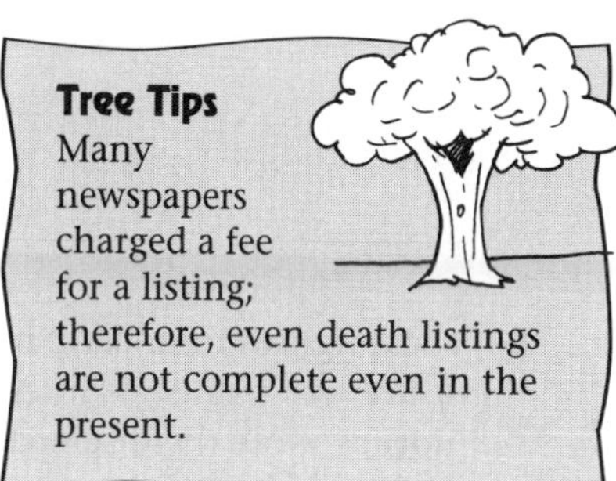

Tree Tips
Many newspapers charged a fee for a listing; therefore, even death listings are not complete even in the present.

The Family Thanks You

In some areas, it was and is popular for the family to publish a card of thanks during the month following the funeral. Watch for these. A pair of examples are shown below.

The family's thank you after the father's death.

CARD OF THANKS

To those who nave ministered unto our husband and father, J. M. Rose, and did all that loving hands could do, and to those who spoke of our aching hearts through the silent language of beautiful floral offerings, we turn with thankful hearts. May God of All comfort and bless you.

Mrs. J. M. Rose and Irl,
Mrs. Thirza Barr,
Mrs. Emma Wick
Mrs. Kannie Fields,
Otis Rose,
C. H. Rose,
R. L. Rose,
Ira Rose,
Harve Rose,
John Rose.

The family's thank you when the mother died.

CARD OF THANKS

We sincerely wish to express our thanks and appreciation to our many friends ana neighbors for their kindness and sympathy to us in the sudden death of our mother.

Mrs. S. E. Wicker, Mrs. J. L. Gields, Mrs. J .R. Barr, R. L Rose, Ira Rose, H A. Rose, O. R. Rose, C. H. Rose, John V. Rose, Irl Rose, Ora E. James.

These figures from early newspapers show two cards of thanks from the same family; one notice was published after the death of the father and the other after the death of the mother. Note the discrepancies in the lists. Some differences might be explained by marriages, but others are clear errors in one or the other list. Research will determine which names are correct. Such discrepancies are common and emphasize the necessity for gathering as many records as possible on the same individual.

The family may have published a notice to mark the anniversary of the death of their family member. Typically, these are brief "In Memoriam" types of notices. They are valuable because they are often signed, providing names of living relatives.

A Baby Was Born!

Some of the 19th-century newspapers published a special column of birth notices or mentioned them in community columns, although they were not prevalent. Columns became more popular in the early and mid-20th century. They were brief: "a daughter Mary was born to John and Martha Smith of Smith Twp." Such a notice might provide you with the first name of the mother if it was unknown (and sometimes even her maiden name), the township, or other small bits of information you did not have.

Tree Tips
Many newspapers now eliminate birth columns; few even retain columns of marriage licenses.

Wedding Vows

Marriage notices were—and still are—popular newspaper fodder. First, perhaps news of the engagement was published, often with photos. Next, the couple may appear in a column of wedding licenses issued. This column usually lists the name of the intended bride and groom, their ages, and perhaps other significant details. After the wedding, there may be an article with a full description of the event and, again, a photo.

The language and details or the editorial commentary in earlier newspapers was much more intimate than we see now. In a description of the wedding of a great-aunt, the newspaper reports "It was intended that the father would give the bride away, but at the last moment he faltered, as it was more than he could do."

Silver and golden wedding announcements generate news items. If you have the marriage date, add 25 or 50 years, determine where they may have been living, and check the newspaper. You may be rewarded with a photo and names and residences of close family members. There may even be a bonus: a wonderful description of the attire, the presents received, details of the original wedding, and relatives who came from afar to share the occasion.

Christenings and More

If you can identify the religion of the family, watch for church items. The baptisms, confirmations, and other church news may provide you with another source of information on your family. Perhaps your grandfather was an elder, or Grandma taught Sunday school.

Love Gone Awry

When a couple separated, the husband sometimes published a notice in order to absolve himself of legal responsibility for the wife's bills. We think of this as a more modern legal maneuver, but it actually was used very early. When Ezekiel Rose and his wife separated, he published a notice: "Whereas Mary Rose, the wife of me the subscriber, has left my bed and board, without any just cause, I therefore caution all persons trusting or in any manner dealing with her on my account, as I will not be answerable for any debt she may contract, or any dealing she may make, after this date." It was signed by Ezekiel Rose in Hampshire County, March 15, 1794, and published in the *Potowmac Guardian and Berkeley Advertiser* of Martinsburg, [West] Virginia, now preserved in the collection of The American Antiquarian Society. Without this notice, you might assume when he left his will in 1818 omitting any provision for a wife that he was a widower, though she actually survived him by ten years.

In the late 19th century, in a moment of poetic inspiration, one husband submitted the following notice to *The Standard* of Jackson County, Ohio: "Mr. W. S. Williams of Illinois, announces that his wife, Ann Eliza, having left his bed and board without cause, he will not be responsible for any debts she may contract."

> "Ann Eliza, Ann Eliza,
>
> Once I loved but now despise her,
>
> And So I no longer prize her,
>
> I will go and advertise her,
>
> For although I'm not a miser,
>
> I won't pay for what she buys her."

Sale of Property

These notices can be charming. And explicit. The executor of an estate is perhaps advertising the deceased's property, or the sheriff is selling a piece at public auction because of debt or taxes due.

In the following figure, the land commonly known as T. Rose's Old Place was advertised for sale in the *Maryland Herald* of Hagerstown, Maryland on 3 March 1819. The description includes details just about impossible to find in other sources.

In a different matter, a lengthy advertisement was published in the issue of 17 September 1817 of the *Adams Centinel* in Adams County, Pennsylvania. Being sold was a:

> *Valuable Grist or Paper Mill Seat or any other kind of Water Works with 18 feet of head and fall, situated on Conowago Creek, in Franklin & Menallen townships, Adams county, three quarters mile from John Arendts Tavern, on the Road leading from Pine Grove to Gettysburg, with a LOT of 12 acres of land whereof 7 are excellent timothy meadow clear—the remainder is well covered with Timber. The improvements are a new two-story log dwellinghouse, with a back shed to it…for terms of sale, apply to the Subscriber living on the Premises.*

THE subscriber offers for sale that well known Public Stand, commonly called T. Rose's Old Place, situated on the Potomac. The Cumberland Turnpike runs through the land nearly a mile, and passes immediately by the buildings.

This is one of the best scites for a Tavern between Cumberland and Hagers-town, being forty one miles from the former and twenty-two from the latter place, and four from Hancock-town. There are about 40 acres of Potomac bottom, 12 acres of which are excellent meadow, and about 60 acres of upland, part cleared, the remainder in wood-land. The improvements are but indifferent. There is a tolerable good spring on the premises, and a run passing through, convenient to the improvements. It is presumed any persons wishing to purchase such property, will come and view it and judge for themselves. It will be divided to suit purchasers if required. The terms of sale will be, one half in hand; the other half in three annual payments.

Advertisement of land for sale.

It was signed by John Mackley. The precise description in the advertisement enabled the family to locate the piece of land.

Legal Notices: The Fine Print

Among newspaper items are the legal notices, those items usually in small print. They include items directed by law to be published to notify possible interested persons of the action. Those items have usually been omitted among modern indexes, which is unfortunate. They can provide valuable leads in your quest.

You Are Hereby Summoned...

When a defendant in a suit or heirs of a decedent cannot be located, the law normally grants permission to publish the summons or citation to give notice to the parties involved. It may be published in more than one newspaper as directed by the court. Stop to examine these. You will readily see their value.

Other Miscellaneous Notices

During the gold rush to the West and other surges of expansion, the newspapers were packed with bulletins such as "John Smith, George Martin and Gregory Morton left last Tuesday to join the train at Huntsville traveling west." Or, "Josiah Martin finished outfitting his team and wagon and left yesterday." The Civil War generated as many items about hometown boys who left for service or news when they wrote home.

Tree Tips
In some areas, paper was scarce during the war years, and the local newspaper may have suspended publication for the duration.

Other notices can be of value. When an extensive search of records of Susquehanna County, Pennsylvania failed to turn up a conclusive record proving that Judson Lysander Gelatt of Nebraska was a brother of James Gelatt, the newspaper came to the rescue. From the *Independent Republican*, Montrose, of March 29, 1880, in a column headed Thomson Borough, an item that "James Gelatt of Susq'a Depot, has bought the house and lot in this place, where his mother lives, of his brother, J. L. Gelatt, who is in Nebraska."

Those Charming Advertisements

Was your ancestor a tailor? A pharmacist? Owned a stable? Look for advertisements. They are charming. The doctor extols the cures reported from the latest herbal wonder; the tailor will tell you that there is no workmanship that matches his. Always make photocopies when you find those advertisements placed by your ancestors. They will add interest when you put together the story of their lives, and the copies will add eye appeal when you illustrate it.

A Letter Is Waiting for...

Letters sent by anxious relatives, or others, often went unclaimed at the post office. The recipient was either unaware that the letter had been sent or he had moved away. The newspaper periodically published the lists. That list might be the only proof you have that your ancestor was supposed to be in the area. In other instances, a worried relative might have written a letter to the editor of the newspaper and inquired about "my brother who I have not heard from in over five years...have your readers heard of him...please have him write to..."

Ethnic and Religious Newspapers

If you cannot find notices, in spite of an exhaustive search of the English language newspapers, the information you seek may be in an ethnic newspaper. Was the family German, and living in a large city? The item may be there. "But I don't read German," you may say. Doesn't matter. Watch for the name; you'll recognize it. If you find a notice, copy it and seek the assistance of a professor or student of the language at the local college or university. You can also seek assistance from an ethnic genealogical society to find others who can translate the notice for you.

The newspapers published by various religious denominations often published very full and descriptive obituaries, as well as christenings and other matters. Look for abstracts and listings at your genealogical library; many of the earlier denominational newspapers have been indexed or items of genealogical significance abstracted.

Flavor the Times

Use newspapers routinely during your search. They will give you a rare opportunity to understand the times in which your family lived. You will soak up a flavor of the area: the bake sales, local pageants, and sports event winners. A strong feeling for the people and an understanding of the community atmosphere that influenced the lives of your family will be yours after reading those pages.

Relative Resources

Gutgesell, Stephen. *Guide to Ohio Newspapers 1793–1973*. Columbus, OH: Ohio Historical Society, 1974.

Hansen, James. "Research in Newspapers." In Loretto Dennis Szucs and Sandra Hargreaves Luebking. *The Source*. Revised ed. Salt Lake City, UT: Ancestry, 1997. pp. 414–438.

Illinois Libraries. Springfield, IL.: Illinois State Library. 70 No. 3–4 (Mar.–Apr. 1988): pp. 131–268.

The Least You Need to Know

- Newspapers are not all the same.
- There's much more than obituaries to help in your search.
- Many newspapers have been indexed by general subjects.
- There are many published inventories to guide you to the locations of newspapers.

Chapter 16

Did Great-Grandpa Carry a Rifle?

In This Chapter

- Determining whether your ancestor served in the military
- Using compiled military service record files
- The value of pension files
- Bounty land awards to soldiers

My husband's great-great-grandfather was born about 1788 and did not marry until 1819. Though he was about 25 and single when the War of 1812 erupted, no family tradition had indicated his service. Pursuing the possibility that he may have served, based only on age and the fact that he was unmarried, I contacted the National Archives. Completing the form they provided with my limited information on his age and places of residence, I requested a *bounty land* file. Imagine my excitement a few weeks later when a packet

Genie Jargon
Bounty land is public land awarded by the federal government, under certain conditions, to veterans for their service in the military.

arrived with copies of papers signed by this ancestor, giving all the details of his service! His widow's documents in the same file gave their marriage, his death, and many interesting sidelights. This success so many years ago convinced me to always seek military files. You, too, will be amazed when you realize the scope of the records that exist if your ancestor had any kind of military service. Compiled service files, pensions, bounty land papers, hospital rolls, draft papers, and many others await your discovery.

The Treasure of the National Archives

For military records before 1900, there is no greater repository than the National Archives. With its principal facility in downtown Washington, D.C., (known as Archives I), and the new facility in College Park, Maryland, (known as Archives II), this repository offers many documents, microfilm, and maps that can assist the researcher. Many (but not all) of the National Archives records on earlier wars have been microfilmed.

Tree Tips
Though the National Archives in Washington, D.C. has all the available microfilm, the Archives branches (see Appendix B) have only selected series. If the rolls you want are not available at an Archives branch, try other major repositories, the commercial microfilm rental vendors, or a Family History Library center.

Study the catalog titled *Military Service Records: A Select Catalog of National Archives Microfilm Publications,* (called hereafter the *Catalog*), widely available in libraries and at all National Archives branches. You will find thousands of rolls of microfilm listed. Some are indexes. Others are service records, unit histories, post returns, pensions, and more. (This catalog is also available on the Internet at http://www.nara.gov.)

The lists of rolls in the National Archives *Catalog* are only the records that have been microfilmed. Others, still in their original form, can be viewed in person in Washington, D.C., or on photocopies ordered by mail.

Let's focus on the Revolutionary War (1776–1783) as a start, then the Civil War (1861–1865), and, finally, bounty land files. You can branch into the various other wars as you continue your search and learn what is available.

The Revolutionary War

Calculate the estimated age of your ancestor during the Revolutionary War. Don't consider 16 and 17 too young; there are many instances of soldiers serving at this age or even younger. Promises by the government to give land (in addition to pay) induced even older men to try to enlist.

The Compiled Military Service Record

Most of the records of the American Army and Navy in the custody of the War Department were destroyed by fires in 1800 and 1814. In a project begun in 1894, abstracts were made from documents purchased by the War Department from a variety of sources. Individual packets were created for each soldier, and the abstracted records inserted. Muster rolls and pay rolls, rank rolls, returns, hospital records, prison records, and other records were examined, and information was extracted to bring together all the items relating to a specific soldier.

A typical *Compiled Military Service Record,* as it is known, gives the rank, military unit, date of entry into service, and whether discharged or separated by desertion, death, or other reasons. It may show age, place of birth, and residence at the time of enlistment. These compiled records are arranged by the war or the period of service, and thereunder by state (or some other designation), then by military unit, and, last, alphabetically by the name of the soldier. Those for the Revolutionary War not only have a microfilmed index, but the actual files also have been microfilmed. Using them requires only that you find a repository with both sets of microfilm.

Lineage Lessons

Indexes to Compiled Military Service Records are available not only for the Revolutionary War, but also for the War of 1812, various Indian wars and disturbances, the Mexican War, the Civil War, and others. Though the indexes have been microfilmed, some of the actual files have not and are only available at the National Archives branches or by ordering photocopies by mail.

Let's Try It Hands-On

Go to a National Archives branch or to a library that has the National Archives microfilm. Look in the *Catalog* for the listings of the Compiled Military Service Records of the Revolutionary War. The *Catalog* lists micropublication M860 with 58 rolls by number, and indicates the range of surnames on each roll.

As shown in the following figure, it is easy to ascertain which roll has the index for the surname you seek. Upon accessing the correct roll, find the soldier's name, and copy all the information shown for him. With that you will be able to find his file. Return to the same *Catalog*; it will point you to a second micropublication, M881, the *Compiled Service Records of Soldiers who Served in the American Army During the Revolutionary War*. Your file is on one of the latter's 1,096 rolls.

Example of roll listings on micropublication M860 by surname.

Roll	Description
1	A–Ange
2	Angi–Ballan
3	Ballar–Bearne
4	Bearnh–Biso
5	Biss–Box
6	Boy–Brown, Joh
7	Brown, Jon–Bur
8	Bus–Cartel
9	Carter–Chp

Let's practice. Searching for John Carter, go to Roll 9 of M860, as seen in the above figure. Find his name in the index on that roll. Copy all the information: regiment, company, everything. Now return to the same microfilm *Catalog* and examine the rolls listed for M881, which contain the files.

As seen in the following figure, the rolls in M881 are arranged by state, thereunder by regiment, and so on, and last by surname. Find the listed roll that matches the data shown by the index for the soldier. If John Carter served in Delaware in the 2nd Regiment of New Castle County, Militia (determined from the index), his record would be on Roll 380 of M881. Now you can find the Compiled Military Service Record file. It may consist of only one card or a number of cards.

Roll listings of micropublication M881, which contains the actual files.

Delaware:	
380	1st Battalion (New Castle County)
	2d Battalion, Militia
	2d Regiment, Militia
	2d Regiment (New Castle County), Militia
	A–G
381	H–W
	7th Battalion, Militia
	Hall's Regiment
382	A–Br
383	Bu–C

A few of the rolls in micropublication M881 for the state of Delaware are shown here to illustrate how the rolls are listed. Match the information you found on your ancestor's indexed entry to determine the roll you need.

Now His Pension File

Don't be too disappointed if the Compiled Military Service Record does not give you as many details as you had hoped. At least you can now document that your ancestor did serve. There are a multitude of additional records from the Revolutionary War, which might supply further information. One of the richest records for genealogical information and interest is the soldiers' pension file. These files can contain valuable information, such as birth date and birthplace, marriages, and other similarly helpful details. Once you discover that your ancestor served in the Revolution, the pension file indexes will reveal whether he or his heirs have a pension file. The Act of 1818, based on financial need, is the first pension act for which the application papers are preserved. As the government became more lenient in requirements, restrictions were lessened in several subsequent acts. In 1832, a general act was passed to award pensions based solely on service.

The complete pension file for each soldier has been filmed. Micropublication M804 of the National Archives consists of 2,670 rolls of alphabetically arranged records titled *Revolutionary War Pension and Bounty Land Warrant Application Files, 1800–1906.* (The dates shown are correct; applications were made by heirs as late as 1906.)

Lineage Lessons

In spite of the ease in using the micropublication M804, (since it is alphabetized), you may find it handy to consult the *Index of Revolutionary War Pension Applications in the National Archives* in book form if microfilm is not readily available. This book has the advantage of being more widely available than the film. It lists all the applicants and their file designations. After you determine from it that your ancestor has a file, then you can search for a repository with the microfilm of the actual pension files.

Micropublication M804 reproduces every paper available in each pension file. Each soldier's file contains two groups: the "selected papers" (certain sheets that the National Archives provides for mail orders), and the remainder of the file, marked as "nonselected." Examine every paper in your ancestor's file; any can contain some important bit of information. The nonselected papers often include additional *affidavits* and forms; also letters from descendants around the 1920s and 1930s, when many (wishing to apply to lineage societies) sought information on their ancestors. These letters, though not a part of the official war record, are nonetheless valuable because they can lead you to locations of descendants. It is best to photocopy the complete file, and read it at your leisure. Otherwise, you might miss valuable clues.

In another micropublication, M805, the National Archives again reproduced the Revolutionary pension files, but in this micropublication only the "selected" portion of the files were filmed. This shorter series was purchased by many libraries that could not afford the lengthier M804 series, or didn't have space to store it. If you find your ancestor on M805, make it a point to re-examine the file in its entirety when you can access M804.

Genie Jargon

An **affidavit** is a written declaration made under oath before a notary public or other authorized official.

Now in Print

Another resource to assist in your search of the Revolutionary War pension files is Virgil D. White's *Genealogical Abstracts of Revolutionary War Pension Files.* The abstracts are in three volumes, with an every name index in a fourth volume. These abstracts do not include every paper in the files, and are not a substitute for examining the complete files. Nonetheless, they are invaluable as search tools. These short abstracts can help you determine if your ancestor did indeed serve.

Tree Tips

The publication by Virgil D. White is particularly useful since these published abstracts are indexed. Your ancestor may have made an affidavit in the application file of another soldier. You would not have found that affidavit without this index, because only the applicants' names are included in the previously mentioned *Index of Revolutionary War Pensions.*

Why Check Further?

Why bother to proceed to the pension file, if you already know from the Compiled Military Service File that your ancestor served? You will experience a connection to your ancestors, as you read the words they spoke in detailing the battles in which they were engaged, and the resultant disabilities and hardships.

You will read about some sad situations, such as that of the widow Rebecca Rose, who at the age of 91 was found in the poorhouse, blind, "nearly naked, entirely helpless," defrauded by two unscrupulous men who filed her pension for her and gave her little of the funds. A man of conscience in the county came to her aid, demanding federal government assistance for this aged widow.

James Rose, the husband of Rebecca, a Virginian, had his share of difficulties, too. In his words he will tell you that he was at Mill Creek when "the picket guard came in great haste, scared nearly to death," bringing a report that thousands of British were coming, just on the other side of Mill Creek Island. "Col. Mazzard having no horses at that time to manage the cannon, commanded the army to hasten to Mill Creek, and draw with them three of the cannons. This soldier [Rose] was one of the number that managed the cannon in the stead of horses, and produced a rupture in his body of which he never has and never will recover by his great exertions in drawing..." Later, he was discharged, and returned to King George County. He left his discharge at the home of a friend and, on a borrowed horse, went to see his relatives in King William County. On the way he was taken up as a deserter "by a company of drunkards" and retained in custody three days before he could get his discharge, "which he procured by giving a man a regimental coat to take the horse back and bring the discharge."

James' troubles weren't over. Soon after, a draft came at King William Courthouse, and he was drafted for another tour. He insisted that he should not be drafted so soon but was told he was liable to be drafted within 24 hours of discharge. His officers kept the discharge, saying he would have it again but this applicant "has never seen it since." Also taken from him and not returned was his due bill (acknowledging what was owed to him). He later received another discharge, but he put it in a pocketbook which was stolen at Flat Swamps. In 1782, he was given a discharge from a tour, but this was destroyed by being washed in a waistcoat. He had served in all four and a half years. Fortunately for the unlucky James, his service was substantiated, and later, a special Act was passed by Congress on his behalf. Similar stories abound. The files are fascinating and will give you a rare opportunity to know your ancestors.

A bonus: Your ancestor may be one of those soldiers who either tore out the pages from the family Bible and offered them in support of the statements, or had the Bible examined and notarized. Those papers in the file may be your only proof of dates and relationships in the family.

The compiled military service record file and the pension file you find are not the only records available for Revolutionary War service. There are many others, but these will get you started.

The War Between the States

The Civil War tore families apart. Brother fought against brother. Families were divided, and many never did heal their differences. Feelings run deep to this day. Be aware of this as you query your family about their Civil War connections. Be sensitive. In one file, a Tennessean, who was faced with a decision whether to stay with the Union or join the Confederacy, moved to Arkansas to join a Union force there. His wife, whose family was staunchly of southern sympathies, refused to accompany him. The files are full of such situations. Often the soldier later took a new wife in his chosen state, (in this case without benefit of a divorce from the former wife, who still refused to live with him). Don't be surprised at what you may find. Remember the times in which these families lived.

It also is not unusual to find records of the same soldier having served on both sides. The 19-year-old who went into town to run some errands for his family was spotted by southern (or northern) recruiters and forced to enter the service. At his first opportunity, he deserted and joined the opposing side, where his sympathies lay. Don't stop when you find the first record of your ancestor; if he was from a border state such as Tennessee, Kentucky, Arkansas, or Missouri, you may find dual records for him.

Lineage Lessons

Don't assume that your ancestor's record showing "deserted" means he was a "coward." There were many reasons for desertion: loyalty to the other side, going home for a few days because of sickness in the family and then returning, and more. He may even have been improperly listed as a deserter when he fell into the hands of the opposing army.

He Wore Gray

Start your search for the Confederate soldier with National Archives micropublication M253, *Consolidated Index to Compiled Service Records of the Confederate Soldiers.* Consisting of 535 rolls, this is arranged alphabetically by surname. When you locate the surname in the index, take down all the information for state, regiment, and so forth.

Once you have the index information, return to the *Catalog*. Look for the micropublication number for the Confederate Compiled Service records of the state from which your ancestor served. The records on the state rolls are arranged by regiment, unit, and so on and last by surname. It should be fairly easy to determine the correct roll. You can then view on the microfilm the entire file for your Confederate ancestor.

An additional micropublication of the National Archives, often overlooked, is M347, titled *Unfiled Papers and Slips Belonging to Confederate Compiled Service Records.* This reproduces an extensive series of papers that the War Department accumulated to interfile with the regular series of compiled service records of Confederate soldiers. It was arranged alphabetically but never interfiled. Examine it, too, for your Confederate ancestor.

The Confederate Pension Records

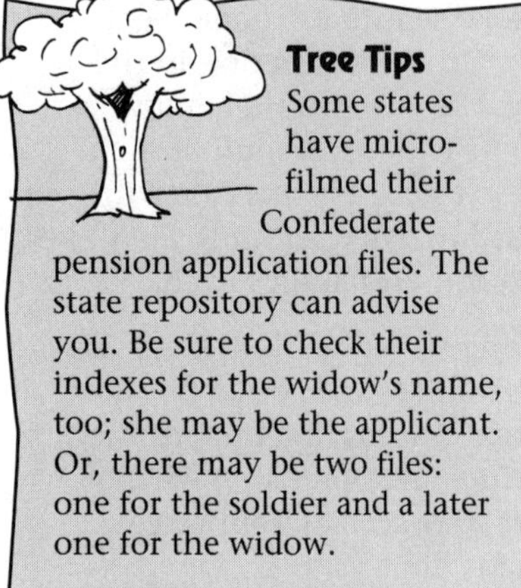
Tree Tips
Some states have microfilmed their Confederate pension application files. The state repository can advise you. Be sure to check their indexes for the widow's name, too; she may be the applicant. Or, there may be two files: one for the soldier and a later one for the widow.

In the years after the war, a number of states granted pensions to veterans of the Confederacy. These were not federal pensions and are not in the National Archives. These pensions were granted by the states to the Confederate soldiers who resided in them at the time of their pension applications. A soldier who served from Louisiana but who lived later in Texas, filed for his pension from Texas. Some states have published indexes to their Confederate pensions. Typically, the indexes are available at the State Archives or State Historical Society of the states granting the pensions. Those same repositories may also hold the originals, so you can order a photocopy.

He Wore Blue

There is no consolidated index to the Compiled Military Service Record files for those who served with the Union. Indexes exist state by state only. In the *Catalog*, look for the state in which the ancestor served; next look for your ancestor's name in that state's list for the proper film number. Copy all information shown for your ancestor—unit, regiment, or anything else, exactly as it appears. That will lead you to either his original record (still in textual form) or to a series of microfilm that contains the file. If you do not find your ancestor but feel sure he served, check the surrounding states.

Once you have located your ancestor and copied the information from the index, determine through the *Catalog* if the actual files have been microfilmed. Some of the Union Compiled Military Service Record files have been filmed, but others (depending upon the state from which the man served) are only available in their original form. You will have to view those unfilmed files personally, or by ordering a photocopy of the file by mail, using the Archives' NATF-80 form.

Obtain the NATF-80 form personally at a National Archives branch, or write to the National Archives (Archives I) in Washington, D.C. and request forms. (See Appendix B.) You cannot use a photocopy of the form, because the Archives uses multiple color-coded copies. Do not send funds when you mail the form. The Archives will advise you first if they have the file, and at that time you will be requested to submit the funds. (An alternate method is to include a credit card number on the form, which speeds the process.)

If He Got a Pension

The chances are good that if he lived long enough, your Union Civil War ancestor applied for a federal pension. Five acts between 1862 and 1907 provided pensions based on Union service. The earlier acts provided for those who were disabled or killed. A widow, children, or a parent who could prove an unmarried son contributed significantly to his or her support may have applied soon after the death of a soldier in service.

To locate a Union pension file, consult National Archives micropublication T288, *General Index to Pension Files, 1881–1934*. This index includes service for the Civil War and, in some instances, earlier service by a Civil War veteran. Other entries in the same film series relate to service in the Spanish-American War, the Philippine Insurrection, the Boxer Rebellion, and those who enlisted in the regular Army, Navy, and Marines. The index is arranged by surname, and then by state from which the soldier served. Be sure to take down all the information: the veteran's name, rank, unit, all the filing dates of applications, the certificate number, and anything else you find. You will need this information, whether ordering the file by mail or viewing it in person at the National Archives.

> **Tree Tips**
> When using the index, if you don't find the soldier under the name you expect, try variations. George Washington Jackson may be listed as George, George Washington, G. W., or just plain Washington. If he was known by his middle name, the names or initials may be reversed, such as Washington G. or W. G.

To order the pension file, fill out Form NATF-80. Send it to the address shown on the form. It will take the National Archives probably one to three months to respond. When they locate the file, they will notify you to send the funds before they send the file. (If you provided a credit card number on the form, this step will be eliminated.) The Archives will not accept your funds until they have determined that they have the file in their possession.

Some of the Civil War Union pension files are in the custody of the Veterans Administration. If that is the case, the National Archives will send you the appropriate VA office address to which to write.

The National Archives will provide only a few papers from the file, perhaps 10–20 sheets, for their minimum $10.00 fee. Because of this, you would not see all the papers in the file. Civil War pension files, for instance, are routinely much larger—40, 50, 100 pages, or even more. If you want to obtain photocopies of the complete file, write on the form that you would like a quotation for the complete file. Be forewarned, however, that because some files are very lengthy, it can be expensive to obtain all the papers.

The Inducement of Bounty Land

Bounty land was awarded by the federal government either as an inducement to serve, as an inducement to remain longer in service, or later, as a reward for service. Government legislation authorized bounty land (that is, a free right to federal land) in 1776, and in subsequent acts, the land and requirements were specified. For the Revolutionary War, the bounty land warrants could be sold. Since it was many years before there was a tract of federal land designated where the soldier could exchange the warrant for land, most soldiers were induced to sell their warrants (usually to speculators), and few actually settled on the land. Because of this, during the War of 1812 restrictions were imposed by the federal government on the disposition of the warrant. The soldier could not sell or assign the warrant (though it could be inherited if he died). This was not changed until 1852 when new federal legislation allowed any unused warrants to be sold.

Lineage Lessons

Many states also provided bounty land for Revolutionary service; information on these is available in Lloyd DeWitt Bockstruck's *Revolutionary War Bounty Land Grants.*

Many early bounty land application files were destroyed in War Department fires in 1800 and 1814. Any papers remaining were combined with the Revolutionary pensions and microfilmed in M804, previously described. Bounty land warrant files for the War of 1812, under early acts of 1811–1816, were microfilmed on M848 of the National Archives on fourteen rolls. The indexes are on the first roll of this series.

The bulk of the bounty land application files, under more lenient acts passed from 1847–1855 that reduced the required length of service for eligibility (and instituted other changes), have not been microfilmed. Nor is there an available index. These files are packed with items of importance genealogically; marriages, Bible records, death records, and many more.

If you ascertain that you had an ancestor who served in the War of 1812, Indian Wars before 1855, or the Mexican War (or any service 1790–1855), fill out a National Archives Form NATF-80, and mark the box shown for bounty land file. These records are filed alphabetically by the Archives in file folders; the National Archives will search for a record when it receives your request. Keep in mind that the last bounty land act was passed in 1855; applicants who filed later were doing so for service prior to the passage of this final act. There is no bounty land for Civil War service (fought 1861–65), because it was fought after the last bounty land act was passed.

Tree Tips

Though the early bounty land application files for the Revolutionary War were destroyed, information from warrant registers and other related items will be found scattered throughout a number of repositories and states. You will become acquainted with these as you conduct your search.

Other Ways to Locate Evidence of Military Service

Your ancestor's gravesite may have a flag or marker indicating service, as might his tombstone. His obituary or death record could mention service. For the Civil War or later, the discharge might be recorded in the courthouse. The 1910 census, which includes a column for Civil War service, could list him; the 1890 special federal Civil War census (discussed in Chapter 10, "Making Sense of the Census") could also list him. County histories are another source, often including rosters of those who served from the county. Lineage society records, many published, will also assist.

Virgil D. White, mentioned previously for his abstracts of Revolutionary pension files, has also published a series of indexes for pension files of other wars, and a variety of other military records. Look for these, too, at your library. And don't overlook state records: the Adjutant General's office; the state library; and special state projects, such as graves registration for soldiers or biographical sketches of all known soldiers of the state. Sources for military service are endless.

Study Chapters 4 through 9 in the *Guide to Genealogical Research in the National Archives,* published by the National Archives in 1982. This publication explains many of the records related to the various wars, including some that have not been microfilmed. It will give you some familiarity with what is available. For another overview of records, consult James C. Neagles, *U.S. Military Records: A Guide to Federal and State Sources, Colonial America to the Present.* Or read Chapter 9 in Ancestry's *The Source.*

There's More?

This introduction to the military files of the National Archives acquaints you with some basic records of two major wars and with bounty land. There are many more files and records available: enlistment papers, Quartermaster records, headstone applications, post returns, applications for military academies, and much more. The *Catalog* will give you an idea of the number of records available. But remember that the *Catalog* lists only the microfilm, which is a small part of the vast records created by military service. The suggested books will lead you to a multitude of additional sources.

There is a fascination with the history of the wars and those who served. You will find information surprisingly abundant once you have started your search. Don't overlook these "because I already know he served." Details on your ancestors—physical description, age, occupation—these and much more are yours for taking the time to understand these amazingly informative records.

Relative Resources

Bockstruck, Lloyd DeWitt. *Revolutionary War Bounty Land Grants: Awarded by State Governments.* Baltimore, MD: Genealogical Publishing Co., 1996.

Cerny, Johni, revised by Lloyd DeWitt Bockstruck and David Thackery. "Research in Military Records." Chapter 9 in Loretto Dennis Szucs and Sandra Hargreaves Luebking, *The Source*, rev. ed. Salt Lake City, UT: Ancestry, 1997.

Guide to Genealogical Research in the National Archives. Washington, D.C.: National Archives, 1982. Chapters 4–9, pp. 71–145.

Index of Revolutionary War Pension Applications in the National Archives. Bicentennial Edition. Rev. and enl. Arlington, VA.: National Genealogical Society, 1976. [Originally compiled by Max E. Hoyt and others, and known as *Hoyt's Index*.]

Military Service Records: A Select Catalog of National Archives Microfilm Publications. Washington, D.C.: National Archives and Service Administration, 1985.

Neagles, James C. *U.S. Military Records: A Guide to Federal and State Sources, Colonial America to the Present.* Salt Lake City: Ancestry, 1994.

White, Virgil D. *Genealogical Abstracts of Revolutionary War Pension Files.* 4 vols. Waynesboro, TN.: The National Historical Publ. Co., 1990.

The Least You Need to Know

- Always seek military records for your ancestors.
- The National Archives has thousands of rolls of filmed military records and thousands of unfilmed files.
- Military records can be as brief as period of service or comprehensive enough to give you three generations of ancestors.
- Such diverse items as physical description, marriages, deaths, Bible records, and others may be found in military records.

Part 5
Making Sense of It All

You're going to collect a whole lot of records before you get through. You'll be cramming files into closets and under beds unless you learn to keep control of the "paper" from the beginning. In this section you'll learn how to keep everything organized before it gets out of hand. You'll record your information with citations and effective numbering systems so it will make sense to you and to others.

You'll learn to make the records "talk" to you so that your ancestors will come alive. They'll no longer be just names in dusty records, but real people with personalities. You'll begin to understand the times in which they lived. You'll become aware of conflicting records and how to make judgments to resolve them.

Chapter 17

Organization: Creating Order Out of Chaos

In This Chapter

- Using binders effectively
- Establishing an expandable filing system
- Using the computer for maximum benefit

It won't be long before you discover the one major problem of genealogy: the amount of paper generated by your research. If you work on several lines, as most researchers do, you will quickly become confused. "Where are the notes from Aunt Mattie's interview," you'll exclaim in despair.

The charts and family sheets that will help record what you find are discussed in Chapter 4. But knowing how to use the charts and family sheets is not enough to keep you from being flattened under a mound of paper. Many genealogists ruefully admit that as they sit at their desks, piles of papers encircle them. You don't want to throw away anything important. "What do I do?" you lament.

Filing the Charts and Sheets

The Pedigree Charts can be stored in a binder numerically, starting with yourself as number 1 on chart 1. You will see that each pedigree chart is assigned a number. As you leave one chart and start another, the new chart is also numbered. File these in a three-ring binder.

> **Tree Tips**
> Invest in a sturdy three-hole punch, available at most office supply stores. You will use it often, as you punch charts and sheets to store in binders.

After filing the pedigree charts, create a series of binders to file the family group sheets you have accumulated. Assign one binder per surname. If the sheets overflow that binder, continue into a second binder, still maintaining the filing system by family name. If you are tracing the family of John Jordan, who married Martha Adams, you would create a binder for the family group sheets of the Jordan family and another for the family sheets of the Adams family.

Filing Systems

Using binders for your charts and family sheets is a start, although you will accumulate considerable additional paper. You want a simple system, easily expanded as your search progresses. Create a set of file folders. Use either standard 8.5 × 11, or legal size 8.5 × 14 folders. Legal size may seem the most desirable, since many document photocopies will be legal size. However, legal size filing cabinets are wider than standard size. That difference in width can be significant if you eventually need two or three filing cabinets.

Now set up a system for filing the "papers"—all those letters, photocopies of censuses, documents, biographies, and so on that you have been systematically gathering. Consider creating files by various categories:

- Family name
- State
- County
- Subject
- Correspondence

If you do not have enough papers in the file to create subfiles (shown in the following figure), don't. Generate new files only as the need arises.

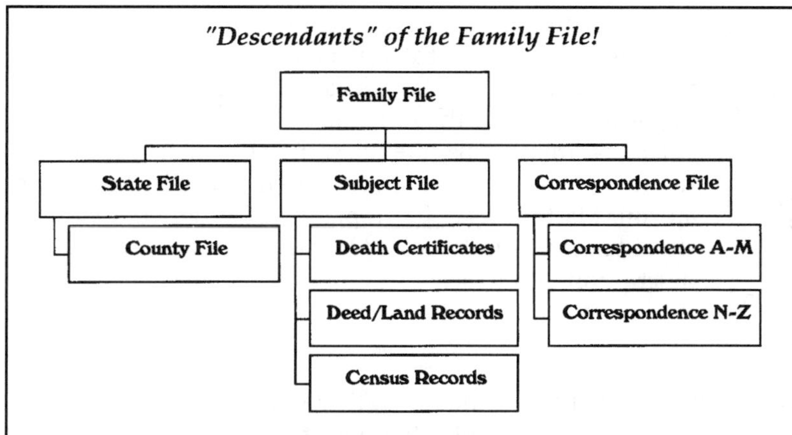

Flow chart of files.

The Name Is Martin

When you start your search, set up family files for each of the surnames you are tracing. In each of these files, insert letters that you write regarding that surname and any documents you find involving that name: the deed, the marriage record, the Bible record. Anything that involves that family will go into that family file.

They called Tennessee home...and North Carolina...and...

If you get deeply involved in one surname, you will find that one file to handle all the paper will not be sufficient. It will not be adequate to simply create a second family file for the same surname. Then you would have to search two family files for the paper you want, and later three, and then four. Resist the temptation to start that second file; instead establish some specialized files, starting with state files.

Suppose you are working on the Martins. This family has become a focal point. The major part of your energy is devoted to them. As is typical of many early families, they lived in several states, defying your erroneous belief that your ancestors were not mobile. Your file is overflowing with censuses of Tennessee, deeds and tax lists from North Carolina, and a raft of papers from Virginia. Now is the time to set up state files. For each state in which you have a particular amount of material (perhaps ten or more items) for the Martin family, create a state file. Label it as "Martin–Virginia" "Martin–Ohio," or "Martin–North Carolina." Also create a "Martin–miscellaneous state file." Anything that does not fit into the first three will go into the miscellaneous state file. When you accumulate sufficient records on another state, perhaps Pennsylvania, create another state file. (At that time you will remove the Pennsylvania records from the miscellaneous state file, and insert them into the new Martin–Pennsylvania file.)

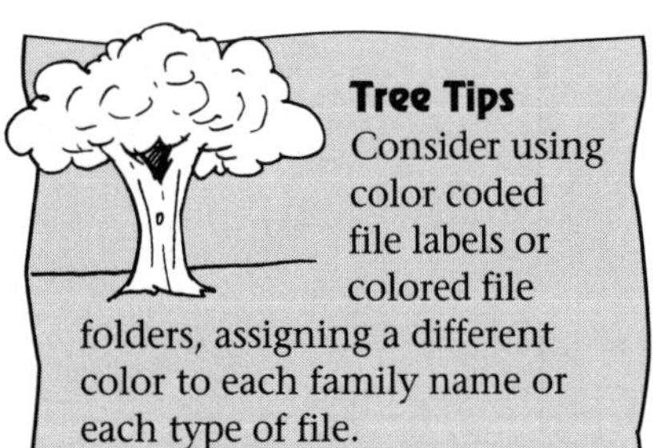

Tree Tips
Consider using color coded file labels or colored file folders, assigning a different color to each family name or each type of file.

When creating the state files, do not label them solely as "Virginia," or "Ohio." Later you may need to establish state files for records of another surname, and it will be confusing. Always include the surname on the label, such as "Martin–Virginia." Be sure the surname is first, followed by the state. The folders will be filed alphabetically. In order for all your Martin files to be properly filed together, their name should begin with the word "Martin," followed by the description of the file.

County Files

As the search progresses, even the state file may not be sufficient. If it gets too full, it will be unwieldy. You have a state file for "Martin–Ohio" but find that your family lived in Pickaway County, Ohio for a long time. They left so many records in Pickaway County that they take up half your "Martin–Ohio" file. Now is the time to create a subfile called "Martin–Ohio–Pickaway County" Move all the items in the Martin–Ohio file that relate to Pickaway County into this new file. Now, when you want to examine the deed to the land in Pickaway County or verify that you have a copy of the estate papers filed in that county, you know immediately where to look.

Remember, when creating the new file for the Pickaway County, Ohio records of the Martin family, it will be labeled: "Martin–Ohio–Pickaway County" to preserve an alphabetical filing system that draws all the Martin files together. Files should always be labeled with the broadest classification first, followed by each of the subject subdivisions in order. If you are breaking files down by 1. surname, 2. state, and 3. county, then the file label should be so marked.

Tree Tips
It will help if you file the certificates in your special file alphabetically by name for easy retrieval. Not enough death certificates to have a file by itself? Name it instead, "Martin–Vital Records" and include birth, marriage, and death records in the file.

Document Files

When you get several of a particular type of document on the surname, you can create a subfile for those specific documents, such as "Martin–Death Certificates." This time you won't do it by geographic location; all of the Martin death certificates will go into this document file. On the family group sheet you maintain on the family, note that the information came from the death certificate. When you want to re-examine the certificate of John Martin, you will know exactly where to find it.

Correspondence Files

At first, you may file correspondence relating to a particular surname in your basic family file, mentioned earlier in this chapter. But if you do considerable research on the family, you'll have correspondence mixed in with your other notes and papers. It is usually best to reserve the family file for research papers: the published biography, the manuscript written by your grandfather 40 years ago, and others. If so, you need a way to handle the filing of correspondence. Create a set of correspondence files. At first you will need only one for the surname: "Martin–Correspondence." As the file gets larger, you can separate it into two files, "Martin–Correspondence A–M" for all your correspondents on the Martin family with surnames A through M, and "Martin–Correspondence N–Z," for the rest. You can break it down even further as needed, such as A–C; D–G, and so on.

Correspondence Cards

In addition to the correspondence files, you need an easy and effective index. One way to keep track of your correspondence, no matter which family it involves, is to keep a correspondence card or log.

The card shown in the following figure can either be a standard 4 × 6 card, or a log on the computer. It will include the name and address of your correspondent, phone numbers (home and office), fax number, and e-mail address. Also include the name of the spouse if known. If a correspondent moves or changes telephone numbers and the phone is listed under the spouse's name, you may need it in order to obtain the new number. Leave room on the card for comments, which should include the specific branch of the family the correspondent is tracing.

The very last line should be "SEE FILE." This is one of the most important items on the card. Here you enter the name of the family file in which you filed their correspondence. If they are tracing the family Martin and you filed their correspondence in the "Martin–Correspondence" file, insert that in the SEE FILE space. The correspondence card will allow you to quickly note where the correspondence is located. If you establish this correspondence card early in your search, you will avoid many frustrations in trying to remember which file holds those letters.

CORRESPONDENCE CARD

Name

Address

City and State Zip

Spouse

Family Traced

County Traced

Phone Work Phone

Fax email

Comments

SEE FILE: Updated:

Sample of a correspondence card.

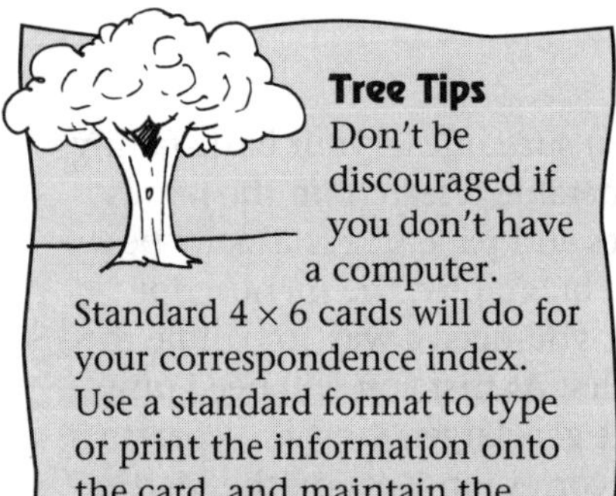

Tree Tips
Don't be discouraged if you don't have a computer. Standard 4 × 6 cards will do for your correspondence index. Use a standard format to type or print the information onto the card, and maintain the cards alphabetically by the name of the correspondent.

If you use a computer, you can easily establish a correspondence log similar to the card shown in the figure. Use a Personal Information Manager, such as *Sidekick*, available at your software store. There are others. You can even set one up using your word processing program. The advantage of having the information on your computer is that you can use the find command of a word processor or the sort command of a database program to locate those who are tracing specific branches of the family. All those tracing the "John and Mary (Smith) Jordan" branch can be quickly found.

Computers Cut Down on Paper

At first you'll keep every scrap of paper. You photocopy a marriage record from a book and photocopy the title page; now you have two pieces of paper in the file. Multiply this many times over, and you'll be overflowing with paper. You need to find a way to reduce the paper. The problem is not limited to providing the space needed to store all the paper. You need to consider that some day others will use the records. Unless your files are condensed sufficiently, others will not want to store them. Even repositories will be reluctant to take them if they are in complete disorder or too voluminous.

The Computer Becomes the Filing Cabinet

File on the computer in the same way you file in file drawers. Set up some computer files by family name, state, county, subject, and correspondence, just as suggested in this chapter. As you have time, take some of your paper notes, copy them to the computer, and then discard the paper copies. There may be certain copies you want to keep, but make your selections carefully. Always keep:

Tree Tips
A good rule of thumb is to transfer to disk all items from books that can be easily accessed again. If the book is rare, or the copy is from an original, (or it is lengthy), keep it.

- Copies of Bible records
- Family notes (written in the hand of an ancestor)
- Photocopies of original documents
- Death certificates and other vital records
- Obituaries from the newspaper

Keep the items that will not be easily replaced, or that you might need to prove your documentation in the future. Items you can discard (after entering the data onto your computer) are items from published books and notes that can be replaced if necessary. If you transfer a marriage record from a book onto your computer and include the full bibliographic citation, you can find it easily again should you need it.

Naming the Computer Files

As you establish computer files and name them, be sure to keep an index to genealogy file names. When naming your computer files, use some designation for each family, and start each file name with that designation. As an example, in the following figure, each of the Martin files starts with "Mar." This allows you to quickly search your computer directory for all your files on that family.

INDEX TO GENEALOGY FILES

File Name	*Description*
MarAlab	Martin–Alabama records
MarBib	Martin Bible Records
MarCorAM	Martin Correspondence, surname A–M
MarDeath	Martin Death Records

Example of an index to organize your computer files.

You may wish to name your files in some other descriptive fashion. Anything will do, as long as you keep an index to them. You won't always remember what they are named. It is best to create a different subdirectory on the computer for each family.

Correspondence Computerized

At first you save every letter and a copy of every response you send. That works fine until you suddenly realize that you have ten thick files of correspondence. To go back and try to reduce the paper is time consuming. Start now, in the beginning, to establish some firm rules for saving correspondence.

There are many ways to store your computer files. The one that works for me is to create correspondence files in the same manner as you would if using file folders. If you start one for correspondence A–M, it will hold the letters and responses to all correspondence with anyone of the surname A through M. If storing the summary on the computer, however, take a few minutes after you answer the letter to transfer the main points to the computer file. As an example, you received a letter from Sandra Williams, in which she sent some information on the Martin family, and asked for assistance. Examining the letter, you might summarize it on the computer as shown on the next page.

Save summary of letter in a computer file, alphabetically by surname of the correspondent.

> WILLIAMS, Sandra, 1111 NoWhere Street, Anywhere, U.S.A. 12345. Wrote July 17, 1997; says grandmother was Agatha Roberts who married Jonathan Martin on 3 April 1863 in Montgomery Co., Va. She thinks Jonathan was son of Roger Martin listed in tax records of the county in 1855 but is uncertain. This couple had: Jeffry b. ca 1866, Martha b. ca 1868, Mary b. ca 1870 (m. John Webster), and Joseph b. ca 1875. They are in 1870 Montgomery Co. census (she doesn't give citation. Wants to know if I have further info.) Wrote to her July 20, 1997: told her I am tracing a Joseph Martin who was born 4 April 1874 in Virginia by his tombstone in Hamilton Co., Ohio. I don't know if he is the same person, but I note that my Joseph named a son Roger Martin. Asked her for the listing she has in 1870, and sent her the 1860–70–80 census of my Joseph Martin. Suggested that we check deed records.
>
> See: MARTIN file.
>
> Updated: July 20, 1997

Now you can discard the three-page letter she sent and your two-page response. You have recorded the essential details. I like to make a printout of the condensation and place it in my correspondence file. You may decide only to keep the summary on the computer, and avoid the filing. If the correspondent writes again, add comments to the condensation. The date at the bottom of the condensation tells you when you last updated the contents of this summary.

You now have the notes in handy form on the computer and you can search them. When someone writes three years from now inquiring about a Roger Martin, you can use your computer program to search the files on your disk. You will find the summarized correspondence involving Roger Martin in a few seconds. If more than one person wrote you about him, you'll find that, too.

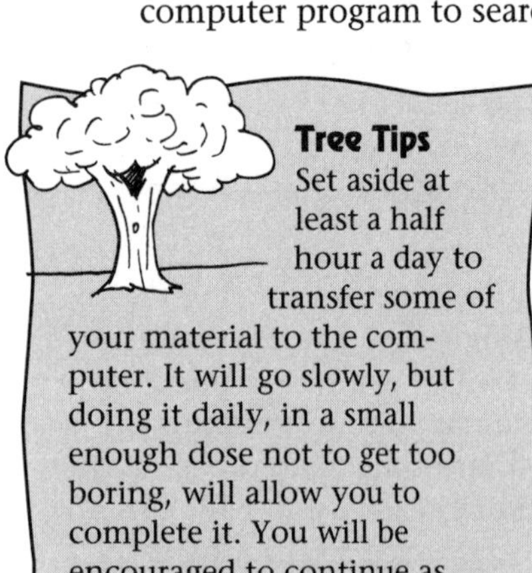
Tree Tips
Set aside at least a half hour a day to transfer some of your material to the computer. It will go slowly, but doing it daily, in a small enough dose not to get too boring, will allow you to complete it. You will be encouraged to continue as you see the space in your filing cabinet grow, and usability of the data increase.

Condensing your correspondent's letter onto the computer at the same time you use the computer to answer the letter will only take a few minutes. It will conserve filing time and eliminate some of the extra pieces of paper that fill your cabinets. And perhaps more importantly, it will make your collection easily usable by others who come after you.

You may want to keep a copy of your own letters on the computer. Either set up a "mail" file to save them, or save them in individual files with unique file names, whichever you prefer.

If you are new to genealogy, establish a good filing system right away and use your computer (if you have one) to facilitate storing and searching. You have an advantage; you can prevent the massive paper problem before it happens. If you have been into genealogy for a while and already have many paper files, allocate some time to get your files on disk. You will be making the collection more usable and valuable for others after you.

The Commercial Products

The filing system suggested in this chapter enables you to easily expand your system as needed with a minimum of cost. However, you may prefer to use one of the commercial products designed to help you store your records in binders. Examine the genealogical periodicals for advertisements. If a regional or national seminar is held in your area, attend, compare the wares of the various vendors, and decide which you prefer.

No matter what system you use, establish it now. Staying organized from the beginning will allow you more time to spend on what you enjoy the most: the search for those elusive ancestors.

The Least You Need to Know

- Creating specific files for "paper" makes for easy retrieval.
- Correspondence cards allow you to readily find addresses and files.
- Condensing correspondence onto the computer has long-range benefits.

Chapter 18

Doing It Right

In This Chapter

- Why citations are necessary
- Numbering systems to organize the compilation
- Approximating dates to assist in planning the search

After careful research you located crucial dates and locations of your family. It wasn't easy. You had to do an exhaustive search to find the information. Now you enter into your compilation: "John Washington Jackson was born 10 April 1857, in St. Louis, St. Louis County, Missouri, and died 5 July 1935 in Springfield, Greene County, Missouri." You look it over, and wonder if you missed something. Indeed you did—the citation is missing! On which record did you base the birth date, and on which did you base the birthplace as St. Louis? It is important to let others know on what the facts are based. Did the facts come from a published 1900 family history? Was the marriage of John Jackson in a book of abstracts? Was his birthplace from the tombstone? *Cite* this in some manner. Those using your records will need this citation if they find that some records conflict. You will assist them in their evaluation by letting them know the source of your statements.

Genie Jargon

To **cite** is to call attention to the proof or source of your information.

Published genealogies in the past commonly lacked almost any citations. Present day standards require a citation for every fact. If you have your grandparents' marriage as 3 May 1885 and the person using your information finds a notation elsewhere that it was 10 May 1887, they can't judge which might be correct unless they know the source of each statement. If they know your date came from the old letter that your grandmother wrote two days after the wedding, and that the 1887 date came from an obituary after her death, they can better judge which might be correct.

It is easy to underestimate the importance of the citation, but others will want to know. You may need a source again, too. You suddenly realize that items you copied from a book of abstracts appear to have a child missing. Did you just omit it when you copied it? You want to recheck. The little green book that was sitting on the shelf of the library is vividly in your mind, but you have now forgotten the title. You return to the library, and they have rearranged everything: The book can't be found. If you had the source citation, you could quickly locate it again through the library catalog. Learn the correct procedures when you first start your search. Later you won't be constantly frustrated as you try to find important records again.

Getting Help with Citing

There are books to help you learn how to cite properly. One of the best and most detailed is *The Chicago Manual of Style.* Another book by the late Richard S. Lackey, *Cite Your Sources,* was compiled for genealogists but doesn't include newer sources, which have become widely used since the death of the author. Look for a book, published in 1997, by Elizabeth Shown Mills. Titled *Evidence! Citation and Analysis for the Family Historian,* it illustrates, simply but effectively, the manner in which the various sources encountered by genealogists should be cited. This includes books, magazine articles, journals, microfilm, manuscripts, and other sources.

Tree Tips

The Chicago Manual of Style not only includes detailed information on preparing citations and referencing, but also other useful information such as manuscript preparation and copy editing, indexing, book design, and other related subjects. Check your library for other similar guidebooks used by colleges and universities.

If you keep in mind that the purpose of the citation is to enable the reader to readily find the same source, it will be easier to remember which items should be included. Basically, the citation for a book must include the complete title of the book, the full name of the author, the city and state where it was published, the name of the publisher, the year published, and the edition (1st ed., 2nd ed. revised, reprint, and so on). None of the components can be omitted for the citation to be complete. The citation for an article must include the full title of the article and the author, in addition to the full title of the magazine or journal, where published, publisher, volume, issue and page numbers, and date of the publication in which it appeared. When citing microfilm, include the series number and roll number, as well as the micropublication title, the specific item and page numbers, and anything else that will help identify it so others can locate the microfilm. Think what you would need to know if you were trying to find the record.

Tree Tips
Some researchers photocopy the title page of the book to prepare the citation. Though this appears to be helpful, it adds expense and adds "paper" to your files. Learn early the correct citation techniques, and write down the details. Be sure to check the reverse of the title pages of books; some of the needed information may be there.

Also cite personal documents, such as letters and photographs. The citation for the letter that Aunt Martha wrote to Cousin Jim in 1910 giving the family history should at least include the date, to whom addressed, by whom, and in whose possession the original letter now resides. If referring to an oral interview, give the date, who was interviewed, by whom, and where. For Bibles, besides the date of publication, be sure to note whether your information is from the original Bible, a photocopy, a handwritten copy, or a typed copy made from the original. This will help in evaluating whether errors may have been made in copying or transcribing. (For fuller examples and illustrations refer to the mentioned manuals.)

You may think, "But I am only doing this for fun." Your diligent search of your ancestors, if not properly cited, could someday puzzle descendants who will wonder upon what the statements were based. A new record could turn up with differing information, and they need to judge it together with the information you preserved. It takes little extra effort to add your sources if done at the time the information is obtained. Your record may be the correct one, but they won't know unless they know where you got your information.

Undocumented data is an immense problem for genealogists. In the past, there was little effort to include citations. Today there is increased interest in restudying earlier records to add details, and to thoroughly document compilations in order to correct prior errors and omissions. You can see a need for this when using a source that gives names and dates but nothing more. A book may show that Mary Gordon was born in 1832 while her tombstone says she was born 1835. Which is correct? You cannot evaluate the validity of the information unless you know the source. Was the information in the published genealogy supplied by Mary herself at the age of 80? Was the tombstone erected by a granddaughter? Knowing the source, you can make a judgment. This applies not only to dates, but to locations, parentage, and other

Tree Tips
The necessity of adding citations is not a reflection on your ability. You may use a record that appears correct when you locate it; another record you didn't even know about may later be found that is in conflict with it. Knowing the source of each statement will help you and others in making judgments.

important details. Sometimes the discrepancy is only an error made in transcribing the handwriting from a document, or a slip made in writing it down. If you know from where it came, you can reexamine the source.

Family Group Sheets Are Convenient, but...

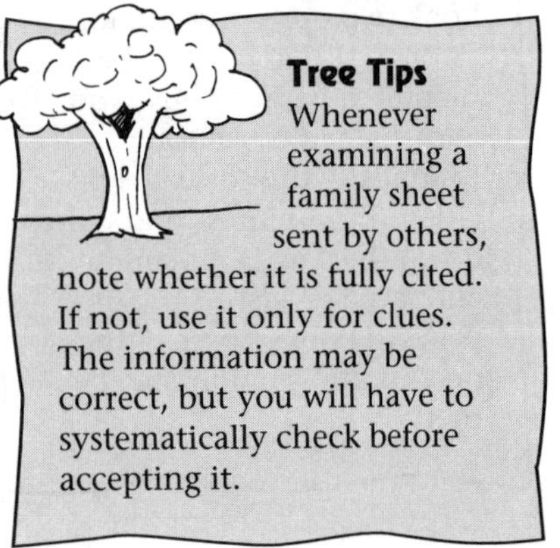

Tree Tips
Whenever examining a family sheet sent by others, note whether it is fully cited. If not, use it only for clues. The information may be correct, but you will have to systematically check before accepting it.

Family group sheets, those forms leaving room for the names and statistics of an individual family, are popular because they are a convenient form of entering data. However, problems exist. Seldom do the forms have sufficient room to enter the sources. Computer programs that are now available often handle the problem by allowing text notes to be included. But those prepared in earlier times, without the benefit of a computer, encouraged the researchers to enter dates and locations without documentation. Genealogists who did attempt documentation normally wrote on the back of the form. Later, when the form was sent to others, perhaps only the front was photocopied.

Put It at the Bottom or at the End?

Once you know that each fact must be cited, where do you put a citation in your compilation? If you are using family group sheets and there is not enough room on the front for the citations, use the reverse side. (Remember to photocopy the reverse, too, if you send copies to others.) Some computer programs allow you to add text or provide special templates for citations.

If you are using a word processor (or a typewriter), you can add your citations in one of three ways:

- In-text citation
- Footnotes
- Endnotes

The in-text citation adds the information immediately following the fact: "Mary Morgan was born 3 April 1846 [*Family Bible, adding the full citation here*]. She died 8 March 1895 [*Death Certificate: adding the full citation here*]." As can be seen, the text is considerably broken up with each of the citations. This method has fallen into disfavor because of the choppiness. The two favored systems are to either footnote the citation or show it in endnotes at the end of the chapter or compilation.

Because many word processing programs can handle footnotes, they are easy to implement. A superscript number is added to the fact and keyed to the footnote that holds the citation. The advantage of footnotes is that the citation remains on the same page as the text. In endnotes, you use the superscript number and key it to an endnote. Each system (footnotes and endnotes) has its advantages. In footnoting you don't have to constantly flip to the end to read the notes. Others prefer endnotes, believing that footnotes can be distracting. It's your decision as to which you want to use.

Use whichever of the three mentioned systems of citation placement that suits you; the important thing is that the citation be there, keyed directly to the fact it is citing. It is not enough just to add a list of "Sources" to the end of the compilation. The person using the data must know specifically which source goes with each fact.

Keeping Track by Numbers

When you start using published genealogies in the library, you will be stumped many times by complicated numbering systems. When faced with a massive listing of descendants in a family, compilers often devise their own system to keep track. Later they decide to print it for the family. Being fully familiar with their own style, they resist any thought of transferring it to a uniformly accepted style. The increased use of computers seems to have encouraged many to create new systems. Often the reader must devote considerable time to understanding a complicated and unique system.

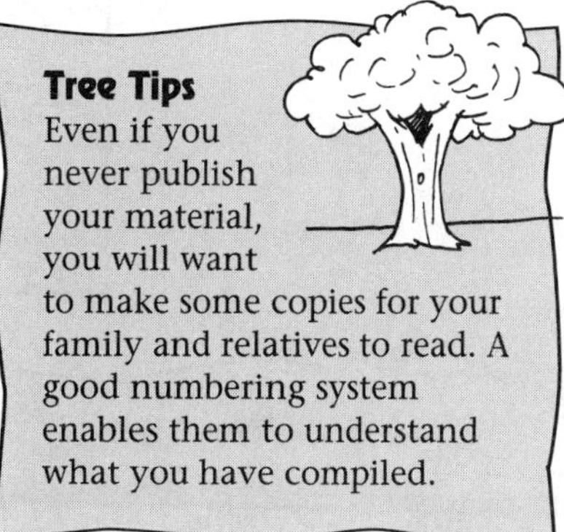

Tree Tips
Even if you never publish your material, you will want to make some copies for your family and relatives to read. A good numbering system enables them to understand what you have compiled.

An excellent publication by Joan Ferris Curran, *Numbering Your Genealogy: Sound and Simple Systems*, will assist you in understanding the basic numbering systems that are widely accepted in the genealogical community. This was first published as an article in the *National Genealogical Society Quarterly* and later offered by the National Genealogical Society as Special Publication No. 59.

Descending Genealogies

The two most widely used and recommended systems are the Register System (developed by the New England Historic Genealogical Society for their *Register*), and the modified Register system used by the *National Genealogical Society Quarterly* (usually referred to as the NGSQ System). They are applied to descending genealogies. This approach normally starts with the immigrant, but if the immigrant's identity is not yet known, it can start from the earliest known ancestor of the family. He is assigned an Arabic numeral 1. The children of number 1 are all given Roman numerals in order of birth. In the Register System, those for whom there is sufficient information to carry forward include the next Arabic numeral in front of the Roman numeral, alerting the reader that more will be found in the section corresponding to that Arabic number.

In the following figure, there is no need to carry child i. to her own section; nothing further is known about her to warrant carrying her forward in the compilation. Mary, child iii. died young (d.y.) and is also not carried forward. More information is known about Jonathan, so he received the next Arabic numeral 2, notifying the reader that there is something further on him in section 2. More details are also known for Ezekiel, so he received the next Arabic numeral, 3. Those Arabic numerals will precede the sections in which further details on Jonathan and Ezekiel are presented.

The Register system of numbering.

1. John^{1} Smith was born 3 April 1788, etc. [include here rest of information on him, events of life, marriage, documents, etc.]

Children; surname SMITH:

- i. Mercy b. 5 Apr. 1808, Richmond, Va., further unknown
- 2. ii. Jonathan b. 18 Mar. 1810, Richmond, Va.
- iii. Mary b. 3 Aug. 1813, Richmond, Va., d.y. 4 May 1814
- 3. iv. Ezekiel b. 22 Dec. 1816, Alexandria, Va.

2. Jonathan^{2} Smith (John^{1}) was born 18 March 1810, Richmond, Virginia, etc.

3. Ezekiel^{2} Smith (John^{1}) was born 22 December 1816, Alexandria, Virginia, etc.

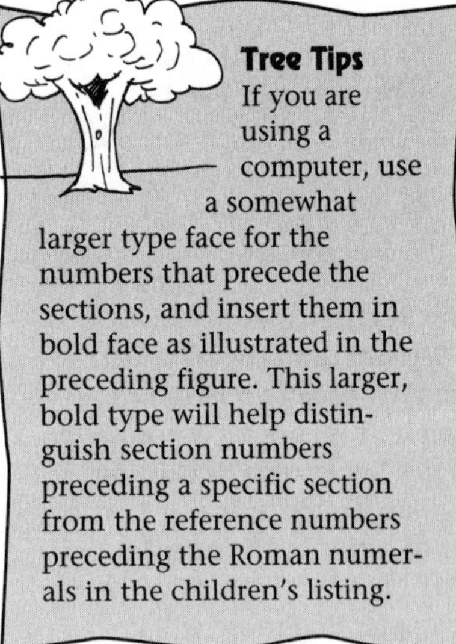

Tree Tips

If you are using a computer, use a somewhat larger type face for the numbers that precede the sections, and insert them in bold face as illustrated in the preceding figure. This larger, bold type will help distinguish section numbers preceding a specific section from the reference numbers preceding the Roman numerals in the children's listing.

Note that generational numbers are also included. John^{1} Smith indicates that he is either the immigrant, or the first identified progenitor in this family. The children who are carried forward are also shown with a generational number in superscript, followed by a "runner" showing their line back to the earliest known progenitor. Let us say you have researched Abraham Smith of the fifth generation. He is carried forward to his own section. The generational runner would be something like: Abraham^{5} Smith (George^{4}, William^{3}, Jonathan^{2}, John^{1}). It is easy to distinguish these generational numbers from the overall numbering of the compilation. They can also be distinguished from any citation numbers you may insert, as the superscript generational numbers are inserted after the first name of the individual, while superscript numbers for citations follow the surname. Thus: John^{2} Smith is referring to John Smith of the 2nd generation. John Smith^{2} would indicate a citation reference.

NGSQ System

The NGSQ System is based on the Register system, but assigns an Arabic numeral to *each* child. A "+" mark in front of the Arabic numeral designates whether the child is carried forward.

As seen in the figure below, the "+" readily identifies the sections that hold further details. Those sections are preceded by the Arabic numeral assigned to that individual, (in larger bold typeface if using a computer).

1. John[1] Smith was born 3 April 1788, etc.

Known children of John Smith and wife Mary Martin were as follows:

2. i. Mercy b. 5 Apr. 1808, Richmond, Va., further unknown

\+ 3. ii. Jonathan b. 18 Mar. 1810, Richmond, Va.

4. iii. Mary b. 3 Aug. 1813, Alexandria, Va., d.y. 4 May 1814

\+ 5. iv. Ezekiel b. 22 Dec. 1816, Alexandria, Va.

3. Jonathan[2] Smith (John[1]) was born 18 March 1810, Richmond, Virginia, etc.

5. Ezekiel[2] Smith (John[1]) was born 22 December 1816, Alexandria, Virginia, etc.

The modified Register System, known as NGSQ System.

Each of these systems has devotees. Those using the Register System find it simple and "clean" in appearance, but most will admit it has a disadvantage. When the compiler must add newly found information on a child whose data was previously unknown, creating a new section for that child's data requires complete renumbering.

Those who prefer the NGSQ System like the advantage of having an Arabic numeral already assigned to each of the children. If more information is located on that child, it is simple to insert a plus before the Arabic numeral, and insert the section in its proper place. (Even those using the NGSQ System have to renumber if they discover the couple had more children than was originally known when the compilation was first numbered.)

Tree Tips

You can devise a way of handling the disadvantage of having to renumber constantly. One way is to insert temporary section numbers such as "3a," and "3b" between section 3 and section 4 to handle the problem of added sections. At some later point you can renumber the whole compilation.

Before They Came

Since the immigrant is numbered with an Arabic 1, you will wonder how to "number" the generations before the immigrant's arrival. You are tracing a family from England and have information on earlier generations. These are handled by assigning the closest pre-American generation as A, the next as B, and so on. If the father of immigrant John Jackson was George Jackson, and his grandfather was William Jackson, this numbering system will show John^{1} Jackson (George^{A}, William^{B}). This immediately conveys that John is the immigrant, his father is George, and his grandfather is William.

The Register System and NGSQ System lay out the family generation by generation. The systems are easy and will become second nature to you. Further details and illustrations can be studied in Curran's *Numbering Your Genealogy*.

Approximating Dates

If an exact date is not known, whenever possible, estimate dates rather than leave them entirely blank. We'll discuss a few of the many ways in which this can be accomplished.

By Date of Will

If John Morgan made his will on 17 April 1853, and on 15 July 1853 the will was presented in court for probate, you know that John Morgan died between 17 April 1853 and 15 July 1853. It's best not to show "died 1853," but specifically that he "died between 17 April 1853 (date of will) and 15 July 1853 (date will proved)." Be as precise as you can in presenting the information if you have the information to do so. It will prevent confusion; when someone finds a record that John Morgan sold a piece of land on 12 February 1853. If you had only entered the date as "ca. 1853" they might have been puzzled, but if you were precise and entered the death as being between the date of the will and the date it was proved (as above noted), they'll realize he was living until at least 17 April.

Rule of Thumb

Studies of countless families living in the 17th and 18th centuries (and earlier) have determined that a good rule of thumb is that children were born two years apart. When you examine the lists of children of your earlier relatives, you may find gaps, but often they can be accounted for because of the death of a child. You know that the couple married in 1816, their first child Amy was born in 1818, Timothy was born in 1822, and Jonathan, the youngest, was born in 1824. When you discover a child Joseph, you can estimate that he may have been born ca. 1820. Do not state it as absolute fact, but include "ca." (*circa*, about) to indicate that it is an approximated date.

Similarly, if you know the marriage date and don't have the birth dates of any of the children, you can approximate their births based on the marriage date. If John Taylor was married in 1838, and had three sons and a younger daughter, you can estimate that the sons were born ca. 1840, 1842, 1844, and the daughter ca. 1846, two years apart. Now that you have some estimated dates, you can make some evaluation of when they may have married, whether any of the sons might have served in the Civil War since they were the right age, and more.

You can also use several census records to provide an approximated date (see Chapter 10 for more on the census). If the age of John is 15 in the 1850 census, 22 in the 1860 census, and 37 in the 1870 census, you can approximate that he was born ca. 1833–1838.

Tree Tips

You not only used the rule of thumb in the example given above, but combined that with the fact that Jonathan was the youngest, and the couple married in 1816. It is often possible to glean clues on the approximate date from several related records.

Choosing Their Own Guardian

Minors had guardians appointed by the court if they had any property due to them. Most states allowed those minors, upon reaching the age of fourteen, to choose their own guardians. If your ancestor is noted in court making that choice, you can estimate that he or she was between the age of 14 and 21. (By the latter age, a guardian would not be necessary if the person was competent.)

Of Age to Marry?

You will find records of those who misrepresented age to get a marriage license; nonetheless, the marriage license can be a gauge for determining age. If the couple applied for the license without the consent of a parent or guardian, assume that they were of age unless other records prove otherwise. The legal age varied by location and time period, but usually the groom had to be 21 and the bride, 18. (The legal age was lower in some areas, especially for the bride.)

Tree Tips

As you progress in your genealogical pursuits, you will turn at times to the laws to determine the legal age for certain matters, in order to best evaluate the ages involved. When doing so, remember that states differed and the laws changed.

Why Bother with Approximate Dates?

The purpose of establishing an approximate date rather than leaving it blank is to better determine the records that can be examined. If you know only that your ancestor William Carr was born in Tennessee, you have nothing on which to determine a course of action. If you know he was born ca. 1791 in Tennessee, you might then research to learn if he served in the War of 1812, if he was listed in the 1820 census of Tennessee as head of a household, and other possibilities.

The Little Children

Always include in your compilations the little children who were stillborn or who died before maturity. They, too, were important in the overall genealogy. They may carry a name that is significant—perhaps named after the mother, grandmother, or other family member. That name may be the clue that triggers a breakthrough. Their ages are important; they can explain gaps in the family groupings. Their burials are important; they may lead to family plots. Lacking any other reason, those children were precious to their families. If you don't remember them, no one will. Even their causes of death can explain a mystery; if the child died of cholera, you may realize why three of the family members disappeared from the records that year.

Genealogy should be fun. And it is. Developing sound techniques does not diminish that fun—it adds to it. Taking the time to do things right from the beginning will save you many headaches later. It will also preserve your information in such a way that you will be proud to share the results with others. You will know you have produced a family history documented to the best of your ability, and that it will be easily understood by those who read it.

Relative Resources

Chicago Manual of Style, The. Fourteenth Ed. Revised and Expanded. (Chicago and London: Univ. of Chicago Press, 1993.)

Curran, Joan Ferris. *Numbering Your Genealogy: Sound and Simple Systems*. Special Publication No. 59. Arlington, Va.: National Genealogical Society, 1992. Originally published as an article by the same title in the *National Genealogical Society Quarterly*. Arlington, Va.: National Genealogical Society. 79 No. 3 (Sept. 1991):182–193.

Lackey, Richard S. *Cite Your Sources*. New Orleans: Polyanthos, 1980.

Mills, Elizabeth Shown. *Evidence! Citation and Analysis for the Family Historian*. (Baltimore: Genealogical Publishing Company, 1997.)

The Least You Need to Know

- Citations are important; they allow others to locate the sources you used.
- Numbering systems should be easy and standard.
- Approximating dates will assist in pointing you in the right direction for the search.

Chapter 19

Gaining Historical Perspective

In This Chapter

- Gather more than the bare facts
- Analyze and interpret the documents
- Interview the oldest relatives
- The Life Story: a practical example

You've been gathering the bare facts about your ancestors: their names, their dates, their locations. So far, so good. But, at this point, they are just shadowy figures. Who were these people whose genes you share? You can connect with them and make them come alive, if only on the pages of your family history. How can you know what life was like for them? Make the records talk to you. Add historical background and visualization so your ancestors become more real.

Take a Fresh Look at What You've Found

By analyzing the records, you will find the information to flesh out your ancestors. You dutifully wrote down the items listed in the inventory taken when your ancestor's estate was probated, and you filed it away. Take it out and look at it again. What does it say to you? Even the arrangement of the inventory can give you clues. Think about how you inventory your possessions for insurance purposes. You start in one room and progress through the house. That is the way most inventories are taken. Stand in the doorway with the appraiser of your ancestor's possessions and look around the room with him.

two beds and bedsteads	tea canister
four sheets four pillows six blanketts	pitcher set
two double coverlets	red plates
one Bureau and stand	one saw
table	two trunks
chest	looking glass
two sets bed curtains	one wash tub
stove	wash board
one set chairs	sugar tub
rocking chair	lard tub
little oven	one flat Iron
one set silver teaspoons	one par hand irons
one set silver tablespoons	one bible and 10 Books
molases can	one cow
sugar bowl	

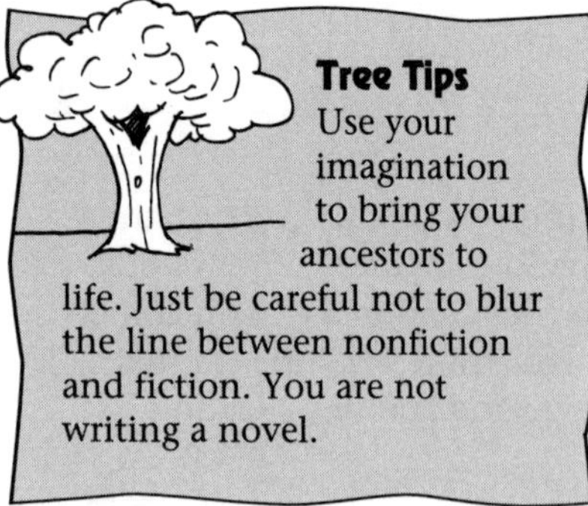

Tree Tips
Use your imagination to bring your ancestors to life. Just be careful not to blur the line between nonfiction and fiction. You are not writing a novel.

The possessions in the preceding list, meager by our standards, probably describe a house with two rooms. One room had two beds complete with bedding and curtains for privacy. The other room was the all purpose kitchen, family, dining, living, laundry room. The looking glass hangs on a nail over the wash tub that was also used for bathing. Picture the saw, leaning against the wall, perhaps next to the stove, and the table set with red plates and silver spoons. Where are the books and Bible? (And who got the Bible with the family records? you wonder.) Outside is one cow, probably kept for milk, cream, and butter.

Expand Your Research

Look for records that give you data to work with. Comparing the New York state censuses of 1855 and 1875, you can learn a great deal about your farming ancestor. For example, suppose that in 1855, an enumerator in Onondaga County mentioned that yields were down one half to one third because of drought and wind, yet your ancestor's crop yields were much better than those of the neighboring farmers. From that you know that either he was a better farmer or he had better land. You learn he harvested 100 pounds of honey; he probably kept bees to pollinate the fruit trees, because he also had 100 bushels of apples and 20 gallons of cider. In 1875, his crop land allocations were quite different. By this time, he was 75 years old, so it is conceivable that he was slowing down. Yet 15 years later a newspaper article remarks that at 90 he is the oldest native born resident of the county and "is an excellent farmer, though nearly blind." These small details enhance the picture you're developing.

Court Records Tell Many Secrets

Read as many abstracts of court records as you can find in the areas where your ancestors lived. Your ancestors' court appearances give you more insight. They appear in court for "unlawful gaming" or because a speculator wants to foreclose on their land. They want water rights, or they are evicting a tenant. There may be statements in their own words.

Divorce records can be quite telling. He accuses her of infidelity; she accuses him of drinking too much and hitting her. After the divorce is granted, they continue to appear in court wrangling over their young daughter. They have joint custody, but neither is happy. The mother says the father does not meet the little girl's train; the father says the mother doesn't send her dressed warmly enough. Reading this, you understand a little more about the bitterness in the family and how the family became estranged.

Treasure Your Ancestors' Enemies!

Disputes create records and provide glimpses of your ancestor that you might not otherwise have. You never know what you'll find. In an 1805 Bourbon County, Kentucky, deed book, Peter Sap releases Thomas Glass from further liability for having cut or bitten off the top part of his ear in "an affray."

You may find something similar to my own discovery: Great-Grandpa's Civil War pension was challenged by a disgruntled townsman who wrote his congressman saying "after coming home they all say he been an auctioneer, if a man is very deaf it does seem to me that a deaf man would make a very poor auctioneer." As a result of this complaint, there was

Tree Tips
Deed books often contain more than land records. They may include the record of an adoption, an apprenticeship, or a livestock brand. Perhaps a bill of sale for "one yoke of oxen, one red and one brindle color, I call one Bill, the other John."

an investigation, including a physical examination that showed the old man to be quite frail, and testimony from numerous townsfolk about Great-Grandpa's fine character. Your ancestor's enemies can be just as important as their friends in generating records for you to find!

Tree Tips
Any time you are examining volumes of original records, take time to look at the beginning and the end of the volume. The notations may be invaluable.

Unexpected Finds

There is much to be said for examining the original records even if you have seen them on film, but especially so if you have only seen the abstracts. Perhaps the record has a notation that the abstracter didn't include. In Wabash County, Indiana, Marriage Book 6, there are three handwritten notes pasted on the inside front cover. The notes were written to the County Clerk by three fathers telling him not to issue marriage licenses to their children. My favorite appears in the following figure:

> Wabash County, Ind. Jan. 11, 1867
>
> Bro. E. Hackleman Dear Sir do not issue a marriage license to Marshall Murray & Mary E. Shortridge without a certificate from me. Mary is underage & I am not being treated as respectfully as could be desired if everything goes off right I will give them a certificate.
> Respectfully
> L. Shortridge [signed]

You may be lucky enough to find a record that is annotated and gives you totally unexpected information: the census taker who marks a name with an asterisk and at the bottom of the page writes "died of drink;" or the assessor who adds comments beside the names on his list: "bankrupt," "left for Kansas," or my favorite "not dead, but asleep."

By scrolling to the end of the Sevier County, Utah, 1870, census roll, I found this notation: "The foregoing number of houses were abandoned by the Whites during the late Indian War of 1865–'6–'7." If your ancestors were in this area at that time, this could well be relevant to their lives, and you'll want to follow up by reading about the events that took place there.

Looking Beyond the Records

Follow every opportunity to learn about the times of your ancestors. All over the United States there are towns and museums creating living history celebrations. Colonial Williamsburg in Virginia, Sturbridge Village and Plimouth Village in Massachusetts,

Strawberry Banke in New Hampshire, Skagway in Alaska, and Columbia in California, are some of the larger ones, but there are many small projects also. For now, attending these is the only kind of time travel we can know. If your ancestor was a blacksmith, visit the re-created blacksmith's shop. Observing the activity will make you realize how much physical strength your ancestor had to possess to pursue this occupation. Visit the kitchen garden where your ancestor grew things for the table and the medicine cabinet. Families had to be self-reliant, and mothers learned the benefits of many herbs for treating illnesses.

Tree Tips
Civil War reenactments have become popular. The participants study hard to make the encampments as authentic as possible. You will get the real flavor of the times by attending one.

Tornado Watch

Weather is a factor in our everyday lives, but it loomed even larger in the lives of our ancestors. Their crops were dependent on the rain. They learned how to prepare for the usual occurrences of harsh winters and blistering summers. It was the unusual that dealt them severe setbacks: the tornado, the hailstorm, or the flood. Families in precarious financial situations were pushed over the edge by bad weather. This can affect your research and may explain why families pulled up stakes and left an area. Reading about the weather can help you interpret the records.

Be a Student of Local and Family History

As you try to complete the pictures of your ancestors' lives, steep yourself in the history of the period and locality. There may be clues there. Reading about the coal mine disaster or the opening of the canal, you may finally understand why your family left the area. The newspaper article in the weekly paper extolling the virtues of Nebraska may explain why they left the fertile land of central Illinois and headed west.

Learn about the churches in the area. Our ancestors were passionate about their religion, and religious upheaval was not uncommon. Arguments over doctrine among the parishioners often caused a dissident group to start another church in different place—down the road, in another county, or in another state.

Search for authors who wrote about life in the areas and times of your ancestors. Authors such as William Faulkner, John Steinbeck, James Whitcomb Riley, Wallace Stegner, Owen Wister, and Willa Cather wrote

Pedigree Pitfalls
Be sure that historical events are relevant to your ancestors before including them in your narrative. The lives of famous people probably touched your ancestors no more than they do yours. But, legislative action, such as the Homestead Act, or events, such as the Gold Rush, may well be important.

fiction and nonfiction about places you can visit today. Published letters or diaries that pertain to your ancestors' experiences give you insight. Look for them.

Illustrate Your Story

Don't be satisfied with just portrait photographs of your ancestors themselves. Collect photographs and maps of the local area. The National Archives in Washington, D.C., has millions of still photographs with an incredible range of topics. There are photographs of military units, photographs documenting the terrible conditions in the Dust Bowl, and photographs of federal projects. The grandeur of national parks and the bleakness of tenements are preserved. On a less sweeping scale, local museums and historical societies tell the stories of their counties. It is there that you'll find the picture of Grandpa self-confidently astride his horse and Grandma posing with the students she taught in the one-room school.

If you know the ship your ancestor came on, see if you can find a picture of it or a similar ship. Maritime museums are a good source for sketches and photographs of old ships.

Historical maps and atlases will help you locate the exact spot of the farm. The atlases may have drawings of local sights, such as the livery stable in the following figure. The caption under the sketch says, "The only first class livery in Morris. Ladies & gent's driving horses a specialty. Particular attention paid to funerals. Good accommodations for farmers." Your ancestors in Grundy County may have patronized this place, but even if they didn't, it was probably a part of the scenery of their everyday life. Again, these enhancements to your narrative may be found locally, at the regional and state level, or at the National Archives and the Library of Congress.

Livery stable sketched in Atlas of Grundy County and the State of Illinois, (Chicago: Warners & Beers, 1874).

Closer to Home

In addition to analyzing the records and reading history books, contact all the relatives you can find. Ask them to look in their attics, basements, and filing cabinets to see if they have some long forgotten piece of family history.

This particular part of your genealogy research depends a great deal on serendipitous finds. From a family you only recently learned existed, you may receive a copy of a letter such as this one written on December 15, 1875, in Bear Grove, Iowa, from Alice Dunn to her cousin Lis Harcourt: [spelling as in the original]

> Dear cousin I received your most welcome letter yesterday and was very glad to hear from you once more. It found us all well. I was at church when I got it. Our father got it from the office and brought it to church and gave it to me…
>
> Well you said you expected my school was out. So it is but I have taken another one but for a longer term than that one. I have taken one for life this time. How is that for high. You know we promised to tell each other when we were going to get married. Well I wrote you a letter and told you to answer it right away and I would tell you something but I guess you did not get the letter from the tone of your letter. I was married on the 18th of November 1875 at home at seven 7 o'clock in the evening and also Willson was married the same day at twelve in the morning. He married a lady by the name of Miss Nora Mason and my name is Mrs. Parsons. I guess you know the rest of his name. I wish you could have been there. We had a real nice time. There was about 30 at the wedding. I will send you a piece of my wedding dresss and tell you how I made it. Well I trimmed the front breadth in knife pleatings and sheared ruffing and the rest of the skirt on down and put it on in box plaiting and put a mould over each plait and made it to trail and looped the skirt. The back bredth were just one yard and three quarters long. I got it in Desmoines city and my hat is white velvet trimmed in drab rep ribbon and drab plume and veil. My veil is one yard and a half long. Come over and see me. I am keeping house now. I live just one mile from fathers. I am going to look for you in one year from now and I want you to be sure and come. I expect it will be your weding tour. Be shure and write me when it is and I will come and then you can come on home with me and we will have some buckwheat cakes and beef juice and dried turkey and boiled frog and old rooster and row potatoes boiled [?] and stewed cake and fried biscuit and stewed onions and baked beets and roasted turnips and other things to numerous to mention. I will send you our picture as soon as we get some taken but do not wait for them but send your picture without delay. John and Willson are going to start for Marion Co this state next week and me and Ed are going to go with them and visit so no more at this time.
>
> Please answer soon. Give my love to all enquiring friends and keep a portion for yourself. From your cousin Alice.

Here is a wonderful glimpse of life. The new bride excitedly telling her cousin about her wedding dress, and detailing the feast they will have when the cousin visits. Notice, also, the genealogical information. Alice gives her husband's name and her brother's as well as that of his bride, and the date of both weddings, and mentions locations.

The Art of the Interview

You want to conduct interviews with everyone still living who knew your relatives and remember the stories that were handed down. Do not delay. Deaths and illnesses may put their recollections and insights forever beyond your reach. Glean all you can from still living family members and their associates. Seek out the stories of their youth.

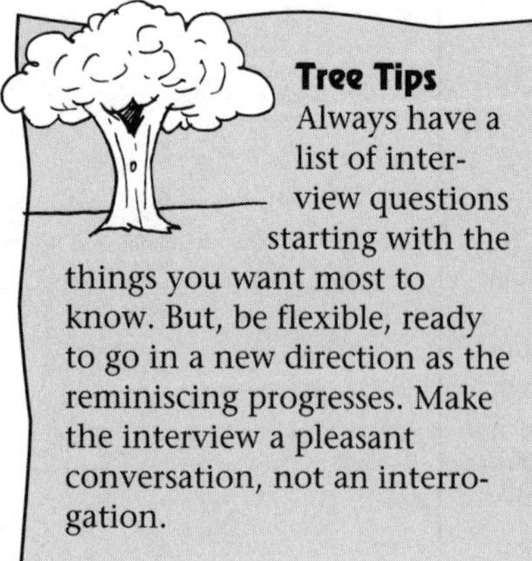

Tree Tips
Always have a list of interview questions starting with the things you want most to know. But, be flexible, ready to go in a new direction as the reminiscing progresses. Make the interview a pleasant conversation, not an interrogation.

You want a general feel for the events and traditions of the family, and you want to know about the individuals. So your questions should be designed with that in mind. You have to be more explicit than "Tell me about yourself and tell me about the family and friends."

The "things" of our ancestors are catalysts for stories. When family treasures are handed down, they are accompanied by tidbits such as "Mama always made potato salad in this bowl," or "My mother won these pearls at the raffle at St. Joseph's, and she wasn't even Catholic." Often the quilts are made from pieces of clothing the family wore. If the stories are from a time beyond the memory of anyone living, be careful in accepting them as completely accurate. The story probably has a kernel of truth, but may have been altered from years of telling.

Tree Tips
Older people often feel self-conscious talking into a tape recorder. Make it unobtrusive so they forget it's there. I had great success in taking my mother 2,000 miles to the town where she grew up. As we drove slowly around, the tape recorder on the dash recorded her excited recounting of past events and people.

Appendix D has suggestions for interview questions. For more help in devising your list of questions, look for books on oral history techniques. Bob Greene's *To Our Children's Children* was written to help you write your own recollections, but the topics and hundreds of questions suggest many avenues for you to explore with your subjects.

We can't know our parents as vigorous young adults the way their contemporaries did, but we can learn about them by interviewing their friends. You will be amazed at the stories their friends share as they reminisce about the good times they had with your parents or the time your mother borrowed the dishes to impress your father's wealthy aunt who was coming to dinner and then forgot to serve the rolls; how your father grew beautiful flowers, but he showed his practical side by planting the daffodils marching along the garden border rather than flamboyantly scattering the bulbs.

Putting It Into Practice

Let's take an example of how you might direct your research to build on the facts you've accumulated, using the previous suggestions of contact with relatives, interpretation of records, and reading historical background.

> Anson Parmilee Stone, born 9 January 1815 in Oneida County, New York, married 14 October 1835 in Vernon, New York to Cornelia Adams, daughter of Isaac Ward Adams and Eunice Webster. She was born in Vernon on 5 May 1812, and was a distant cousin of the Presidents Adams. Her grandfather Abraham Webster was brother of Noah Webster, the lexicographer. Anson died 14 March 1852 in Ft. Atkinson, Jefferson County, Wisconsin, and is buried there at the Lake View Cemetery. Cornelia died 16 February 1882 in Ft. Atkinson, and is buried with him. They had five children, the three oldest born in New York in 1837, 1839 and 1842, and the two youngest born in Ft. Atkinson, Wisconsin in 1845 and 1850.

The preceding contains the facts. But we want to know more. One of the first items that might interest us is the trip from New York to Wisconsin sometime between 1842 and 1845 (based on ages of children.) What took them there? How did they travel?

Contact and Interview Living Relatives

Following the suggested pattern of research, interviews were conducted with all the grandchildren who were living when this research was undertaken in the 1960s. They were exhaustively interviewed about their recollections, and each scoured his or her own collection of family material. A handwritten paper was found in Anson's son Marsena's hand, stating that "Father went ahead out west, to grow up with the country, and he bought a farm, 200 acres, one half mile from Ft. Atkinson and built a small house and a large barn, split rails and fenced in the farm..." Anson sent word to his wife Cornelia to bring the family, and in 1844, according to the same writer, they joined him making the trip from New York to Milwaukee. Said Marsena, "[Father] sent for Mother, Emory, Newton and little me, we followed up on a sailing scooner across the lakes. Newt told me when I had grown up that we had a terrible squally time crossing the lakes and I squalled so loud and long that he and Em put their heads together to throw me over board, but Mother never gave them a chance. Theres no one that walks on earth like a mother..."

Use the events in the lives of your ancestors to trigger a search for interesting sidelights. The event mentioned in Marsena's letter led to a study of travel via the Great Lakes in the period when many left the New York area for parts west. Cornelia and her children took part in the great sailing era that had begun about 1834. The three boys, ages seven, five, and two, were no doubt enthralled with the billowing sails of the schooners crowding the Great Lakes, while Cornelia was preoccupied with trying to keep them from falling overboard.

Check Records for More Details

The events of Anson and Cornelia's lives were chronicled through the records. Census listings were examined; Anson was a farmer. County records were searched for his estate record. His will revealed that he was in "a very infirm state of health" when he made it in 1852. He left his wife Cornelia in control until the oldest child became 21. He added that she was to treat each in a manner as "nearly equal as possible" but "always giving those that are the most needy and unfortunate the preference." He desired that his estate be sold and the family maintained from the funds. He specified that funds were to be for support and education.

His obituary confirmed his parentage and his birth, and his age at death as 37. It added that at age 14 he joined the Methodist Episcopal Church, and served as class leader and steward most of the time until his death. He died of pulmonary consumption (tuberculosis).

Begin to Know and Understand

Now we start to understand this family and the lives they led. We sense the struggle of the family: moving from New York to Wisconsin and then having the father die before reaching forty; the young mother, nursing her sick, contagious husband, then left alone to raise five children and keep the farm going. Researching the land sales, we find Cornelia sold the farm in pieces for their maintenance, following Anson's instructions. She kept some of the land and, in 1860, was listed as a farm widow. In 1880, although no longer on the farm, Cornelia was still in Ft. Atkinson, living with her school teacher daughter.

To continue the story of the family's life, the lives of the children were followed, too. The son Marsena served in the Civil War, opening a new study area for details to add to his life story. The children began marrying, and some moved to Illinois, Missouri, and, ultimately, California when the transcontinental train was connected. (The historical events surrounding the completion of the train route also provided fascinating details.) Another son became a doctor and went to Montana, while a third became a dentist and headed to Alaska. Cornelia had done well, seeing that they were educated. The family continued to make its way, and then adventure and the far west beckoned the children, just as it had their parents.

Writing the Story

Writing your family history is more than a mere rearrangement of the family group sheet into a narrative paragraph, but you need not be a professional writer to complete the picture. If you have difficulty, write brief sections with the goal of piecing it all together. Try writing it as a letter to some other family member. Once you get started the words will tumble out because you are so eager to tell what you have found.

Never think that your writing must be polished and of publishing caliber to be worthwhile. Think of how excited you are to find *anything* written by your ancestors. What your reader wants are the details that perhaps only you can supply. A bonus of writing about your ancestors is that you will quickly see what you are missing and what events you want to investigate.

Your ancestors were ordinary people, making choices good and bad, raising wayward teenagers, caring for elderly parents. These stories are about them: real people coping with real problems and successes. They are as much a thread in the fabric of history as the important personages in the history books.

Tree Tips
Many books can give you ideas of how to craft the stories you're telling. One of the best is Lawrence Gouldrup's *Writing the Family Narrative*. He includes an annotated bibliography of books written about families. The books he lists are examples of various approaches.

Relative Resources

Gouldrup, Lawrence P., Ph.D. *Writing the Family Narrative*, Salt Lake City, UT: Ancestry Inc., 1987.

Greene, Bob, and D. G. Fulford. *To Our Children's Children*. New York, NY: Doubleday, 1993.

The Least You Need to Know

- Genealogy is more than a family group sheet.
- Reconstruct your ancestors' lives by interpreting their records.
- Look for records that amplify and expand the dry statistics you've accumulated.
- Read historical fiction and nonfiction about the people, places, and events of your ancestors' times.
- Interview your elderly relatives now.

Chapter 20

Resolving Discrepancies

In This Chapter

- What to do when the data conflicts
- Creative thinking to find data
- Customs that impact your research
- How the calendar change affects your research
- Understanding evidence

As your research progresses, you might begin to notice that your information doesn't agree. Dates don't seem to work out correctly, or you seem to have two children in the family with the same names. You can't find someone you are sure was in a certain place. "What's happening here?" you may wonder.

To solve these mysteries and others, you need strategies to deal with conflicting data and lack of information.

When the Information Doesn't Agree

The census says Great-Grandpa was 9 in 1870, but the 1900 census says he was born in 1860. His tombstone says he was born 4 April 1861. The Bible record in his father's pension file has 7 April 1861. Which is correct?

First, recheck your notes and sources to be sure you didn't make a mistake. Then, analyze the information you have collected. Evaluate the sources from which you collected the information. Ask these questions and apply the answers to your problem:

- Was the information from a published source or from an original document?
- If from a published source, what do you know about its reliability?
- Who supplied the information? Was there anything to be gained or lost by giving false information?
- Was the document created at the time of the event?
- Have you misinterpreted something because you are unfamiliar with a custom, an abbreviation, or the use of certain words?

Published sources with unsubstantiated data cannot be counted on to provide you with accurate information. The facts in them must always be corroborated with other sources. Even reliable published sources can have errors. There are many steps to publication, and at any point, mistakes can be made, particularly in dates.

Tree Tips

An abstract is only as good as the abstracter. Whenever possible, confirm the information by looking at the original documents.

Who supplied the information? It is unwise to depend solely on the information given to the census taker. You don't know who answered the questions. Was it the head of the household? A child? A neighbor? Maybe the census taker thought he knew the answers, so he didn't bother to ask. Maybe Grandma shaved a few years off her age not wanting Grandpa to know she was older than he thought, or she didn't want her neighbor, the census taker, to know how old she really was. Human nature hasn't changed over the years; mistakes, both honest and deliberate, are made.

The accuracy of the date on the tombstone depends on the knowledge of the informant and the skill of the stone cutter. The Bible record, if made near the time of the event by someone who was an eyewitness, is probably the most accurate of the records in the preceding conflict among the dates on the tombstone, census, and Bible record.

When the family seems to have had two or more children with the same name, consider the possibility that one child died and a subsequent child was given the same name (a common custom). Or that the family was German and used the same first name for all the boys, distinguishing them by giving them a different second, or middle, name.

Perhaps you have read an abbreviation as Jas. and assumed that was James, when actually the abbreviation was Jos. for Joseph. Or you couldn't figure out why the place of birth for so many people was "do." When you learn that "do" was an abbreviation used for "ditto," you go back to the record and find the actual birth place that was dittoed.

Don't Get Counted Out

You are certain your family was in the county at the time the census was taken, but you cannot find them. What could be the reason?

- Have you tried all the variant spellings?
- Do you have the right county in the right state? Many states have counties with the same name. Do you need to look in the parent county? County boundaries change. (See Chapter 12 for information on parent counties.)
- If you're working with Soundex, did you code the name correctly?
- Were the Soundex cards filmed out of order? This is a more common occurrence than you would expect. Check throughout the microfilm roll to see if the cards have been slipped into the wrong sequence.
- Are you looking at the right roll of microfilm? It is surprisingly easy to pull the wrong film out of the drawer.
- Are you in the right place on the film? There may be more than one county on the film, and if the family you're looking for is in Hardin County and you didn't scroll through Hancock, but started looking at the first county on the roll, you're in the wrong place.
- Do you have the right page? Often, more than one page number is on the sheet, and it may be difficult to figure out whether the index referred to the typed number, the small handwritten number, the large handwritten number, or the stamped number. Try them all.
- Did you check the end of the county enumeration? Occasionally, the census pages stuck together as they were filmed, but the mistake was caught in time to film the missed pages at the end of the county.

It is possible that you have done everything correctly and still can't find the family. Before you give up, consider that the indexer may have made a mistake. Names are misinterpreted and sometimes alphabetized incorrectly, or are omitted. Some censuses have been indexed by several organizations; check to see if another index to the same census includes your missing ancestor.

If, after all this, your ancestor remains elusive, there is one more avenue. Go through the census pages one by one looking at every name. This is definitely tedious work, but if you have exhausted all the other possibilities, this may be the only way to find the listing. It is best to attempt this method when you are rested and fresh, and to stop when you realize your scanning of the pages has become a blur. Note where you stopped checking, and start there another time. Continue this process until you have examined the entire county.

Maybe They Were Missed

Keep in mind that your ancestor may not have been enumerated. Many people, especially those on the frontier, were suspicious of the government. They were conveniently not home when the census taker stopped by. Or, if living with another family, your ancestor may have skedaddled out the back door when the census taker walked in the front door. Or, the census taker, tired, cold, and wet after traipsing farm-to-farm for several hours on his final route, decided not to visit the family living two more miles down the road. Or, having visited the homestead once and finding no one there, he didn't return. Your ancestors may have been in transit when the census was taken at their old residence, and arrived at their new location after the census was finished there.

Several families might share one dwelling. If the enumerator does not know that and the information is not volunteered by the family being interviewed, the other families in the dwelling may not be on the census.

Maybe They Were Listed Twice

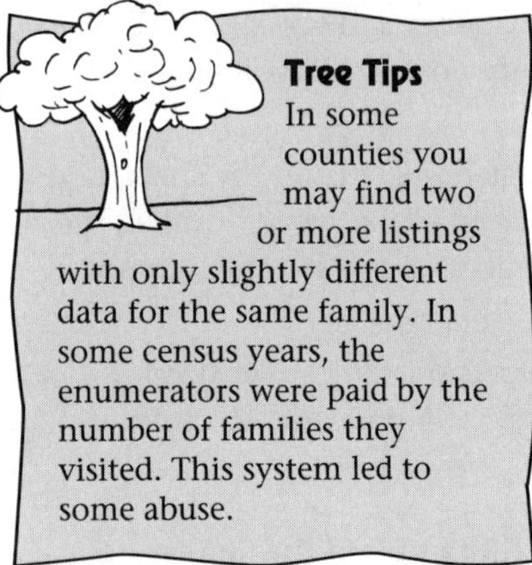

Tree Tips
In some counties you may find two or more listings with only slightly different data for the same family. In some census years, the enumerators were paid by the number of families they visited. This system led to some abuse.

You found two listings so similar that it makes you wonder if you've found the same family, or the same individual, twice in the same census year. Perhaps you have. The census taker was instructed to enumerate everyone living in the household on the day that he visited, and he had several weeks (in some census years as many as nine months) to get to every household in his district. If the Holmeses are enumerated in their Wisconsin county the day the census taker stops by, and two months later moved to live near her parents in Illinois and were there the day the census taker arrived, the Holmeses could conceivably be listed twice; once at their home in Wisconsin, and once at their new home in Illinois.

The Data Doesn't Conflict; There Isn't Any Data!

Your ancestor just seems to appear in town with his wife and children, and you have no idea from whence he came. Start looking at the records created by his neighbors. Families did not move alone. They came with their friends and relatives. They came because of discord in their old church or because they wanted more land or new opportunities.

Remember how difficult overland travel was through uncleared lands and over the mountains. Might they have come to the area by water from another area or through a natural mountain pass? Could they have crossed an ice-frozen lake in the winter to get to a new territory? Do their deeds tell you where they lived prior to now? Or perhaps county histories detail a migration of an ethnic or religious group from another county.

If you can't find a burial where you expect it, one of several things may have happened. Elderly parents may have moved closer to their children in another county. Widows and widowers, who moved to be near sons or daughters, may die in the new county but be shipped back to the original home to be buried next to a spouse.

Everything Is Relative

The mobility of our modern society would astound our ancestors. When the United States was primarily a rural society, the marriage pool for young men and women consisted of their neighbors within walking or horseback distance. Young men and women married the other young men and women they grew up with and saw at church and family gatherings. "Older men" of 25 waited for the beautiful 14-year-old to reach marriageable age. Because the marriage pool was so limited, first cousins married in areas where the law permitted. (This custom of the past is no longer allowed.)

Families became intertwined when a brother and sister married a sister and brother from the same family, or two sisters of one family married two brothers of another. These situations made their offspring "double cousins."

Many women died in childbirth, leaving a widower with several young children and perhaps a tiny infant to raise. He was eager to marry again, if only to have help with the children and sometimes married a sister of his dead wife. Aunt Rachel became a stepmother to her nieces and nephews.

> **Tree Tips**
> Remember your ancestors' options for a partner were limited. If you can't find the maiden name of your ancestor's wife, look for families in his immediate neighborhood with female children to see if you can find some approximate candidates. Look for more records of those families to see if they will lead you to the right young woman.

Happy New Year—25 March

When the glossy new calendars start arriving in December, it probably doesn't occur to you that New Year's Day was not always 1 January. Furthermore, it may not be obvious how this can affect your genealogical research.

Calendars were developed to make sense of the natural cycle of time: days and years from the solar cycle, months from the lunar cycle. It took some experimentation before folks got it right. There are many calendars, but for right now, we need be concerned only with the *Julian* and *Gregorian* calendars.

The Julian calendar resulted from Julius Caesar's reformation of the system to conform more closely to the seasons. The Gregorian calendar was Pope Gregory XIII's solution for the gradual problem that had developed with the Julian calendar: Over time the calendar was 10 days off the natural solar cycle. To compensate, the Gregorian calendar dropped 10 days from October in 1582. And to keep this problem of extra days from reoccurring, one day was added to February in every year divisible by 4.

The Gregorian calendar was adopted by different nations at different times. It was generally adopted by Britain and her colonies in 1752. The day added to the calendar every four years (Leap Year) meant that the calendar was now 11 days out of sync with the solar cycle. To take care of this, the system was adjusted so that the leap day is dropped from every century mark not divisible by 4. Instead of dropping 10 days in October, the British dropped 11 days in September and changed the New Year from 25 March to 1 January. Why do you need to be aware of this interesting bit of trivia? The calendar change makes dates in the months of January, February, and up to 25 March, prior to 1752, subject to *double dating*.

Genie Jargon

Double dating is the practice of giving dates, from 1 January, through February, to 25 March before 1752, two dates to represent the old and the new calendar, for example 23 January 1749/50. This may alternately be shown as 23 January 1749 O.S. (old style) or 23 January 1750 N.S. (new style).

George Washington's birthday, 11 February 1731, under the old calendar became 22 February 1732 under the new calendar, and would be expressed as 22 February 1731/32. This doesn't actually change the date of his birth, merely the way it is expressed. In 1731, February was almost the end of the year because 1732 began on 25 March. After the year 1752 there are two things to contend with: the dropping of 11 days, and the change of the beginning of the year from 25 March to 1 January.

The calendar change affects your research because it is sometimes hard to determine whether the dates are meant to be old style or new style. You may think that the change was not significant enough to make a difference in your research, but it does. If you find records that indicate Abraham was born on 27 March 1741 and his younger sister Ruth was born on 23 March 1741 you may think there is something wrong. In reality, it is likely correct, because 23 March of 1741 in the old style calendar followed 27 March 1741 by about 12 months.

The change in calendar can also explain the seemingly erroneous court item that shows the will was dated 3 December 1740, and proved in court 1 January 1740. "That can't be," you think. But it can, and was, because 1 January 1740 followed 3 December 1740 (expressed as 1 January 1740/41). Once you understand this, you need to show it in your records, or others will think you have erred. The best way to show it is: The will was dated 3 December 1740, proved in court 1 January 1740/41. Be sure to use a slash and not a dash; it is the slash that clarifies you are referring to the double dates caused by calendar changes.

Don't just convert the date with no explanation. If you do prefer to express it in new style (N.S.), show it as "1 January 1741 N.S." so that others understand under which calendar the date is given.

It is important to interpret carefully when faced with dates that were shown in months. This prevalent Quaker custom was also used by some others. A date of "30 9ber 1741" (or "30 9 mo 1741") is 30 November 1741, based on the calendar of the time in which the first month was March and the ninth month was November. It is best, in extracting records that are expressed in months, to write them in your abstract as shown in the original record. If you want to show it also as it would be under the present calendar, add that in brackets. For example: John Betts was born, according to the Quaker Monthly Meeting record, 30 9ber 1741 [30 November 1741 N.S.].

Tree Tips
Though the difference of 11 days can explain some records (he died on the 3rd of the month but was not buried until the 13th), genealogists should not convert dates to account for the 11-day difference unless the old style date would cause confusion. If it does, change it, but indicate the date has been conformed to the new style calendar. Or, leave it as is and explain the seeming discrepancy.

Rushing to Conclusions

Other things besides conflicting or missing data and new dating systems can throw off your research. Pay attention to the clues. If you find William and Mary on the 1860 census with three children and on the 1870 census you find William and Polly with five children, don't assume that Mary and Polly are one and the same, even though you know that Polly is a nickname for Mary. They may indeed be the same woman, but analyze the record. Is the woman on the 1870 census approximately 10 years older than on the 1860 census? Are their birthplaces the same? Are the children's ages consistent with one marriage, or is there a gap between numbers three and four, or four and five? If the older children are teenagers and the younger a three-year-old, there might have been two marriages.

The will you find for James makes bequests to "my wife" and "my children," all named. Don't assume that the named wife is the mother of these children. She may be the mother of all of them, some of them, or none of them, but this wording does not tell you.

How about the census record? You found your ancestor John Matson listed as age 30, and with him is Mary, 28, and children George, 5; Martha, 3; and Sally, 1. You write in your records, "John Matson was born ca. 1820, married Mary—born ca. 1822, and had children George, born ca. 1845; Martha, born ca. 1847; and Sally, born ca. 1849." What's wrong? You have just assumed that Mary was his wife! It is likely that she was indeed his wife, but the 1850 census does not include relationship. If further examination of the family records proves to be perplexing, consider the possibility that his wife died. Perhaps a relative (most likely a sister) came to help out with the small children until he remarried, and it was she who was living with him in 1850. (It is even possible that the head of the household is not the father of the named children. They could be nieces and nephews; if not, they are probably related in some other manner. Keep this possibility in mind if the census doesn't match other known records of the family.)

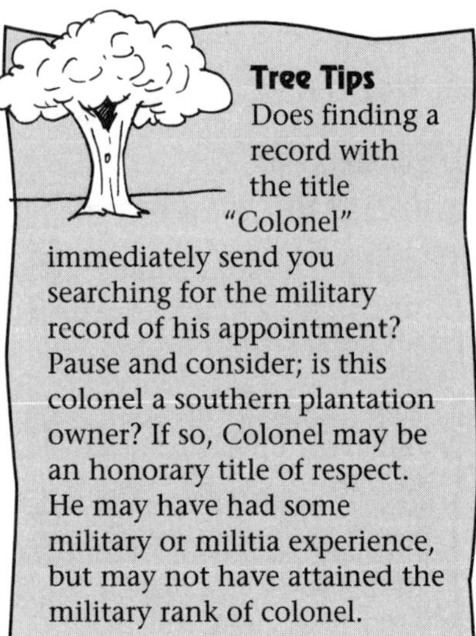

Tree Tips

Does finding a record with the title "Colonel" immediately send you searching for the military record of his appointment? Pause and consider; is this colonel a southern plantation owner? If so, Colonel may be an honorary title of respect. He may have had some military or militia experience, but may not have attained the military rank of colonel.

You find two men with the same name, except one is designated Senior, one Junior. Don't assume they are father and son. Junior and senior might have been used to distinguish individuals in the community with the same name. They may be father and son, but it is just as likely that they are cousins, uncle and nephew, or totally unrelated. The only thing you know for sure is one is older and one younger. Additionally, when "Senior" dies, "Junior" may be promoted to Senior, further confusing us as we try to determine the correct line. If a man with the same name came into the area who was older than the original inhabitant, the town might designate the original resident as John Smith I, and call the new resident John Smith, 2nd.

You discover a will in which John refers to his "now wife." It could mean that he was married previously. But, it usually means nothing more than designating his wife at the time of the will (rather than a woman he might marry after the will was signed).

Theories of Relativity

Sooner or later, usually sooner, you are going to find records that suggest there are two people with the same name in the same place, only one of whom is your ancestor. How to sort them out?

One method is to write each thing you have found on a 3 × 5 card or in a table in a word processing or database computer program. Then sort the cards or data to connect the events with each other, watching for inconsistencies and contradictions. Remember that you are not researching a name, but a person. Look for associates, occupations, church affiliations, anything that will develop identities for the people you found who happen to have the same name. Look at their neighbors.

Deed: Thomas Dunn in 1822 sold 100 acres in Decatur County, Indiana. Land adjoins that of Robert Johnson and William Ballard.

Census: Thomas Dunn, farmer, 1850 census in Decatur County, Indiana, age 30, wife Elizabeth, children James and Elizabeth.

Military: Thomas Dunn served in War of 1812.

Will in probate file: Thomas Dunn's will, dated 20 July 1852, probated 1852; bequests to wife Sarah, son James, daughter Elizabeth; witnesses to will were Robert Johnson, William Ballard. Admitted to probate in December, 1853.

Begin to build a mini-biography for these men. The Thomas Dunn who sold land in 1822 cannot be the Thomas Dunn, age 30 on the 1850 census because he would have been two years old in 1822. The Thomas Dunn age 30 on the 1850 census can't be the Thomas Dunn who served in the War of 1812 because he wasn't born yet, but the Thomas Dunn who sold land may have been the same one who served in the War of 1812. The Thomas Dunn whose will was probated in 1852 may be the same man who sold land because the witnesses to his will owned land adjoining the land he sold in 1822. Who are the neighbors of the Thomas Dunn on the 1850 census? Are there any Johnsons or Ballards?

Your problem may be more difficult than this, but the approach is the same. Sort out what you have, and make the connections.

Based on the Evidence...

In the preceding example, the *evidence* is the deed, the military record, the census record, and the will. They are all useful in proving or disproving that there are two Thomas Dunns.

You will often be faced with three or four records of a specific event, all differing. The Bible shows Hattie was born 3 February 1851. Her tombstone shows her birth date as 3 February 1852. Her death certificate, filed in 1915, gives her birth as 3 February 1852. Which to pick? Do you decide that since two records showed 3 February 1852, that is the correct date?

Genie Jargon

Evidence is the information offered as proof of a fact relating to a lineage or relationship.

Consider three questions: *WHO* gave the information; *WHY* did they give it; and *WHEN* did they give it? The answers will assist in determining which is the most likely date.

It is not unusual to see the death record, obituary, and tombstone all showing the same date, even if the date is incorrect. It is likely that the same person supplied the information for all three. If that person had the date wrong, all three records will be in error. Fall back on WHO. Was it someone who was in a position to have the correct information? Or was it a daughter who never knew that her mother fudged her birth date all those years?

Consider the Bible. When was the Bible published? If the title page on the Bible was 1848, and the family entries start with the marriage of the parents in 1849, followed in the same handwriting by the births of the children, it seems likely that the couple acquired the Bible when they were married and subsequently added births as the children were born. Because that was done close to the time of the event (answering the WHEN question) and by someone in a position to have the correct information, it would appear to be correct.

We then ask WHY. In this case, there doesn't appear to be any reason the Bible date might be purposely entered incorrectly. (On the contrary, if a record was being provided to establish a pension, or social security, and did not jibe with other records, you might consider the WHY important.)

Proving the Case

There are basically three ways to build a case in genealogy. You can build it with pieces of direct evidence, pieces of indirect evidence (sometimes referred to as circumstantial evidence), or a combination of both. When the records conflict, each piece of evidence must be weighed and evaluated for authenticity, applying the criteria of "Who" created the record, "When" it was created, and "Why" it was created. Additional factors are weighed, such as whether it is an original record or a copied record. All evidence must also be examined with an understanding of the time period in which it was created because customs and laws changed. For the case to stand, you must do a thorough study, and all evidence must point in the same direction. Learning to evaluate evidence is essential for arriving at sound conclusions to link your generations of ancestors. Greenwood's *Researcher's Guide to American Genealogy* and Noel C. Stevenson's *Genealogical Evidence* will help you understand, as will Milton Rubincam's *Pitfalls in American Genealogy*.

Relative Resources

Greenwood, Val D. *The Researcher's Guide to American Genealogy*. 2nd ed. Baltimore, MD: Genealogical Publishing Co., 1990.

Rubincam, Milton. *Pitfalls in American Genealogy*. Salt Lake City, UT: Ancestry Publ., 1987.

Stevenson, Noel C. *Genealogical Evidence*. Laguna Hills, CA: Aegean Park Press, 1979.

The Least You Need to Know

- When the data conflicts, weigh the evidence.
- Write mini-biographies to sort out individuals with the same name.
- Don't read more into the records than is there.

Part 6
Expanding Your Horizon

Now you're really hooked, and starting to look at all the things you'd like to have: books, magazines, equipment. There are even national conferences, regional seminars, institutes, and courses. Where to spend your money!?

You'll also learn a bit about sources that won't be your first line of attack, but you'll need as you dig deeper. Records on orphans, the naturalization process—these and much more await your discovery.

Finally, with some strategies for success and some words of caution, you are well on the road to many happy years of climbing your family tree!

Chapter 21

Spending Your Money Wisely

In This Chapter

- ➤ Analyze your needs
- ➤ Allocate your expenditures
- ➤ Gradually acquire references

Your genealogical education is a life-long process. Everything you learn leads to areas where you need to delve more deeply. Much of what you want to know is available without cost through public libraries, but there are also many educational opportunities for which there is a charge. You start wondering how you can afford to acquire all the knowledge and resources you need. Don't despair; there are many values for your money.

Just as you apportion your money for the necessities of life, budget for your interests. Consider these five areas:

- ➤ Education, classes, and basic reference materials
- ➤ Memberships and subscriptions
- ➤ Services
- ➤ Resources including books, tapes, computer software, and Internet access
- ➤ Luxuries, such as the books you constantly consult at the library and CD-ROMs that save you time

Readin', Writin', and 'Rithmetic

Tree Tips
Regional conferences are not on a regular schedule. Watch for announcements of them in your region. The dates and locations are published in the genealogical magazines and sometimes posted on the bulletin boards of libraries.

Seek every opportunity to attend classes and lectures on genealogy. Become familiar with the names of outstanding genealogists, and look for opportunities to hear them lecture. Read their published articles.

In addition to the seminars sponsored by your local genealogical society, there are regional and national seminars and conferences. Attending the conferences will give you new ideas for solving your problems, help you hone your skills, introduce you to new materials, and connect you with others who share your enthusiasm for genealogy.

The National Genealogical Society (NGS) and the Federation of Genealogical Societies (FGS) each sponsor a national conference in a different location every year. The NGS conference usually takes place in May or June; FGS in August or September. These conferences run for three or four days, and feature five or six simultaneous lectures every hour by top genealogists and lecturers. The topics are wide-ranging: military files, land records, problem solving, ethnic research, newspapers, courthouse research, and methodology, to name a few.

Tree Tips
The syllabi in themselves are good references for future research. As you tackle a new problem, see if there were any lectures pertaining to it, and check the bibliographies. They can give you ideas of where to look for information. Even if you have not attended a conference, you might find the syllabus helpful. Your genealogical library may have a copy available.

Your conference registration includes a syllabus, a thick volume with material submitted by the lecturers. The material ranges from a few paragraphs to a detailed outline of the lecture, including bibliographies, maps, special instructions, and more.

Networking

Networking is a vital part of the national conferences. In talking to your table mates at lunch or relaxing during a break, you may find you share a common research problem or possibly even an ancestor. Many attendees have made connections from such contacts.

Exhibits

National conferences often draw 2,000 or more attendees. In addition to the lectures, one of the attractions is the exhibit area where vendors sell everything from rare books to

T-shirts with genealogical messages. You'll find genealogical supplies such as charts alongside materials for preservation such as acid-free paper. Books (new and used) and maps are big sellers. There are vendors who specialize in European maps and some who concentrate on books about New England. The major genealogical book publishers stock booths with their new releases along with a selection of older titles. Genealogical bookstores bring hundreds of books.

Computer programs are popular, as are CD-ROMs. Some vendors specialize in photo restoration. Large genealogical societies sponsor booths, recruiting members and selling publications.

Hands-On

At both the regional and national conferences, there are hands-on workshops that allow you to develop and practice skills important to your research. Workshops on land platting are popular. This skill can be crucial to solving genealogical problems of many kinds. Practical experience under the guidance of knowledgeable, patient instructors makes the techniques easier to acquire.

Occasionally, there are workshops devoted to abstracting and handwriting, as well as workshops on how to complete successful lineage society applications. In the latter, the emphasis is on the types of evidence needed to establish your line and suggested sources for finding that evidence.

Computer workshops concentrate on specific genealogy programs, explaining many of their features, or on general topics, such as learning to use the Internet for genealogical research. Sometimes there are computer labs where you can see commercial demonstrations of programs and try before you buy.

Institutes

For a week of saturation in genealogy, attend one of the various genealogical institutes. Rather than a series of unrelated lectures, the institutes usually offer one or more tracks of related subjects. For instance, at the Institute of Genealogy and Historical Research at Samford University, Birmingham, Alabama, there may be tracks for beginning genealogy, intermediate and advanced methodology, records of the South, military records, genealogical writing, and others.

Some tracks are offered yearly; others periodically. The National Institute of Genealogical Research, Washington, D.C., is held at the National Archives and concentrates on genealogical materials available in the National Archives. Currently, other institutes are held in Texas, Illinois, and Utah. Some genealogists return to these institutes year after year, taking advantage of the variety of courses offered each time.

Staying Independent

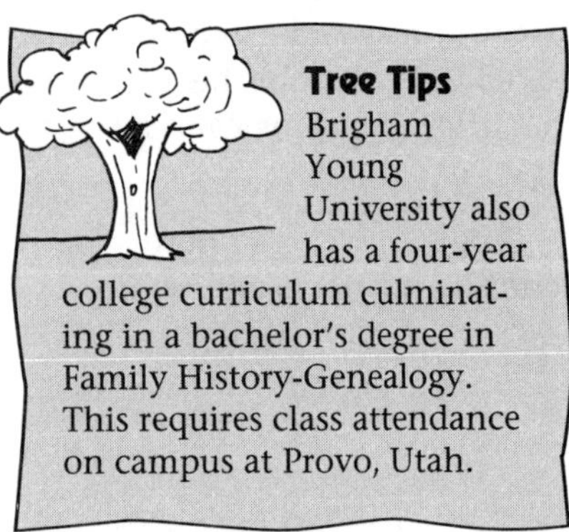

Tree Tips
Brigham Young University also has a four-year college curriculum culminating in a bachelor's degree in Family History-Genealogy. This requires class attendance on campus at Provo, Utah.

In-depth lessons that you can do at your own pace are the attraction of home study courses. You miss the interaction of classroom instruction, but home study may fit better into your time and budget. The National Genealogical Society has an accredited and highly rated home study course, American Genealogy: A Basic Course. Completing the lessons gives you a good grounding in how to find and record your sources, maintain your records, and evaluate your evidence. Brigham Young University offers numerous courses of independent study, such as Oral History Interviewing, Latin for Genealogists, Germanic Sources, and Hispanic Family History.

Be a Joiner

Allocate part of your genealogy budget to society memberships and subscriptions. You will usually benefit from belonging to at least three organizations: one local, one state or regional, and one national. As you become aware of more areas where your ancestors lived, consider joining societies there. The newsletters and journals you receive as part of your membership dues are a part of the continuing education process that is so essential to successful genealogy.

Consider subscribing to some of the premier genealogical journals that publish the results of scholarly work. Even if the information presented has nothing to do with the surnames you are researching, the methodology used is important and may eventually help you solve a problem. Genealogists often develop an interest in obscure records or subjects; the articles they write about those interests may lead you to new sources. Journal articles can alert you to newly published abstracts or compiled genealogies.

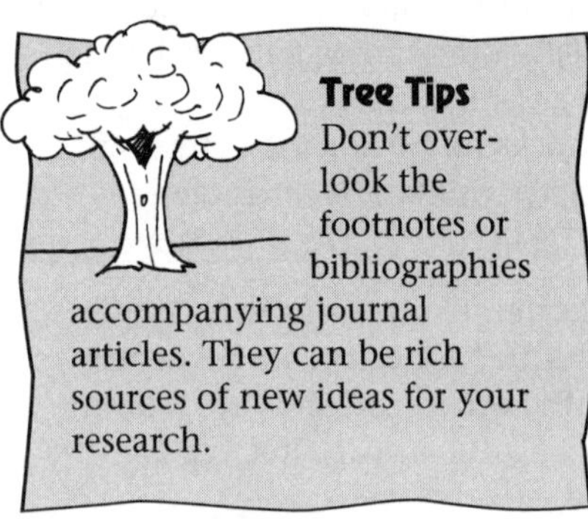

Tree Tips
Don't overlook the footnotes or bibliographies accompanying journal articles. They can be rich sources of new ideas for your research.

An important part of all journals is the book review section with its evaluations of recently published books. The books may pertain to a specific region, a family, general reference, related topics, or other area of interest. Reading the reviews may suggest books that would be useful in your research—and some to avoid.

In addition to the scholarly journals, there are popular publications with articles of general interest. They often include question-and-answer columns on different topics, such as ethnic research, computers, or a particular geographic location. Other periodicals focus on one subject, such as computers or Irish genealogy.

Are You Being Served?

Genealogists use many fee-based services that are quite reasonable but add up to substantial amounts over time. Budget for photocopying, postage, loans of books or films through interlibrary loan or rental companies, and, if you have a computer, an Internet provider.

Occasionally, you may need professional help with a stubborn problem. Or it may be more economical to hire a researcher than to travel to a distant area. In some counties, the officials are too busy with the daily work of the county to engage in research, so they maintain a list of researchers for your convenience. Many archives and libraries maintain lists of researchers. They also have copies of the *Directory of Professional Genealogists* (published by the Association of Professional Genealogists) and the *Certification Roster* (published by the Board for Certification of Genealogists). Lists of accredited genealogists for specific geographic areas can be obtained by writing to the Family History Library in Salt Lake City.

Before hiring genealogical help, you should know what to expect. The Association of Professional Genealogists publishes a brochure, *So You're Going to Hire a Professional Genealogist.* It has tips on how to find a professional, how to evaluate the credentials, and what to expect in the way of costs and results. Request the free brochure by sending a SASE to the Association of Professional Genealogists, P.O. Box 40393, Denver, CO 80204-0393, or download it from the APG Web site, http://www.apgen.org/~apg.

Developing Your Home Support System

Add to the references and resources you keep handy at home. Tapes, books, catalogs, computer programs, and CD-ROMs can all advance your research from the comfort of home.

Most national conference lectures, and some regional ones, are taped. Although you miss the visual parts of the lectures, the tapes are nonetheless useful aids for your education. Conferences since August 1991 are available on tape from Repeat Performances of Hobart, Indiana. Write for their catalog and order tapes relevant to your particular interest.

Adding to Your Library

Build your collection little by little. Start with some basic guidebooks, and as you progress in your research, add to your collection. You may find that there is one particular book you regularly consult at the library; consider investing in a copy for your own bookshelves. When you find a particular area where you are doing a great deal of research, you will probably want to purchase books about that area—not just genealogical books, but histories.

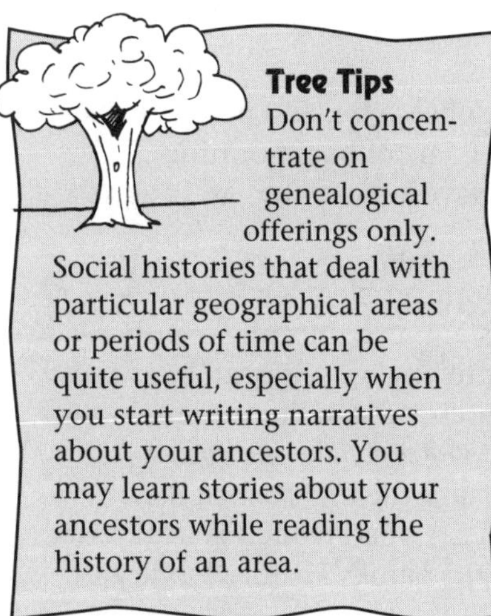

Don't concentrate on genealogical offerings only. Social histories that deal with particular geographical areas or periods of time can be quite useful, especially when you start writing narratives about your ancestors. You may learn stories about your ancestors while reading the history of an area.

Although new editions may render previous ones obsolete, much of the methodology will be the same. Good used bookstores are worth checking regularly for books about your particular interest.

If you find you have an interest in a particular ethnic group, look for books in that field. There are numerous books on many aspects of Jewish genealogy, as well as on Italian, German, Russian, Scottish, and so on. One way to learn about these is by attending lectures or studying the bibliographies in the syllabus of a conference or those in articles in journals. If your library has the selected book, review it there; consider purchasing the book if you think you will use it often.

Bookstores

There are several large booksellers that specialize in genealogical materials. Their owners and managers are genealogists who understand the needs of the field. Some specialize in books that are not generally thought of as genealogy books, but are aids to your understanding the laws, customs, and conditions that influenced your ancestors' behavior. Although these books are available through larger bookstores, particularly those specializing in university press publications, if you are not aware that they exist or don't know the titles or authors, you would have to browse the shelves to find them.

Don't overlook the major societies and archives. Many of them publish historical books and finding aids for their collections. North Carolina Archives, National Archives, New England Historic and Genealogical Society, National Genealogical Society, and Illinois State Genealogical Society are only a few with publications.

Booksellers, and many societies and archives, advertise in genealogical publications. Look for them and send for their catalogs or reach them through their Internet addresses.

Feeding Your Computer More Software

Numerous programs have been developed by genealogists for genealogists to help in record keeping and research. Among the most widely used genealogy database programs are Family Tree Maker, Personal Ancestral File (PAF), Reunion, Ultimate Family Tree, and The Master Genealogist. Some genealogists find that more than one database program is useful; they may like the style of reports in one but prefer another for ease of data entry. Because all major genealogy programs incorporate a standard data transfer utility, it is possible to use two programs without re-entering data.

Mapping programs are useful in genealogical research for converting a typed legal description of land to a graphic representation. Two programs currently on the market that enable you to plat the land are DeedMapper and Black Oak Mapper.

As CD-ROM drives become an integral part of computers, more and more information is published on CD-ROMs. They take advantage of one of the things that computers do best—searching through mountains of information. As with any publication, however, be wary. Many CD-ROM compilations are incomplete or have errors, just as many printed indexes do.

Budgeting for Genealogical Luxuries

All these resources can move into the luxury category as genealogy takes hold of your life. You find you want to attend all the conferences and institutes and load up on memberships, subscriptions, books, tapes, and computer programs. You'll covet the latest multivolume indexes available on CD-ROM. You'll buy into the reasoning that a copier and even a microfilm reader will save you time and money. If you don't have a computer, you'll want one. If you have a computer, you'll want multimedia and a scanner.

Before you go on a spending spree, study your budget. Be an informed consumer, first buying the essentials that will help you become a skilled researcher. Ask yourself, "Will this purchase add to my genealogical skills and knowledge?" "Will it help me trace my ancestors?" Later, you can contemplate the purchase of the "big ticket" items.

Relative Resources

There are so many resources to tell you about in this chapter that we've broken them into categories, as you see below.

Computer Programs

Black Oak Mapper. Black Oak Systems, 7472 Mt. Sherman Rd., Longmont, CO 80503-8678.

DeedMapper. Direct Line Software, 71 Neshobe Rd., Newton, MA 02168.

Family Tree Maker. Broderbund Software, P.O. Box 6125, Novato, CA 94948.

Personal Ancestral File (PAF). Salt Lake Distribution Center, 1999 W. 1700 South, Salt Lake City, UT 84104.

Reunion. Leister Productions, P.O. Box 289, Mechanicsburg, PA 17055.

Ultimate Family Tree. Palladium Interactive, Inc., 743 E. Franklin St., Ste. B, Spencer, IN 47460.

The Master Genealogist. Wholly Genes Software, 6868 Ducketts Ln., Elk Ridge, MD 21277.

Conferences

Brigham Young University Conferences and Workshops, 136 Harman Bldg., Provo, UT 84602.

Federation of Genealogical Societies, P.O. Box 830220, Richardson, TX 75083-0220.

National Genealogical Society, 4527 17th St. N., Arlington, VA 22207-2399.

Institutes

Genealogical Institute of Mid-America, Continuing Education, University of Illinois, Springfield, IL 62794-9243.

Institute of Genealogical Studies, P.O. Box 25556, Dallas, TX 75225-5556.

Institute of Genealogy and Historical Research, Samford University Library, Birmingham, AL 35229-7008.

National Institute on Genealogical Research, P.O. Box 14274, Washington, DC 20044-4274.

Salt Lake Institute of Genealogy, Utah Genealogical Association, P.O. Box 1144, Salt Lake City, UT 84110.

Independent Study

Brigham Young University, Provo, UT 84602.

"American Genealogy: A Basic Course," National Genealogical Society, 4527 17th St. N., Arlington, VA 22207-2399.

Directories

Kersten, CGRS, Elizabeth Kelley and Kathleen W. Hinckley, CGRS eds. *1997–1998 Directory of Professional Genealogists*. Denver, CO: Association of Professional Genealogists, 1997. [P.O. Box 40393, Denver, CO 80204-0393.]

Certification Roster. Washington, D.C.: Board for Certification of Genealogists, 1997. [P.O. Box 14291, Washington, DC 20044.]

Tapes

Repeat Performances, 2911 Crabapple Lane, Hobart, IN 46342.

The Least You Need to Know

- Budget for your genealogical needs.
- Make classes and books your first priorities.
- Always ask yourself if the purchase will contribute to your genealogical knowledge.

Chapter 22

Discovering Less Used Sources

In This Chapter

- County records not to be missed
- Federal records with genealogical information
- Hundreds more federal records
- Ethnic records

Previous chapters have discussed the fundamental records for your research: federal population censuses, deeds, wills, estates, Revolutionary War records, Civil War records, and bounty land. Those alone will keep you busy for some time. As you gain experience, you'll learn to think in terms of, "What other records might tell me more?" Once you embark on a course of research, you'll eagerly devour new sources of information.

The records you'll need to solve your advanced research problems are often somewhat obscure. There are good reasons for some records to be used less often: Many are unindexed; their genealogical value may not be well known; or they may not be filmed and, therefore, are not available unless you travel or hire a researcher. Nonetheless, being aware that certain records exist may eventually be your key to a seemingly impossible problem.

County Records

Within the counties are numerous records with genealogical information besides the ones discussed in Chapter 13. Chances are, some of them have been filmed, although each county has many more records still in their original form. Before you head out to the county to check on these records, go to your nearest Family History Center and check the catalog to see what has been filmed for your county of interest. Always remember, however, that errors can occur, and a filmed series may be incomplete.

Guardianships

Guardianship and orphan records are important to genealogists. They are usually found in the county probate court records. When a decedent left an estate that required administration or probate and left minor children as heirs, the court appointed a guardian to act in the children's interests. Sometimes children in the same family had different guardians. The children may have been from different marriages, or there may be so many children as to make it impractical for one person to care for them all. If you find a child selecting a guardian rather than the court assigning one, usually that child is over the age of 14 but under 21. Children older than 14 could legally make their own selection.

Pedigree Pitfalls

If you see the word "infant" in guardianship or other records, do not assume that the child is a baby. In law, an infant is any minor under the age of majority, usually 21 for males and 18 for females.

When you find the record of a guardian having been appointed or selected, don't stop there. Guardians appear in court records regularly, reporting on income and expenses in administering the affairs of their charges, or perhaps protesting the management of a farm or business in which the charge has an interest. When the child came of age, a final accounting was submitted to the court. If that record survives, it might provide more information on your ancestor.

If a child inherited property from a deceased mother, the father (or someone else) might have been appointed as guardian for the child's interests. The records created by a child inheriting from a deceased mother's estate can provide you with the maiden name of the mother. Someone might have petitioned to be guardian for children "entitled to distributive shares of the estate of their grandmother Catherine Carter by reason of the death of their mother Elizabeth Shimmin."

Orphans, Apprentices, and the Poor

Orphans were not always children without parents. Sometimes, they were children with one parent who could not support them. As with the other poor, the county often accepted responsibility for them. Orphans were sometimes sent to institutions known as workhouses, almshouses, poor houses, or asylums. Look for county records of the poor. These may be orphan records, poor house records, pauper records, or apprentice records.

These records are seldom microfilmed. Records of the institutions under some form of governmental jurisdiction may be at the county or state level. The records of privately run orphanages can be difficult to locate; they may be in historical societies, university libraries, or private collections, or they may no longer exist.

Poor children were often sent out by their parents as apprentices to learn a trade. A father without the means to provide for all his children might designate in his will that one or more of the children should be apprenticed to a specific trade. The master who took on an apprentice was usually obligated to feed, clothe, and educate the child until a certain age, and perhaps required to give him a suit of clothes, a small sum of money, and a Bible when released.

Acting on Behalf

Powers of attorney can contain marvelous genealogical information. Seek them out when you visit the courthouse. Though they are sometimes recorded in the deed books, often they are a separate set of books with their own index, or each book may be individually indexed.

Powers of attorney were often given by individuals who were settling land transactions at some distance from their residences. The individual who inherited property in another state and wanted to sell it might not have been willing or able to travel to that state. He often appointed someone to act on his behalf. The document appointing an agent, usually a relative or close friend, might provide details of what is being sold.

Genie Jargon
A **power of attorney** is a legal document allowing someone else to act on an individual's behalf.

In Kentucky, in 1807, Hugh Rose, "a native of Amherst Co., Virginia, now a surgeon in the 1st Regiment of Infantry," gave power of attorney to two individuals to convey property that was part of his father's estate, and "my Sister Paulina's Estate who died Intestate and without an heir, also my properties…left by my grandfather Robert Rose, left to his sons, John, Hugh, Henry, Patrick and Charles…"

The document was executed in New Orleans where Rose was stationed. Look at the details: his birthplace; his current residence and occupation; the location of the property; the names of his grandfather, uncles, and sister. The information is important in and of itself, but it also gives many leads to continue the research.

Taxing Matters

Tax records are important to genealogists. There were poll taxes, a tax on all free white males in a community, and property taxes, both real and personal. Personal property tax records can document the existence of ancestors who owned no land. First, they verify that an individual was in a particular place at a particular time. If the person remained there, he should appear on the tax rolls year after year. Property tax rolls reflect the acquisition or divestiture of land. The tax information may guide you to more records. If an individual disappears from the tax rolls, you'll know that he reached an age (or condition, such as blindness or poverty) of exemption from tax, died, or left the area. Any one of those reasons is valuable to your research.

Tax records are best used, not in isolation, but in a series. If you find your ancestor on a tax list, follow him year by year back to his first appearance and forward to the year he disappeared from the roll. There may be some gaps in the existing records, but try to follow your ancestor throughout the rolls. Occasionally, abstracts of tax records are published and indexed, but original tax records are not indexed.

Wave the Flag—Vote!

If your ancestor participated in the political process, you may find voter registration records. These records may be in the county along with current registrations, or they may have been transferred to the state archives. Voter registration information varies from state to state but can include such vital information as birth date, marital status, residence, telephone number, citizenship data, and physical description. More current registration rolls have residence and telephone number, and may have party affiliation and social security number. Accessibility to voter registers depends upon the laws of the state in which you are researching.

Swearing Allegiance

Naturalization records are often neglected as a source of information because they are difficult to locate. Continual tinkering with laws governing naturalization results in confusion as to the naturalization process, where the records are, and what they might contain. For many years, any court, (federal, state, county, or local), could accept the declaration of intention to become a citizen and grant citizenship once the individual had fulfilled the requirements. Since 1906, naturalization proceedings have taken place in federal courts. A new book by Christina K. Schaefer, *Guide to Naturalization Records of the United States*, is a county-by-county guide to available records and, though not complete, will assist you in locating these important records.

Genie Jargon
Naturalization is the legal process for an individual of foreign birth to become a citizen.

Because of continual changes in the law, no blanket statements covering naturalization can be made. But, generally, the citizenship process began with the *declaration of intention*, or *"first paper,"* in which the alien stated a desire to become a citizen and renounced allegiance to his native country. When the prevailing residency requirement was fulfilled, the alien went back to court, petitioned for citizenship, and took an oath of allegiance to the United States. The first paper was usually filed in a court near the alien's residence, although until 1906 any court could accept it. The petition and final certificate could be in a completely different state because the alien had moved. In some instances, the alien's wife and children automatically became naturalized when the husband received his certificate.

> **Genie Jargon**
> The **declaration of intention** or **first paper** is a sworn statement by an alien that he intends to become a citizen.

Prior to 1906, when the Bureau of Immigration and Naturalization was established, there was no uniformity in naturalization records. After 1906, standard forms were developed, and the resulting records can yield important information and even photographs. See Chapter 6 for an example of a standardized declaration of intention. Records pertaining to naturalizations after 1906 will be with the Bureau of Immigration and Naturalization Service and in the courts.

Good sources for information on naturalization are Ancestry's *The Source* and Greenwood's *Research in American Genealogy*. Information on microfilmed naturalization records is in the micropublication catalogs of the National Archives, as well as in *The Guide to Genealogical Records in the National Archives* and *The Archives: A Guide to the Field Branches of the National Archives*. Another helpful booklet is John J. Newman's, *American Naturalization Processes and Procedures 1790–1985*.

Good News, Bad News

Always ask yourself how your ancestor came in contact with the federal government. Almost everyone interacts with the federal government at some time, if only during census enumeration. There are hundreds of federal records to help with your research. That's the good news. The bad news is many are not microfilmed and must be used in Washington, D.C., or at the various Archive branches. The original records that exist at the branches usually pertain specifically to the district that branch serves.

The Settling of America

Among the many federal land records are the homestead records. The Homestead Act of 1862 was instrumental in settling the West. Many of our ancestors submitted papers and fulfilled the requirements to claim the allotted 160 acres. The case files created by these claims have valuable genealogical information. Any citizen (or person who had filed papers to become a citizen) over the age of 21 could claim 160 acres of unoccupied, available federal land. The individual had to live on the land for five years while cultivating it and building a home. Women, as well as men, were homesteaders, so don't overlook your female ancestors.

The case files for the homestead lands vary, but nearly all have valuable genealogical information, such as the age and address of the person applying for the land, family members, descriptions of the land, house, crops, and testimony of witnesses. For a

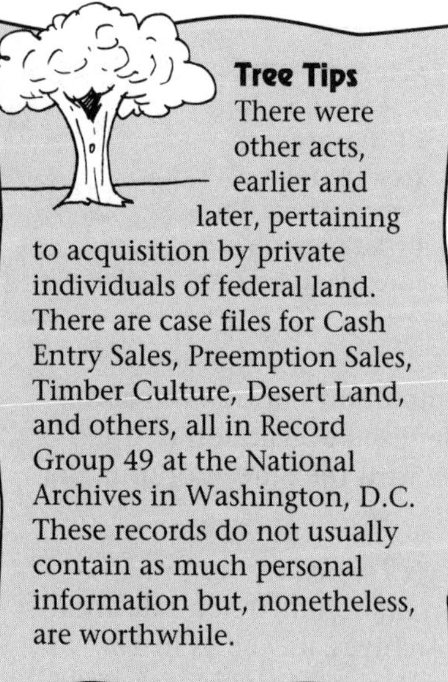

Tree Tips
There were other acts, earlier and later, pertaining to acquisition by private individuals of federal land. There are case files for Cash Entry Sales, Preemption Sales, Timber Culture, Desert Land, and others, all in Record Group 49 at the National Archives in Washington, D.C. These records do not usually contain as much personal information but, nonetheless, are worthwhile.

naturalized citizen, you'll find information about the immigration, such as date and port of arrival, and date and place of naturalization. Some files even have copies of discharge from Union service in the Civil War, because a subsequent act gave special privileges to those veterans.

Homestead files are in two series: one for completed land entries and one for canceled land entries. Both are useful. The completed land entry files are in the custody of the National Archives in Washington, D.C., in Record Group 49. The canceled land entry papers are scattered among a variety of repositories, but they can yield clues to why the requirements were not fulfilled.

For help in understanding and locating homestead and other land records, read Sandra Luebking's chapter, "Land and Tax Records," in Ancestry's *The Source*, and "Government Land: Colonial and American," in Greenwood's *Research Guide to American Genealogy*. Also, refer to Wade Hone's *Land and Property Research in the United States*.

Passport Records

Although passports were not required until World War I, (except for a brief period during the Civil War), many individuals obtained them as a little extra protection. This was especially true for male immigrants who were afraid of being conscripted into the military service in their country of origin if they journeyed there. Immigrants to the United States did return to the "Old Country" on occasion. They returned to visit relatives, marry, take a child to see his grandparents, or, perhaps, to bring a family to the United States. Later passport records are more complete, but you will usually get some personal information from older ones. Two micropublication series to check are the Register and Indexes for Passport Applications 1810–1906, M1371, and Passport Applications 1795–1905, M1371.

The Mail Is Here

Most villages had a post office, even if it was only a tiny back room in the general store, and a local resident was employed as the postmaster. *The Records of Appointment of Postmasters, 1832–30 September 1971*, Micropublication M841, is available at the National Archives and all field branches. The appointment registers are arranged by state, then county, then post office. For each post office, the registers contain the dates of establishment and discontinuance, and the names and dates of postmaster appointments. Earlier appointments are on *Records of Appointment of Postmasters, October 1789–1832*, Micropublication M1131, available at the National Archives in Washington, D.C. Rather than being arranged by state and county, these records are an alphabetical list of all post offices.

There is usually no genealogical information in these records, but the dates prove residence in a specific area, and knowing that an individual was a postmaster adds interest to the family history.

Defending the Country

The military records discussed in Chapter 16 are just the tip of the iceberg. The National Archives contains many more. The National Archives catalog *Military Service Records: A Select Catalog of National Archives Microfilm Publications,* will give you ideas of records to check. One series of particular interest is the *Registers of Enlistments in the United States Army, 1798–1914,* Micropublication M233. The men listed there were in the Regular Army, and this series may be the only information you will find on their service. The information varies but may include time and place of enlistment, age at enlistment, place of birth, civilian occupation, physical description, and unit or regiment to which assigned. There is no index to these files, but they are arranged chronologically and then alphabetically by the first letter of the surname. If you suspect your ancestor served in the Regular Army, check the films for the appropriate time period. In some cases, specific birth places are given, such as Circleville, Pickaway County, Ohio, or Baden, Germany. Others only give a state or country, but even that may be new information for you.

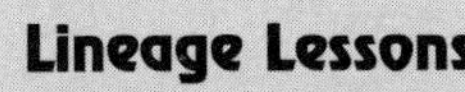

Lineage Lessons

Sometimes a less used record can lead you indirectly to information on your ancestor. The files of your ancestor's comrades may be more enlightening than those of your ancestor, pointing you to the town or county from which these friends enlisted. The abstracts for the compiled service records (M881, *Compiled Service Records of Soldiers who Served in the American Army During the Revolutionary War,* discussed in Chapter 16) were taken from records that are on microfilm: *Revolutionary War Rolls, 1775–1783,* M246, and *Numbered Record Books Concerning Military Operations and Service, Pay and Settlement of Accounts, and Supplies in the War Department Collection of Revolutionary War Records,* M853. Use these rolls to spot the friends who served with your ancestor, and check their files.

On the High Seas

Immigrants usually arrived by ship, and may have come into any number of port cities: New York, Boston, Baltimore, Philadelphia, New Orleans, Key West, Mobile, Charleston, Savannah, New Bedford, New Haven, Providence, San Francisco, Galveston, Seattle, Port Townsend (WA), Gulfport, Pascagoula (MS), and others.

Passenger arrival lists were originally created for customs, and they contain less information than those created as a result of immigration laws beginning in 1882. Because so many of the passenger lists are not indexed, to use them you need to know the ship and or date of arrival, often the very information you are seeking. Nonetheless, it is worthwhile to learn about these records. Even the early customs lists are useful because they usually give age, occupation, country of origin, and place of intended settlement. You may find the whole family traveling together, and they may be accompanied by other relatives or friends. Be careful, however, of accepting the information on these lists without further confirmation. On a ship sailing from Liverpool in 1858, the country of origin for all the passengers is listed as Great Britain when, in fact, they were from many European countries.

Records amassed after passage of immigration laws are more useful. The immigrants were asked many questions, such as whether they had been in the United States before, if they were going to join a relative (and if so, the relative's name, address, and relationship). Their answers were duly noted on the immigration passenger lists. Later, the lists included a physical description and the name and address of the nearest relative in the immigrant's home country.

Consult Michael Tepper's *American Passenger Arrival Records* or Greenwood's *Research in American Genealogy* for good discussions of passenger lists. Also helpful is John P. Colletta's *They Came in Ships.*

More Taxes

Before there was a federal income tax, the federal government reached into your ancestors' pockets several times. The surviving tax lists contain little or no genealogical information, but they can give you a glimpse of the economic status of your ancestor. The first direct tax was a 1798 tax on real property and slaves. The National Archives has the Pennsylvania lists (*United States Direct Tax of 1798: Tax Lists for the State of Pennsylvania,* M372), which are organized in a complex geographic division. The other surviving lists (Connecticut, Delaware, District of Columbia, Maine, Maryland, Massachusetts, New Hampshire, Rhode Island, Tennessee, and Vermont) are in various repositories.

Easier to use are the Internal Revenue Assessment Lists for the Civil War Period. To pay for the Civil War, taxes were levied on various businesses and licenses. Carriages, yachts, billiard tables, and gold and silver plate were also taxed. In 1865 one of my collateral relatives was taxed $10 each for his licenses as a claims agent, insurance agent, real estate agent, and retail dealer. He was taxed $25 as a retail liquor dealer, and assessed $1.00 each for his carriage and two gold watches and $4.00 for his piano. No genealogical information here, but you can get an idea of his economic status from the tax list.

Still More Federal Records

The scope of federal records with genealogical information is mind boggling. Just glancing through the *Guide to Genealogical Research in the National Archives* will give you lots of ideas. Some of the records of the federal government will be useful to you only after you have done a great deal of research in other sources. Some of them can be used early in your search if you have access to them. This selected list (in no particular order) gives you an inkling of the kinds of records that might be useful at some point in your research:

- Bureau of Indian Affairs
- Bureau of Refugees, Freedmen, and Abandoned Lands
- Southern Claims Commission
- U.S. Marshals
- U.S. Coast Guard
- Seamen's Protection Certificates
- Department of the Interior
- U.S. Treasury
- Bankruptcy
- Birth, Death, and Marriages at U.S. Army Posts
- Diplomatic Records
- Records of the Continental Congress
- Veterans Homes
- Amnesty and Pardon Records
- Japanese Evacuations

Use the finding aids discussed in this chapter to locate records in the listed categories. At any time, you can ask assistance of the consultants available at the National Archives in Washington, D.C., either by writing or calling that facility.

Federal records will be at the National Archives in Washington, D.C., and in College Park, Maryland, or at one of the field branches. (See Appendix B for a list of the branches.) Also, some repositories and film rental companies have purchased copies of National Archives' micropublications. The big drawback to using federal records is that many of them are not on microfilm. You will have to go to the National Archives or one of its branches, or hire a researcher to look at the records for you.

Archival research is somewhat different from other kinds of research. Because of the vastness of the federal records, there are no overall indexes. Records are organized as they were when the originating federal agency used them.

The Archives has published many useful guides to its records. There are micropublication catalogs, preliminary inventory lists created by the archivists, and guides such as those listed at the end of this chapter. Write to the National Archives to obtain a copy of its free leaflets, "Using Records in the National Archives for Genealogical Research" and "Select List of Publications of the National Archives and Records Administration." In your library, consult the three volumes of Robert B. Matchette et al., *Guide to Federal Records in the National Archives of the United States*. This includes valuable information on hundreds of subjects, presented by their Record Group classification. The *Guide* is also available on the Internet at http://cliio.nara.gov:70/inform/guide.

Ethnic Records

When you learn that your ancestor was part of a particular ethnic group, your research will be enhanced by seeking special resources. Start with Ancestry's *The Source* to see if there is a chapter on your ethnic interest. The chapter on immigration lists dozens of resources on ethnic groups from Albanian to French, Swedish, and Welsh. Look for special topic books, such as Ryskamp's *Finding Your Hispanic Roots*, Carr's *Guide to Cuban Genealogical Research,* or Rottenberg's, *Finding Our Fathers: A Guidebook to Jewish Genealogy*. New books by ethnic specialists appear regularly; watch for ones applicable to your field. Search for the collections of religious denominations and periodicals devoted to various nationalities.

Numerous federal government records exist that pertain to particular groups, especially Native Americans and African Americans. Chapter 11, "Records of American Indians," and Chapter 12, "Records of Black Americans," in *Guide to Genealogical Research in the National Archives,* describe them. Many are on microfilm, and the National Archives has published catalogs listing them.

Genealogists who specialize in ethnic groups, whether racial, national, religious, linguistic, or cultural, often lecture at national conferences. Many presentations have been taped by Repeat Performance and can be ordered.

Be Alert for New Sources

It is beyond the scope of any book to give you in-depth coverage of every record available for genealogical research. Be on the lookout for new-to-you sources of information. Regularly review Ancestry's *The Source* and Greenwood's *Research in American Genealogy*. Read constantly, and attend any classes you can. Check the back issues of the journals. Search for manuscript collections.

Rich sources of genealogical information are everywhere, mostly in records not created with genealogy in mind. Whatever the source of the records—county, state, or national—the approach is the same. Check the holdings of the Family History Library to see if they are on film, examine the numerous sources of microfilmed and original records of the National Archives, look for published abstracts, and visit the counties where your ancestors lived.

Relative Resources

Carr, Peter E. *Guide to Cuban Genealogical Research.* Chicago, IL: Adams Press, 1991.

Colletta, John P., Ph.D. revised ed. *They Came in Ships.* Salt Lake City, UT: Ancestry, 1993.

Greenwood, Val D. *The Researcher's Guide to American Genealogy.* 2nd ed. Baltimore, MD: Genealogical Publishing Co., 1990.

Guide to Genealogical Research in the National Archives. Washington, D.C.: National Archives, 1982.

Hone, E. Wade, *Land and Property Research in the United States.* Salt Lake City, UT: Ancestry, 1997.

Matchette, Robert B., et al. *Guide to Federal Records in the National Archives of the United States.* Washington, D.C. National Archives and Records Administration, 1995. 3 vol.

Newman, John J. *American Naturalization Processes and Procedures 1790–1985.* N.p.: Indiana Historical Society, 1985.

Rottenberg, Dan. *Finding Our Fathers: A Guidebook to Jewish Genealogy.* Baltimore, MD: Genealogical Publishing Co., 1986.

Ryskamp, George R. *Finding Your Hispanic Roots.* Baltimore, MD: Genealogical Publishing Co., 1997.

Schaefer, Christina K. *Guide to Naturalization Records of the United States.* Baltimore, MD: Genealogical Publishing Co., 1997.

Szucs, Loretto Dennis and Sandra Hargreaves Luebking. *The Archives: A Guide to the Field Branches of the National Archives.* Salt Lake City, UT: Ancestry, 1988.

Szucs, Loretto Dennis and Sandra Hargreaves Luebking. *The Source: A Guidebook of American Genealogy.* Revised ed. Salt Lake City, UT: Ancestry, 1997.

Tepper, Michael. *American Passenger Arrival Records: A Guide to the Records of Immigrants Arriving at American Ports by Sail and Stream.* Updated and enlarged. Baltimore, MD: Genealogical Publishing Co., 1993.

Microfilm Catalogs (also available on the Internet at http://www.nara.gov)

American Indians: A Select Catalog of National Archives Microfilm Publications. Washington, D.C.: National Archives Trust Fund Board, G.S.A. 1984.

Black Studies: A Select Catalog of National Archives Microfilm Publications. Washington, D.C.: National Archives Trust Fund Board, G.S.A. 1996. [Updated]

Immigrant and Passenger Arrivals: A Select Catalog of National Archives Microfilm Publications. Washington, D.C.: National Archives Trust Fund Board, G.S.A., 1983.

Genealogical and Biographical Research: A Select Catalog of National Archives Microfilm Publications. Washington, D.C.: National Archives Trust Fund Board, G.S.A., 1983.

Military Service Records: A Select Catalog of National Archives Microfilm Publications. Washington, D.C.: National Archives Trust Fund Board, G.S.A., 1984.

National Archives Microfilm Resources for Research: A Comprehensive Catalog. Washington, D.C.: National Archives and Records Administration, 1996. [Tapes]

For tapes of lectures, write for a catalog from Repeat Performance, 2911 Crabapple Lane, Hobart, IN 46342.

The Least You Need to Know

- ➤ There are many sources beyond the basic ones for genealogy research.
- ➤ Less often used records can be in the county, state, National Archives repositories, or in private, public, or university libraries.
- ➤ Rich sources may not be on microfilm, but remain in their original form at the custodial repository.

Chapter 23

Some Final Words

In This Chapter

- Success suggestions
- Aspiring to credentials
- Avoiding commercial traps
- Enjoying the research process

We hope you've caught our enthusiasm for genealogy and are ready to discover your roots. Before you rush off pell-mell in search of you ancestors, however, we have some "do's and don'ts" and some words of caution.

Ten Strategies for Success

Keep these things in mind as you begin the journey to find your ancestors:

1. Start with yourself and work backwards. Starting from your "origins" will lead you astray.
2. Examine all the family mementos and papers within your own family. Scrapbooks, family Bibles, photographs—every item can hold clues that will help you identify your family.

3. Interview relatives. Take complete notes. Consider taping or videotaping interviews to preserve the stories and voices.
4. Try to find previously unknown relatives who may have family documents. Use Internet forums, telephone directories, and query sections in genealogical periodicals.
5. Search the records in the towns and counties where your ancestors lived. Courthouses, cemeteries, local libraries, and museums can have information on your family.
6. Examine federal census records, available at National Archives branches and many public and private libraries. Finding the family in the federal census provides considerable information.
7. Use library resources. Examine records in the state archives and state libraries where your family lived. Inquire about special indexes created and maintained by these repositories.
8. Examine other federal records, especially military files and pension files. If you have worked a family branch back to the immigrant, search the ship passenger lists.
9. Establish a record keeping system that works for you. Use charts, forms, and files to keep track of the papers you collect. If you have a computer, become familiar with the programs available for storing family data.
10. Use creative thinking and new or less used sources to solve difficult problems.

Ten Things to Avoid

In conjunction with the rules for success, the following "don'ts" help prevent mistakes and make your genealogy research more fruitful.

1. Don't just accept all the family traditions without careful investigation.
2. Don't accept family sheets or records that have no documentation for the facts. Useful as clues only, they must be substantiated with records.
3. Don't limit yourself to the current spelling of a name. Remember, names were spelled phonetically; your ancestors may be listed under a variety of spellings.
4. Don't neglect to write down in detail where you get information. The source, whether a family member, book, photograph, microfilm, or tombstone, needs to be cited in such a manner that it can be located again.
5. Don't make assumptions on nationality or accept the family tradition of nationality without further investigation. Names were Americanized or otherwise changed. Family traditions often mix the nationality of the husband's line and the wife's line.
6. Don't press reluctant family members for details. Give them time to consider your interest and project. Later, they may tell you more.

7. Don't neglect to get photocopies of the old letters, Bibles, and other family papers still available. And don't fail to get the items identified while there are family members who remember.
8. Don't put off visits to elderly relatives.
9. Don't overlook any record that might have some mention of the family. Often the clues to identify a family's origin come from an obscure source: a receipt, a voting register, or a letter written in 1875.
10. Don't be satisfied with names, dates, and events. Learn about the people and their times: their occupations, their personalities, and their physical appearances.

Reaching Beyond the Basics

As your genealogical expertise develops, you may aspire to certification or accreditation. These credentials are sought, not only by those who wish to take clients, but by genealogists eager to do the best possible work. They take the opportunity to measure their skills against the high standards set by the Board for Certification of Genealogists or the Family History Library.

Whether or not you are interested in adding credentials to your name, it's good to get a taste of genealogy's alphabet soup.

Certification

The Board for Certification of Genealogists (BCG) certifies in five categories. Applicants in each category prepare transcripts, abstracts, interpretations, and research plans for documents furnished by the Board. They submit essays on materials pertinent to their chosen specialties, as well as several research reports done in the course of their work. Additional materials appropriate to the categories are also included in the application.

A brief description of certification categories (as taken from "Genealogical Certification, Who? What? Why? How?" published by the Board for Certification of Genealogists) follows.

Certified Genealogical Records Specialist (CGRS) The CGRS searches original and published records, understands all sources of a genealogical nature relating to the chosen areas of specialization and provides accurately detailed information concerning the contents of the records examined.

Certified Genealogist (CG) The CG is proficient in all areas of genealogical research and analysis, is qualified to resolve pedigree problems of sundry types, and is experienced in the compilation of well-crafted family histories.

Certified American Indian Lineage Specialist (CAILS) The CAILS conducts research to determine descent from a historical Indian tribe indigenous to North

America and is well versed in the pertinent materials and applicable standards within this specialized field.

Certified American Lineage Specialist (CALS) The CALS reconstructs a single line of descent and prepares hereditary society applications. The work of a CALS is based upon sound knowledge of pertinent resources and a skilled appraisal of the authenticity and acceptability of both original source records and compiled printed material.

Certified Genealogical Instructor (CGI) The CGI plans and conducts a full course of genealogical instruction, covering all aspects of genealogical methodology and sources. The CGI must also pass requirements for CG.

Certified Genealogical Lecturer (CGL) The CGL gives public addresses of an educational nature on specific genealogical topics or on related subjects pertinent to the tracing of family relationships. The CGL must also pass requirements for CGRS or CG.

Accreditation

The Family History Department of the Church of Jesus Christ of Latter-day Saints (the Mormons) tests and awards the designation of Accredited Genealogist (AG) in specialized geographic areas. Examinations are given in Salt Lake City, Utah. Although sponsored by the church, accreditation is not limited to church members, but is awarded to anyone passing the examination.

Sorting the Wheat from the Chaff

Certified or accredited genealogists adhere to codes of ethics, and that is some assurance for the reliability of their services. Unfortunately, there are other individuals and companies who take advantage of the curiosity many have about their family histories. Many eager people have been duped by misleading ads and fraudulent products.

Beware the Generic Family History

You may be tempted by the allure of various advertisements that promise "a family history of [your name] in America with origins of the surname, coat of arms, and every individual in the United States with your name," or other ads touting books with information about your forebears and why they immigrated to the New World. Don't be misled. It is not *your* family history, or anyone else's family history. These publications are usually nothing more than paragraphs of general information that could apply to any family, followed by a list of names, addresses, and phone numbers taken from widely available sources.

Coats of Arms

Coats of arms are another area of confusion to family history researchers. Coats of arms do not belong to specific surnames or families. In most cases, those who advertise that they can provide "your" coat of arms are only providing a copy of a coat of arms that was granted to one individual in times past. They deceive or mislead when they claim you are entitled to a particular coat of arms because it belongs to your surname. If you are interested in coats of arms, read Part 5, Chapter I, "Heraldry," in Rubincam's *Genealogical Research: Methods and Sources*.

"I Know a Shortcut..."

Modern technology makes it possible and practical for companies to amass huge collections of unrelated data. Some companies claim that you can now find your ancestors with a few clicks of a computer mouse. In that raw data, you may find individuals with the same names as your ancestors but no proof that they are the individuals you are seeking. Good genealogy requires the researcher to go beyond indexes, beyond undocumented lists. There are some shortcuts in genealogy, but there are no shortcuts to proving that you have discovered *your* ancestors.

> **Pedigree Pitfalls**
> Use database collections of names only as clues for further research. No matter the source of the names, whether submitted by family researchers or culled from state and federal records, confirm with careful research that individuals with the same names you are researching are in fact your specific ancestors.

Legitimate genealogy shortcuts come through innovations, such as using the Internet to search a distant library's card catalog so that you can order the book through interlibrary loan or seek it out on your next visit to that library. Indexes and the full text of books and journals on CD-ROMs make information searches go much more quickly. Technology continues to provide new tools to cut your research time, but there is no substitute for the systematic, thorough research necessary to prove a line.

"We're Related to..."

Something about human nature seems to make us want to claim important historical figures as ancestors. If you know that George Washington had no descendants, you can easily dismiss any pedigree you find that claims him as an ancestor. You should also be skeptical of pedigrees that go back to Charlemagne, Julius Caesar, or even Adam and Eve. Proving relationships beyond the time of surnames and record keeping is problematic. When you begin genealogy research,

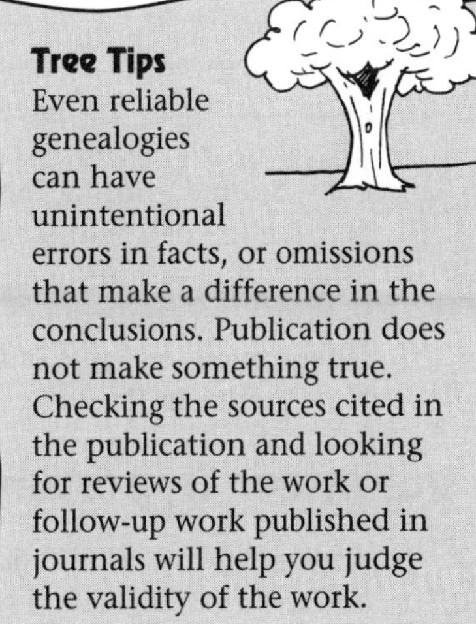

> **Tree Tips**
> Even reliable genealogies can have unintentional errors in facts, or omissions that make a difference in the conclusions. Publication does not make something true. Checking the sources cited in the publication and looking for reviews of the work or follow-up work published in journals will help you judge the validity of the work.

you may be unaware of published genealogies and reference works that have been generally dismissed as unreliable. This is not to say that you should be suspicious of all published work. It means that you should evaluate material based on the evidence presented to support the claims.

Wrapping It All Up

Your enthusiasm builds as you discover the continuity of history told through the fascinating stories of your ancestors. Keep the excitement growing by perpetual learning, becoming a volunteer, and sharing your finds with family and friends.

New books are published every year. "Lost" records are discovered in the dim and dusty recesses of courthouses and other repositories. Journal articles track a previously unknown family or correct a published genealogy. Read the book reviews for ideas of sources. Catalogs from the booksellers often lead you to books you were not aware of. Proprietors of genealogical bookstores are most likely genealogists themselves. They have a wide range of knowledge about books for genealogists, particularly books about their special interest areas.

Restudy Your Notes and Data

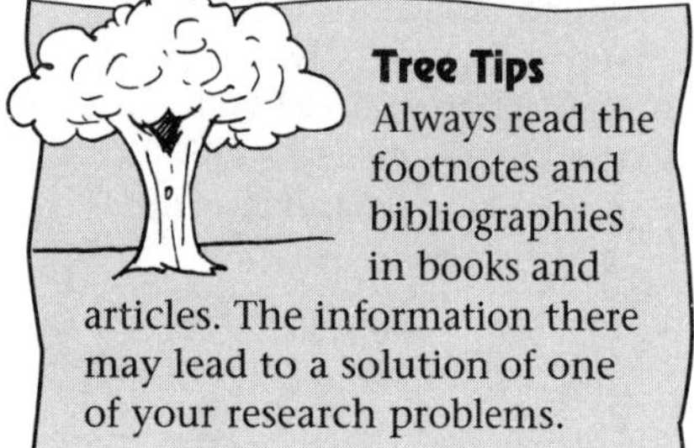

Tree Tips
Always read the footnotes and bibliographies in books and articles. The information there may lead to a solution of one of your research problems.

Continually restudy your data and your notes. Genealogy is usually done in fits and starts. Refresh your memory as you start to work on a line once again. Even when working on the same line continuously, it is easy to overlook a connection. Notes made one year and not referred to again for several more become stale, but they can contain the missing link you're so eager to find.

The Promise of Technology

Technology continues to make it easier to keep track of and share data. Computer programs can help you determine the gaps in your family history. Just a few years ago, genealogy was done by hand with charts painstakingly drawn for each person wanting a copy. Shared information was often incomplete and completely lacking documentation because the person disseminating the information ran out of energy before getting it all sent off to a distant relative. Writers promised to send more details soon but never found the time to complete the task. Copy machines have changed all that. Copiers are everywhere; even residents of very small towns usually have access to one somewhere nearby. Now there is little excuse for sharing undocumented or partial data.

Volunteer Opportunities

Genealogy can be a life-long interest. You'll continually learn new facts, new techniques, and new sources. You'll tie in to the network of genealogists all over the world who have a common interest and are willing to share their materials and knowledge. Give a little back by volunteering for a genealogical organization or repository. There is always work to be done, whether it's typing the newsletter, raising funds, arranging for speakers, or lobbying officials to preserve and keep open to researchers the records needed by family historians.

One of the best ways to learn the records of a repository or library and to give back to the field at the same time, is to donate some time to shelve books, answer questions, catalog, or develop finding aids. The jobs are endless. By volunteering, you'll discover resources you might not have found on your own. As you get acquainted with the other volunteers, you may find help with your research. At the very least you'll meet people with the same interests with whom you can exchange ideas.

Enlighten Your Friends

Your friends probably know what genealogy is. Now that genealogy is better known, there is not so much confusion about the word *"genealogy."* But when we started doing genealogy, many thought we said *"geology"* and would mention that they, too, liked collecting rocks. Even when your friends know what genealogy is, their eyes will glaze over if you begin to recite every detail of the fascinating-to-you search for your own ancestors. (You'll be disappointed to learn that even some members of your own family will have the same reaction!)

Instead, amuse your friends and relatives with the tidbits you are sure to find in your adventures, and impress them by explaining what a *cousin once removed* is. Of course, first you have to understand about cousins! When my daughter was three years old, she came home from a family gathering and squealed delightedly to my mother, "I met a cousin, and she's been removed twice!"

She was a little young to understand, but now she knows the relationships. The children of your aunts and uncles are your first cousins. Your children and your first cousins' children are second cousins. Your first cousins are your children's first cousins once removed. That is, they are one generation away from the individual. It's that simple. The age of the individuals does not matter. Whether your first cousin is older or younger than you, you are of the same generation. Your children are one generation away, or removed, from your generation and that of your first cousin. Cousins are cousins because they have ancestors in common; first cousins have grandparents in common. Your children's great-grandparents are the grandparents of their cousins once removed. If this still seems confusing to you, take a look at Jackie Smith Arnold's *Kinship: It's All Relative*. The charts there will help you to understand.

In the course of your research, don't be blind to the unique, the funny, and the outrageous—the records are full of surprises. The interesting snippets you find may not be about your own family. Some avenues you will never pursue, but they will set you to wondering. Why did two ships, which left Bremen, Germany, the same day and arrived in New York on the same day, each have a man overboard on the same day? What was the weather at sea the day these two men were lost? Did they jump or did rough seas send them over the edge? What happened to the three stowaways on another ship who were put ashore at Halifax before the end of the journey? As you scan the census looking for your ancestors, don't be in such a hurry that you miss someone like Constant Agony, age 65, or the baby named Jehovah, beside which the census taker had placed an editorial comment in the form of an exclamation point. Isn't your curiosity piqued by the deed for Marcus Baron Steuben Isaac Henry Fielding Lewis Pleakenstalver? The records hint at many stories. Genealogy is occasionally tedious, but it is never boring.

Remember most of all that tracing a family is fun. It strengthens family ties, reconnects lost branches, and forges new friendships. Enjoy the journey.

Relative Resources

Arnold, Jackie Smith. *Kinship: It's All Relative.* Baltimore, MD: Genealogical Publishing Co., 2nd ed., 1996.

Wagner, Sir Anthony, "Heraldry," *in Genealogical Research: Methods and Sources.* Washington, D.C.: American Society of Genealogists, 1960.

Addresses

Board for Certification of Genealogists, P.O. Box 14291, Washington, D.C. 20044. Write for certification information. Fee for directory: *Certification Roster.*

Accredited Genealogists, Family History Library, 35 North W. Temple St., Salt Lake City, UT 84150. Write for accreditation requirements. Send an SASE for a list of accredited genealogists in a particular state or country.

The Least You Need to Know

- Searching for your roots is a step-by-step process.
- Be skeptical of exaggerated claims to instant family history.
- Genealogy is an exciting life-long pursuit.

Major Genealogical Repositiories and Libraries by State

Following is a list of the major genealogical repositories in each state. Other repositories with genealogical collections also exist in each state. The listed address is the mailing address. If the actual location differs from the mailing address, it is listed in brackets.

Alabama

Alabama Department of Archives
624 Washington Ave.
Montgomery, AL 36130

Birmingham Public Library
2100 Park Place
Birmingham, AL 35203

Samford University Library
800 Lakeshore Dr.
Birmingham, AL 35229

Alaska

Alaska State Archives and Library
141 Willoughby Ave.
Juneau, AK 99801-1720

Arizona

Arizona State Archives
1700 W. Washington St.
Phoenix, AZ 85007

Arizona Historical Society
949 E. Second St.
Tucson, AZ 85719

Arkansas

Arkansas History Commission
One Capitol Mall
Little Rock, AR 72201

California

California State Archives
201 N. Sunrise Ave.
Sacramento, CA 95561

California State Library
914 Capitol Mall
Sacramento, CA 95814

California State Library
Sutro Branch
480 Winston Dr.
San Francisco, CA 94132

Colorado

Colorado State Archives
1313 Sherman St., I-B20
Denver, CO 80203

Denver Public Library
Social Sciences and Genealogy
1357 Broadway
Denver, CO 80203

Connecticut

Connecticut State Library
231 Capitol Ave.
Hartford, CT 06106

Connecticut Historical Society
1 Elizabeth St.
Hartford, CT 06105

Delaware

Delaware Bureau of Archives
Hall of Records
Dover, DE 19901

The Historical Society of Delaware
505 Market St.
Wilmington, DE 19801

District of Columbia

Library of Congress
Humanities and Social Sciences Division
Thomas Jefferson Building, Room LJ G42
Washington, DC 20540-4660

Daughters of the American Revolution Library
1776 D St., N.W.
Washington, DC 20006-5392

District of Columbia Archives
1300 Naylor Court, N.W.
Washington, DC 20001-4255

Martin Luther King, Jr. Memorial Library
Washingtonian Division
901 G St., N.W.
Washington, DC 20001

Florida

Florida State Archives and Library
R. A. Gray Building
500 South Bronough St.
Tallahassee, FL 32399-0250

P. K. Yonge Library of Florida History
University of Florida
Gainesville, FL 32611

Georgia

Georgia Department of Archives
330 Capitol Ave., S.E.
Atlanta, GA 30334

Georgia Historical Society
501 Whittaker St.
Savannah, GA 31498

Hawaii

Hawaii State Archives
Iolani Palace Grounds
Honolulu, HI 90813

Hawaiian Historical Society
560 Kawaiahoa St.
Honolulu, HI 96813

Hawaii State Library
1390 Miller St., Box 2360
Honolulu, HI 96804

Idaho

Idaho Library and Archives
450 North Fourth St.
Boise, ID 83702

Illinois

Illinois State Archives
Archives Building
Spring and Edwards
Springfield, IL 62756

Illinois State Library
Second and Capitol Streets
Springfield, IL 62756

Illinois State Historical Library
Old State Capitol
Springfield, IL 62701

Newberry Library
60 West Walton St.
Chicago, IL 60610

Indiana

Indiana State Library
140 North Senate Ave.
Indianapolis, IN 46204

Indiana State Archives
Commission on Public Records
140 North Senate Ave.
Indianapolis, IN 46204

Indiana Historical Society
315 West Ohio St.
Indianapolis, IN 46202

Allen County Public Library
Historical Genealogy Department
900 Webster St.
Fort Wayne, IN 46802

Iowa

State Historical Society of Iowa
Library and Archives
600 East Locust
Des Moines, IA 50319

Kansas

Kansas State Historical Society
Archives Division
6425 SW Sixth Ave.
Topeka, KS 66615-1099

Kentucky

Kentucky Department for Archives
[300 Coffee Tree Rd.]
P.O. Box 537
Frankfort, KY 40602-0537

Kentucky Historical Society
[300 West Broadway]
P.O. Box 1792
Frankfort, KY 40602

Filson Club Library
1310 S. Third St.
Louisville, KY 40205

Louisiana

Louisiana Division of Archives
[3851 Essen Lane]
P.O. Box 94125
Baton Rouge, LA 70804

Louisiana State Library
[760 Third St.]
P.O. Box 131
Baton Rouge, LA 70821

Maine

Maine State Archives
Capitol House Station 84
Augusta, ME 04333-8598

Maine State Library
State House Station 64
Augusta, ME 04333

Maine Historical Society Library
485 Congress St.
Portland, ME 04101

Maryland

Maryland State Archives
350 Rowe Blvd.
Annapolis, MD 21401

Maryland Historical Society
201 West Monument St.
Baltimore, MD 21201

Massachusetts

New England Historic Genealogical Society
101 Newbury St.
Boston, MA 02116-3087

American Antiquarian Society
185 Salisbury St.
Worcester, MA 01609

Massachusetts State Archives at Columbia Point
220 Morrissey Blvd.
Boston, MA 02125-3384

Michigan

State Library of Michigan
717 West Allegan St.
Lansing, MI 48909

Burton Historical Collection
Detroit Public Library
5201 Woodward Ave.
Detroit, MI 48202

Minnesota

Minnesota Historical Society and Archives
345 West Kellogg Blvd.
St. Paul, MN 55102-1906

Mississippi

Mississippi Department of Archives
[100 South State St.]
P.O. Box 571
Jackson, MS 39205

Missouri

The State Historical Society of Missouri
1020 Lowry St.
Columbia, MO 65201

Missouri State Archives
[600 West Main]
P.O. Box 778
Jefferson City, MO 65101

Montana

Montana Historical Society and Archives
[225 North Roberts]
P.O. Box 201201
Helena, MT 59601-1201

Nebraska

Nebraska State Historical Society
[1500 "R" St.]
P.O. Box 82554
Lincoln, NE 68501

Nevada

Nevada State Library and Archives
Division of Archives and Records
100 North Stewart St.
Carson City, NV 89701-4285

New Hampshire

New Hampshire Archives
71 South Fruit St.
Concord, NH 03301

New Hampshire Historical Society
30 Park St.
Concord, NH 03301

New Hampshire State Library
20 Park St.
Concord, NH 03301

New Jersey

New Jersey State Archives
State Library Building
185 West State St., CN-307
Trenton, NJ 08625-0307

New Jersey State Library
State Library Building
185 West State St., CN-520
Trenton, NJ 08625-0520

New Jersey Historical Society
230 Broadway
Newark, NJ 07104

New Mexico

New Mexico Commission of Records
404 Montezuma Ave.
Santa Fe, NM 87501

Special Collections
[Albuquerque Public Library System]
423 Central Ave., N.E.
Albuquerque, NM 87102

New York

New York State Archives
The State Education Department
Cultural Education Center, 11-D40
Empire State Plaza
Albany, NY 12230

New York State Library
Cultural Education Center, 7th Floor
Empire State Plaza
Albany, NY 12230

New York Genealogical and Biographical Society
122 East 58th St.
New York, NY 10022-1939

The New York Public Library
5th Avenue and 42nd Street
New York, NY 10018

North Carolina

North Carolina Division of Archives
109 East Jones St.
Raleigh, NC 27611

North Carolina State Library
109 East Jones St.
Raleigh, NC 27611

North Dakota

State Historical Society of North Dakota (and Archives)
Heritage Center
612 East Boulevard Ave.
Bismarck, ND 58505

North Dakota State Library
Liberty Memorial Building
604 East Blvd.
Bismarck, ND 58505-0800

Ohio

Ohio Historical Society
1982 Velma Ave.
Columbus, OH 43211

State Library of Ohio
Genealogy Division
65 South Front St.
Columbus, OH 43215

Western Reserve Historical Society
10825 East Blvd.
Cleveland, OH 44106

Oklahoma

Oklahoma Historical Society
2100 North Lincoln Blvd.
Oklahoma City, OK 73105-3298

Oklahoma Department of Libraries
200 N.E. 18th St.
Oklahoma City, OK 75105

Oklahoma City Public Library
131 Northwest Third St.
Oklahoma City, OK 73102

Oregon

Oregon State Archives
800 Summer St. NE
Salem, OR 97310

Oregon State Library
Summer and Court Streets
Salem, OR 97310

Oregon Historical Society Library
1230 S.W. Park Ave.
Portland, OR 97205

Genealogical Forum of Oregon, Inc.
1410 S.W. Morrison, Suite 812
Portland, OR 97205

Pennsylvania

Pennsylvania State Archives
[3rd and Forster Streets]
P.O. Box 1026
Harrisburg, PA 17108-1026

State Library of Pennsylvania
[Commonwealth Avenue and Walnut Street, Room 102]
P.O. Box 1601
Harrisburg, PA 17105-1601

The Historical Society of Pennsylvania Library
1300 Locust St.
Philadelphia, PA 19107

Rhode Island

Rhode Island State Archives
337 Westminster St.
Providence, RI 02903

Rhode Island Historical Society
121 Hope St.
Providence, RI 02903

South Carolina

South Carolina Department of Archives
[1430 Senate St.]
P.O. Box 11669
Columbia, SC 29211-1669

South Carolinian Library
University of South Carolina
Columbia, SC 29208

South Dakota

South Dakota State Historical Society
Cultural Heritage Center
900 Governors Dr.
Pierre, SD 57501

Tennessee

Tennessee State Library and Archives
403 Seventh Ave., North
Nashville, TN 37243-0312

Lawson McGehee Library
East Tennessee Historical Center
Mailing address: 314 West Clinch Ave.
Knoxville, TN 37802-2203
[Located at: 500 West Clinch Ave.]

Texas

Texas State Library
State Archives and Library Building
P.O. Box 12927
Austin, TX 78711-2927

Dallas Public Library
1515 Young St.
Dallas, TX 75201

Clayton Library
5300 Caroline
Houston, TX 77004

Utah

Family History Library
35 North West Temple
Salt Lake City, UT 84150

Utah State Archives
Archives Building, State Capitol
Salt Lake City, UT 84114

Vermont

Vermont Historical Society Library
109 State St.
Montpelier, VT 05609-0901

Vermont State Archives
State Office Building
[Located at: 26 Terrace St.]
109 State St.
Montpelier, VT 05609-1101

Virginia

The Library of Virginia
800 East Broad St.
Richmond, VA 23219-1905

Virginia Historical Society
[428 North Blvd.]
P.O. Box 7311
Richmond, VA 23221

Jones Memorial Library
434 Rivermont Ave.
Lynchburg, VA 24504

Washington

Washington State Archives
[1120 Washington St. NE]
P.O. Box 40238
Olympia, WA 98504

Washington State Library
[415 15th Ave. SW]
P.O. Box 42460
Olympia, WA 98504

West Virginia

Archives Library
Division of Culture and History
1900 Kanawha Blvd. East
Charleston, WV 25305-0300

West Virginia and Regional History Collection
West Virginia University Library
Colson Hall
Morgantown, WV 26506

Wisconsin

State Historical Society of Wisconsin
816 State St.
Madison, WO 53706-1488

Wyoming

Wyoming State Archives
Barrett Building
Cheyenne, WY 82002

National Archives

NARA (Archives I), in Washington, D.C., is the main National Archives center. NARA (Archives II), in College Park, Maryland, now holds many records useful to genealogists, such as the maps in the cartographic department. The others listed are the regional branches.

NARA (Archives I)
700 Pennsylvania Ave., NW
Washington, DC 20408-0001
(201) 501-5400

NARA (Archives II)
8601 Adelphi Rd.
College Park, MD 20740-6001
(301) 713-6800

National Archives-New England Region
380 Trapelo Rd.
Waltham, MA 02154-6399
(617) 647-8100

National Archives-Pittsfield Region
100 Dan Fox Dr.
Pittsfield, MA 01201-8230
(413) 445-6885

National Archives-Northeast Region
201 Varick St., 12th Floor
New York, NY 10014-4811
(212) 337-1300

National Archives-Mid Atlantic Region
900 Market St.
Philadelphia, PA 19107-4292
(215) 597-3000

National Archives-Southeast Region
1557 St. Joseph Ave.
East Point, GA 30344-2593
(404) 763-7477

National Archives-Great Lakes Region
7358 South Pulaski Rd.
Chicago, IL 60629-5898
(773) 581-7816

National Archives-Central Plains Region
2312 East Bannister Rd.
Kansas City, MO 64131-3060
(816) 926-6272

National Archives-Southwest Region
501 West Felix St., P.O. Box 6216
Fort Worth, TX 76115-0216
(817) 334-5525

National Archives-Rocky Mountain Region
Building 48
Denver Federal Center, P.O. Box 25307
Denver, CO 80225-0307
(303) 236-0817

National Archives-Pacific Southwest Region
24000 Avila Rd., P.O. Box 6719
Laguna Niguel, CA 92607-6719
(714) 643-4241

National Archives-Pacific Sierra Region
1000 Commodore Dr.
San Bruno, CA 94066-2350
(415) 876-9009

National Archives-Pacific Northwest Region
6125 Sand Point Way, NE
Seattle, WA 98115-7999
(206) 526-6507

National Archives-Alaska Region
634 West Third Ave., Room 012
Anchorage, AK 99501-2145
(907) 271-2441

Abbreviations and Acronyms Commonly Used in Genealogy

a.	acre or acres
A.G.	Accredited Genealogist
a.k.a.	also known as
abt.	about
acct.	account
admr.	administrator, administratrix
ads.	adversus; the opposite of versus
ae, aet	aged
aft.	after
ante	before, prior to
APG	Association of Professional Genealogists
ASG	American Society of Genealogists
assn.	association
atty.	attorney
b.	born
b.p, b.pl.	birthplace (do not confuse with bp. for baptism)
B.L.Wt.	Bounty Land Warrant
B.L.M.	Bureau of Land Management
BCG	Board for Certification of Genealogists
bef.	before
betw.	between
bk.	book
bp.	baptized (do not confuse with b.p. for birth place)
bro.	brother
bur.	buried
ca.	about (circa)
CAILS	Certified American Indian Lineage Specialist
calc.	calculated
CALS	Certified American Lineage Specialist
cem.	cemetery
cert.	certificate, certified
CG	Certified Genealogist
CGRS	Certified Genealogical Records Specialist
Ch., ch.	church; children
chr.	christened
co.	county; Company
d.	died
D.B.	deed book

d.s.p.	died without issue (*decessit sine prole*)
d.y.	died young
DAR	Daughters of the American Revolution
dau.	daughter
d/o	daughter of
decd.	deceased
deft.	defendant
dept.	department
desc.	descendant
disch., dischd.	discharge; discharged
Dist.	District
div.	divorce; division
d-m-y	day, month, year
do	ditto, the same
doc.	document
est.	estate; estimate
exec.	executor, executrix
f., fem.	female
f/o	father of
fa.	father
FASG	Fellow, American Society of Genealogists
ff.	and following pages
FGS	Federation of Genealogical Societies
FHL	Family History Library
fn.	footnote
FNGS	Fellow, National Genealogical Society
FUGA	Fellow, Utah Genealogical Association
g.s.	gravestone
GAR	Grand Army of the Republic
gdn.	guardian
GJ	*Genealogical Journal*
grdau.	granddaughter
grdsn.	grandson
h., hus.	husband
h/o	husband of
IGI	International Genealogical Index
Ind. Ter.	Indian Territory
inf., Inf.	infant; Infantry
int.	intestate; interred
inv.	inventory; invalid
J.P.	Justice of the Peace
LC	Library of Congress
LDS	Church of Jesus Christ of Latter-day Saints
lic.	license
m.	male, married, month, mother
M.G.	Minister of the Gospel
m/o	mother of
mat.	maternal
ms., mss.	manuscript; manuscripts
n.d.	no date
n.f.r.	no further record found

n.p.	no place
n.publ.	no publisher [shown]
N.S.	New Style date
NARA	National Archives and Records Administration
NEHGR	*New England Historical and Genealogical Register*
NEHGS	New England Historic Genealogical Society
NGS	National Genealogical Society
NGSQ	*National Genealogical Society Quarterly*
nr.	near
NSDAR	National Society Daughters of the American Revolution
NYGB	New York Genealogical and Biographical Society
NYGBR	*New York Genealogical and Biographical Society Record*
O.S.	Old Style date
obit.	obituary
P.A.	power of attorney
pat.	paternal; patent
plt., pltf.	plaintiff
poss.	possible, possibly
PR	probate record
prob.	probable/probably; probate
pub.	published
R.	Range (land description)
R.G.	Record Group
rec.	record
rem.	removed
res.	resides, residence
s.	son
s/o	son of
sec.	section
sic	thus
soc.	society
T.	Township (land description)
TAG	*The American Genealogist*
TR	town record
twp.	township
UGA	Utah Genealogical Association
unm.	unmarried
unpub.	unpublished
V.R.	vital records
V.S.	vital statistics
vs.	against (versus)
w.	wife
warrt.	warrant
w/o	wife of; without
wid.	widow; widower
yr.	year

Appendix D

Worksheets

The worksheets in this appendix are examples of forms used to organize your genealogy research. Use the research calendar and the correspondence log to keep a running summary of what you have accomplished. The research calendar shows you at a glance the records you have checked in reference to a particular surname and problem. Looking at the list, you can quickly determine whether or not you have searched a particular record and what the results were. The research calendar is meant to be an overview of your work, rather than the place for detailed notes. The correspondence log is a record of your letter writing. Scanning the list, you can quickly see to whom you've written and what the response was. For more on these two forms, see Chapter 3.

Use the pedigree chart as a sketch of your bloodline. Here is where you record the bare bones statistics on your ancestors. Once you have filled in the chart with what you know, you can develop a research plan to find the missing information. The family group sheet is the form used to record more detailed information for the people on your pedigree chart. Family group sheets are the foundation for organizing the information you collect. Complete at least two family group sheets for each individual on your pedigree chart. On one family group sheet the individual appears as a child and on another as a mother or father. (An individual with more than one marriage should have a family group sheet for each marriage.) Pedigree charts and family group sheets are not the end products of your research. They are tools to help you organize your findings. See Chapter 4 for more on pedigree charts and family group sheets.

Also included is a checklist of questions for interviewing relatives. You'll think of others as you devise your own lists for each interview you conduct. See Chapters 2 and 19 for more on interview techniques.

Surname

RESEARCH CALENDAR

Search focus (brief statement of research problem)

Date	Repository/call no.	Source	Findings

CORRESPONDENCE LOG

Date Sent	To Whom	Request	Reply Date	Results (Positive, Negative, Burned)

CHART NO. ______

PEDIGREE CHART

Prepared by ____________
Address ____________
City and State ______ **Zip** ______
Date Prepared ____________

No. 1 on this Chart is # ______ on Chart # ______

1. ____________
Born
Where
Married When
Died
Where

____
Name of Husband or Wife

2. [Father of No. 1]
Born
Where
Married When
Died
Where

3. [Mother of No. 1]
Born
Where
Died
Where

4. [Father of No.2]
Born
Where
Married When
Died
Where

5. [Mother of No. 2]
Born
Where
Died
Where

6. [Father of No. 3]
Born
Where
Married When
Died
Where

7. [Mother of No. 3]
Born
Where
Died
Where

8. Con't on Chart #____ [Father of No. 4]
Born
Where
Married When
Died
Where

9. Con't on Chart #____ [Mother of No. 4]
Born
Where
Died
Where

10. Con't on Chart #____ [Father of No. 5]
Born
Where
Married When
Died
Where

11. Con't on Chart #____ [Mother of No. 5]
Born
Where
Died
Where

12. Con't on Chart #____ [Father of No. 6]
Born
Where
Married When
Died
Where

13. Con't on Chart #____ [Mother of No. 6]
Born
Where
Died
Where

14. Con't on Chart #____ [Father of No. 7]
Born
Where
Married When
Died
Where

15. Con't on Chart #____ [Mother of No. 7]
Born
Where
Died
Where

FAMILY GROUP SHEET

NO. ____

HUSBAND [Full name]			SOURCES: Brief listing.
BORN	AT		No.
CHR.	AT		No.
MAR.	AT		No.
DIED	AT		No.
BURIED AT			(Complete source citations on reverse)
FATHER	MOTHER [Maiden Name]		
OTHER WIVES			
RESIDENCES		RELIGION	
OCCUPATION		MILITARY	
[Use separate forms for each marriage]			

WIFE [Full maiden name]	
BORN	AT
CHR.	AT
DIED	AT
BURIED AT	
FATHER	MOTHER [Maiden Name]
OTHER HUSBANDS	

Sex	Children	Day-Month-Year	City/Town County State	REF. No.
	1.	b.	at	Ref.
	Spouse:	m.	at	Ref.
		d.	at	Ref.
	2.	b.	at	Ref.
	Spouse:	m.	at	Ref.
		d.	at	Ref.
	3.	b.	at	Ref.
	Spouse:	m.	at	Ref.
		d.	at	Ref.
	4.	b.	at	Ref.
	Spouse:	m .	at	Ref.
		d.	at	Ref.
	5.	b.	at	Ref.
	Spouse:	m.	at	Ref.
		d.	at	Ref.
	6.	b.	at	Ref.
	Spouse:	m.	at	Ref.
		d.	at	Ref.
	7.	b.	at	Ref.
	Spouse:	m.	at	Ref.
		d.	at	Ref.
	8.	b.	at	Ref.
	Spouse:	m.	at	Ref.
		d.	at	Ref.
	9.	b.	at	Ref.
	Spouse:	m.	at	Ref.
		d.	at	Ref.
	10.	b.	at	Ref.
	Spouse:	m.	at	Ref.
		d.	at	Ref.

PREPARED BY		OTHER MAR. OF CHILDREN
Address		Use reverse for additional marriages
City and State	Zip	
Date Prepared:		

b.=born m.=married d.=death ch.=christening List references at top and use ref. numbers on items. Use reverse if necessary.

Interviewing Your Relatives

You need to know names, dates, and locations, but if you suddenly bombard your relative with only those questions, they will become flustered. Or worse yet, lose interest. Try to fit those questions in among the ones that trigger the reminiscences. Much of the information you'll find in your search will pertain to your male ancestors. During interviews, make a special effort to elicit information about your female ancestors.

It is not likely that you will have time to ask all your questions, so decide which ones are most important to you. But don't be too rigid. Through the natural course of the conversation, you may get answers to questions you didn't think to ask or were hesitant to ask. And the answer to one question could lead to something you'll want to explore further. The following questions will get you started with your own list; you'll think of others. (See Chapters 2 and 19 for more tips on interviewing.)

- ❑ What was Grandpa's full name? Was he named for anyone else? What was he called? How did he get that nickname?
- ❑ When and where was he born? Was it a small town? A farming community? Do you know what took the family there?
- ❑ What was his father's name?
- ❑ What was his mother's maiden name?
- ❑ Did Grandpa have brothers and sisters? What were their names? When were they born; where were they born? Who did they marry?
- ❑ Where were the various towns in which the family lived? Did they like moving around? Were they following the available work? Just adventurous? Did other relatives move with them?
- ❑ What were the names of Grandpa's aunts and uncles? Did they live nearby? Were there often large family gatherings?
- ❑ What did Grandpa look like? Did he have a beard? Was he big-framed?
- ❑ Does anyone have any photos of him? Did he resemble anyone else in the family?
- ❑ What did Grandpa do to earn a living? Did he like it? Did any of the children follow in his footsteps?
- ❑ Where is he buried? Have you ever been there? Is there a tombstone?
- ❑ Did Grandpa ever serve in one of the wars? Does anyone have his uniform or other paraphernalia from the war?
- ❑ What church did he attend? Did he attend with Grandma? Was he active in the church?
- ❑ Did he have a trade? A hobby? Did he like gardening? Did he have any pets?
- ❑ Did he own land? Was it cultivated for crops? Did he like working on it himself?
- ❑ What was his nationality? Did he speak with an accent?

- ❑ Does anyone in the family have possessions that were handed down? Do you know the stories about the items?
- ❑ Tell me about your holiday dinners. Were birthdays celebrated? What kinds of gifts did you give and receive?
- ❑ What did the family do for recreation? Did anyone have a special hobby?
- ❑ How was the family's health? Robust or sickly? Allergies? Home remedies?
- ❑ Did they embrace newfangled ideas and technologies? When did they get their first automobile, electricity? Did they have indoor plumbing?
- ❑ What is the origin of the family expressions? Did the family have any traditions?
- ❑ Were they involved in politics, civics? Belong to any clubs?
- ❑ What were their attitudes toward religion, race, liquor?
- ❑ Did anyone play a musical instrument? Have artistic talent?
- ❑ Was anyone athletic?
- ❑ Is there some family trait that seems pervasive?
- ❑ What about you—how did you meet your spouse? How did you decide on a wedding date?
- ❑ What was your school like—one room in the country or a brick building in the city? Were you a good student?
- ❑ Who were your best friends, and what did you do together?
- ❑ What was your favorite age? Why?
- ❑ Did you get along well with your siblings? Your cousins?

Census Forms

The following pages contain forms for the 1800–1920 censuses. These forms can be photocopied and used to enter information you extract from microfilm.

1800–1810 CENSUS — UNITED STATES

State ______ County ______ City ______ Call No. ______

Page	Head of Family	Free White Males					Free White Females					All Others	Slaves	Remarks
		Under 10	10–16	16–26	26–45	45 & Over	Under 10	10–16	16–26	26–45	45 & Over			

1820 CENSUS — UNITED STATES

State __________ County __________ City __________ Call No. __________

Page	Head of Family	Free White Males						Free White Females					Foreigners not naturalized	Agriculture	Commerce	Manufactures	Free Colored	Slaves	Remarks
		Under 10	10–16	16–18	16–26	26–45	45 and over	Under 10	10–16	16–26	26–45	45 and over							

1830-1840 CENSUS – UNITED STATES

STATE | COUNTY | CITY | CALL NUMBER

Page	HEAD OF FAMILY	FREE WHITE MALES													FREE WHITE FEMALES													Slaves	Free Colored	Foreigners Not Naturalized
		Under 5	5-10	10-15	15-20	20-30	30-40	40-50	50-60	60-70	70-80	80-90	90-100	Over 100	Under 5	5-10	10-15	15-20	20-30	30-40	40-50	50-60	60-70	70-80	80-90	90-100	Over 100			

1850 CENSUS – UNITED STATES

STATE				COUNTY				TOWN/TOWNSHIP						CALL NUMBER	
Page	Dwelling Number	Family Number	NAMES	Age	Sex	Color	OCCUPATION, ETC.	Value—Real Estate	BIRTHPLACE	Married Within Year	School Within Year	Can't Read or Write	Enumeration Date	REMARKS	

1860 CENSUS — UNITED STATES

STATE | COUNTY | TOWN/TOWNSHIP | P.O. | CALL NUMBER

Page	Dwelling No.	Family No.	NAMES	Age	Sex	Color	OCCUPATION, ETC.	Value—Real Estate	Value—Personal Property	BIRTHPLACE	Married In Year	School In Year	Can't Read or Write	Enumeration Date	REMARKS

1870 CENSUS – UNITED STATES

STATE | COUNTY | TOWN/TOWNSHIP | P.O. | CALL NUMBER

Page	Dwelling No.	Family No.	NAMES	Age.	Sex	Color	OCCUPATION, ETC.	Value—Real Estate	Value—Personal Prop.	BIRTHPLACE	Father Foreign Born	Mother Foreign Born	Month Born In Year	Month Married In Year	School In Year	Can't Read or Write	Eligible To Vote	Date of Enumeration

1880 CENSUS – UNITED STATES

STATE	COUNTY	TOWN/TOWNSHIP	CALL NUMBER

Page	Dwelling Number	Family Number	NAMES	Color	Sex	Age Prior to June 1st	Month of Birth if Born in Census Year	Relationship to Head of House	Single	Married	Widowed	Divorced	Married in Census Year	Occupation	Miscellaneous Information	Cannot Read or Write	Place of Birth	Place of Birth of Father	Place of Birth of Mother	Enumeration Date

MICROFILM ROLL NUMBER	1900 CENSUS – UNITED STATES			
STATE	TOWN/TOWNSHIP		SUPV. DIST. NO.	SHEET NUMBER
COUNTY	CALL NUMBER	DATE	ENUM. DIST. NO.	PAGE NUMBER

LOCATION				NAME		PERSONAL DESCRIPTION									NATIVITY			CITIZENSHIP			OCCUPATION		EDUCATION						
Street	House Number	Dwelling Number	Family Number	of each person whose place of abode on June 1, 1900, was in this family	Relation to head of family	Color	Sex	Month of birth	Year of birth	Age	Single, married, widowed, divorced	Number of years married	Mother of how many children	Number of these children living	Place of birth	Place of birth of father	Place of birth of mother	Year of immigration to United States	No. of years in U.S.	Naturalization	Type	Number of months not employed	Attended school (months)	Can read	Can write	Can speak English	Home owned or rented	Home owned free or mortgaged	Farm or house

1910 CENSUS – UNITED STATES

STATE	COUNTY	TOWN/TOWNSHIP	ENUM. DIST. NO.	PAGE NO.

LOCATION				NAME		PERSONAL DESCRIPTION							NATIVITY		
STREET NAME	HOUSE NUMBER	VISITATION NUMBER	FAMILY NUMBER	OF EACH PERSON WHOSE PLACE OF ABODE ON APRIL 15, 1910, WAS IN THIS FAMILY	RELATION TO HEAD OF HOUSE	SEX	RACE	AGE	SINGLE/MARRIED/ WIDOWED/DIVORCED	NUMBER OF YEARS PRESENT MARRIAGE	NO. OF CHILDREN BORN THIS MOTHER	NUMBER OF THESE CHILDREN LIVING	PLACE OF BIRTH OF THIS PERSON	PLACE OF BIRTH OF FATHER	PLACE OF BIRTH OF MOTHER

1910 CENSUS – UNITED STATES (CONTINUED)

STATE	COUNTY	TOWN/TOWNSHIP	ENUM. DIST. NO.	PAGE NO.

NAME	CITIZENSHIP			OCCUPATION					EDUCATION			HOME OWNERSHIP						
							IF EMPLOYEE											
OF EACH PERSON WHOSE PLACE OF ABODE ON APRIL 15, 1910, WAS IN THIS FAMILY (FROM OTHER SIDE OF THIS FORM)	YEAR OF IMMIGRATION TO U.S.	NATURALIZED/ALIEN	NATIVE LANGUAGE	TRADE OR PROFESSION	NATURE OF BUSINESS	EMPLOYER/EMPLOYEE/ SELF-EMPLOYED	EMPLOYED/ UNEMPLOYED	WEEKS OUT OF WORK IN 1909	ABLE TO READ	ABLE TO WRITE	ATTENDED SCHOOL SINCE SEPT 1, 1909	OWNED/RENTED	OWNED FREE/ MORTGAGED	FARM/HOUSE	NO. OF FARM SCHEDULE	UNION/CONFEDERATE VETERAN	BLIND	DEAF AND DUMB

1920 CENSUS — UNITED STATES

STATE		SUPERVISOR'S DISTRICT #	SHEET NO.
COUNTY		ENUMERATION DISTRICT #	
TOWNSHIP OR OTHER COUNTY DIVISION	NAME OF INCORPORATED PLACE	WARD OF CITY	
NAME OF INSTITUTION	ENUMERATED BY ME ON THE ________ DAY OF ____________, 1920	ENUMERATOR	

PLACE OF ABODE				NAME	RELATION	TENURE		PERSONAL DESCRIPTION				CITIZENSHIP			EDUCATION		
STREET, AVENUE, ETC.	HOUSE NUMBER OR FARM	NUMBER OF DWELLING HOUSE (VISITATION ORDER)	NUMBER OF FAMILY (VISITATION ORDER)	OF EACH PERSON WHOSE PLACE OF ABODE ON JANUARY 1, 1920, WAS IN THIS FAMILY	RELATIONSHIP TO HEAD OF HOUSEHOLD	HOME OWNED OR RENTED	IF OWNED, FREE OR MORTGAGED	SEX	COLOR OR RACE	AGE AT LAST BIRTHDAY	SINGLE, MARRIED WIDOWED, OR DIVORCED	YEAR OF IMMIGRATION TO U.S.	NATURALIZED OR ALIEN	IF NATURALIZED, YEAR OF NATURALIZATION	ATTENDED SCHOOL ANYTIME SINCE SEPT. 1, 1919	ABLE TO READ	ABLE TO WRITE
1	2	3	4	5	6	7	8	9	10	11	12	13	14	15	16	17	18

STATE											
COUNTY	**1920 CENSUS — UNITED STATES**							SUPERVISOR'S DISTRICT # / ENUMERATION DISTRICT #		SHEET NO.	
TOWNSHIP OR OTHER COUNTY DIVISION	NAME OF INCORPORATED PLACE						WARD OF CITY				
NAME OF INSTITUTION	ENUMERATED BY ME ON THE ______ DAY OF ______, 1920						ENUMERATOR				
NAME	**NATIVITY AND MOTHER TONGUE**							**OCCUPATION**			
OF EACH PERSON WHOSE PLACE OF ABODE ON JANUARY 1, 1920, WAS IN THIS FAMILY (from other side of form).	PLACE OF BIRTH OF EACH PERSON AND PARENTS OF EACH PERSON ENUMERATED. IF BORN IN U.S., GIVE STATE OR TERRITORY. IF FOREIGN BIRTH, GIVE THE PLACE OF BIRTH, AND, IN ADDITION, THE MOTHER TONGUE.						ABLE TO SPEAK ENGLISH	TRADE, PROFESSION, OR PARTICULAR KIND OF WORK DONE.	INDUSTRY, BUSINESS, OR ESTABLISHMENT IN WHICH AT WORK.	EMPLOYER, SALARY OR WAGE WORKER, OR WORKING ON OWN ACCOUNT.	NUMBER OF FARM SCHEDULE
	PERSON		FATHER		MOTHER						
	PLACE OF BIRTH	MOTHER TONGUE	PLACE OF BIRTH	MOTHER TONGUE	PLACE OF BIRTH	MOTHER TONGUE					
5	19	20	21	22	23	24	25	26	27	28	29

Selected Definitions of Terms As They Apply to Genealogy

abstract Summary of a document that retains every important or pertinent detail.

administration Decedent's estate for which there is no will.

administrator Person appointed by the court to handle the estate of one who died without a will.

affidavit Written declaration made under oath before a notary public or other authorized official.

age of majority Legal age of adulthood; varies from area to area.

ancestor Person from whom one is descended.

ascendant chart Starts with individual and moves back through the generations of all his or her ancestors.

banns Announcement, usually in church, of an intended marriage.

beneficiary One who benefits from a provision made by another, usually in a will.

bounty land Federal land awarded by the federal government for military service.

CD-ROM Compact disk, read only memory; disk used in a computer compact disk drive.

census Official count that often includes related information to be used for government planning; *population* census—a count of people.

Christian name First (and middle) name; the name given to a child at birth or baptism. Also called *given* name.

citation Formal notation of the source of information.

cite Call attention to the proof or source of information.

Civil War census Special 1890 federal census taken of Union veterans of the Civil War.

collateral relative Someone with whom you share a common ancestor, but not a direct line.

consideration Asset given by the buyer of a property to the seller of the property; may or may not be monetary.

consolidated index Index combining the indexes of several sources.

county clerk Clerk of the court handling particular documents and transactions in a courthouse.

county seat Town or city that is the administrative center for a county.

decedent Deceased person.

declaration of intention Sworn statement by an alien that he intends to become a citizen.

deed Legal document used to transfer title.

descendant chart Chart that starts with an individual and comes down through the generations listing the individual's descendants.

double dating Practice developed because of calendar changes: dates from 1 January to 25 March before 1752 are shown with both the old calendar year and the new calendar year; for example, 23 January 1749/50. The first depicts the year under the old calendar, the second the year under the new calendar.

dower Portion of an estate allotted by law for a widow.

drop chart Connects two people, one of an earlier generation and one of a later generation, showing their link generation by generation.

emigrant Person who departs from one country to establish permanent residence in another (see also *immigrant*).

Enumeration District Area assigned to census taker for counting.

enumerator One who makes a list, usually for census or tax purposes.

estate The whole of one's possessions, especially the property and debts left by a person at time of death (or the possessions of a minor, incompetent person, or other in need of protection by a court process).

et al Shortened from *et alii*, "and others."

et ux. Shortened from *et uxor*, "and wife."

evidence Information offered as proof of a lineage or relationship.

executor Person appointed by the testator to handle an estate after the testator's death.

family association Membership group descended from a particular ancestor or group of ancestors.

family group sheet Form used to record information on a family unit.

family traditions Stories handed down from generation to generation, usually by word of mouth.

forum An electronic meeting place on the Internet where messages can be exchanged.

gazetteer Geographical dictionary.

genealogy The account, or history of descent, of a person or a study of a person's family.

given name First (and middle) name; the name given to a child at birth or baptism. Also called *Christian* name.

grantee Buyer of property.

grantor Seller of property.

infant Person who has not reached the age of majority.

immigrant Person who comes to a country from another to establish permanent residence.

indentured servant One who entered into a contract binding himself/herself into the service of another for a specified term, usually in exchange for passage.

instant (inst.) Indicates that the date referred to was in the same month as a previously mentioned date.

interlibrary loan System in which one library lends a book or microfilm to another library for the use of a patron.

intestate One who dies without a valid will.

lineage society Organization whose members are directly descended from particular ancestors (such as Revolutionary War or tavern keepers).

LSASE (or L.S.A.S.E.) Long Self Addressed Stamped Envelope (usually a #10 envelope).

maternal ancestor Ancestor on the mother's side of the family.

memorabilia Items with a significance to the family.

micropublication Microfilm or microfiche, or series of microfilm or microfiche.

Mortality Schedule Special federal censuses that list those deceased within a certain prescribed period (usually June 1 of the previous year to May 31 of the current year); sometimes accompany a federal census.

mortgage Pledge to repay money borrowed.

mug book Slang term for county (or town) history, containing, among other items, biographies; often accompanied by pen sketches or photographs.

muster roll List of all personnel (officers and enlisted) in a military unit; includes name, rank, absences, money owed, and more.

NGSQ numbering Genealogical numbering system modified from the *Register numbering* system; gives each child an Arabic numeral, and uses a + before each child carried forward.

naturalization Legal process for an individual of foreign birth to become a citizen.

necrology List of persons who died within a certain time frame; collection of obituaries.

orphan In early times, an infant under the age of majority who had one or both parents deceased, commonly used when the father was deceased but the mother was living (though in some instances the mother was the deceased parent); now, usually, one whose parents are both deceased.

parent county County from which a new or present day county was formed.

paternal ancestor Ancestor on the father's side of the family.

patronymics Names derived from a father's name, usually the father's given name, or from the paternal side of the family.

pedigree chart Shows the lines of your direct ancestors.

personal property Individual's belongings excluding land (see *real property*).

power of attorney Legal document allowing someone else to act on an individual's behalf.

probate Process of legally establishing the validity of a will.

progenitor The founder or first person in a line of descent.

query section In a genealogical publication, refers to a specific section of the magazine set aside for submitted inquiries.

real property Refers to land (see *personal property*).

Register numbering Genealogical numbering system developed by the New England Historic Genealogical Society for its *Register;* uses an Arabic numeral preceding each child to be carried forward in the compilation.

repository Physical location where things are placed for safekeeping; this could be a museum, library, archives, or courthouse.

SASE (or S.A.S.E.) Self Addressed Stamped Envelope.

sexton Caretaker responsible for burials and maintenance of a cemetery.

Soundex Indexing system based on the phonetic sound of the consonants in a surname.

sponsors People vouching for the suitability of the applicant to be admitted to a lineage society; also those who sponsor a child at baptism.

testator Person making a will.

topographical map Detailed, precise description of a place or region with graphic representations of the surface features.

transcribing The act of faithfully duplicating the exact wording, spelling, and punctuation of an original document.

transcript Word-for-word exact copy of the text in a document.

ultimate (ult.) In giving dates, refers to the previous month.

vault Steel-lined room designed to prevent destruction of records, such as that found in courthouses.

vertical file Collection of resource materials, usually pamphlets, letters, or clippings, often found in libraries.

vital record Record relating to birth, marriage, and death.

will Legally executed document declaring how a person wishes his or her possessions to be disposed of after death.

witness On a document, one who swears that a signature was made in his or her presence.

Index

Symbols

A

B

F

G

H

I

J-K

L

M

O

S